MODULA–2

Text and Reference

John B. Moore

Kenneth N. McKay

University of Waterloo
Waterloo, Ontario

PB805   384

A RESTON BOOK
PRENTICE-HALL, INC., ENGLEWOOD CLIFFS, NEW JERSEY 07632

Library of Congress Cataloging-in-Publication Data

MOORE, JOHN B., (date)
  Modula-2 text and reference.

  "A Reston book."
  Includes index.
    1. Modula-2 (Computer program language)
  I. McKay, Kenneth N., (date). II. Title
  QA76.73.M63M66 1987   005.26   86-15056
  ISBN 0-8359-4683-5

Editorial/production supervision
  and interior design: Elena Le Pera
Cover design: John B. Moore and Kenneth N. McKay
Manufacturing buyer: Ed O'Dougherty

A Reston Book
© 1987 by Prentice-Hall, Inc.
A Division of Simon & Schuster
Englewood Cliffs, New Jersey 07632

Printed in the United States of America

10 9 8 7 6 5 4 3 2 1

ISBN 0-8359-4683-5   025

Prentice-Hall International (UK) Limited, *London*
Prentice-Hall of Australia Pty. Limited, *Sydney*
Prentice-Hall Canada Inc., *Toronto*
Prentice-Hall Hispanoamericana, S.A., *Mexico*
Prentice-Hall of India Private Limited, *New Delhi*
Prentice-Hall of Japan, Inc., *Tokyo*
Prentice-Hall of Southeast Asia Pte. Ltd., *Singapore*
Editora Prentice-Hall do Brasil, Ltda., *Rio de Janeiro*

To Our Mothers

Eleanor Moore and Mary E. McKay

CONTENTS

PART I - Values and Data Structures

PART III – The System Interface

CHAPTER 12: Low-Level Facilities

PART IV – Appendices

Preface

Modula-2. Modula-2 is a significant new programming language. It is rapidly gaining widespread acceptance for several reasons. Among the foremost of these are:

o   It builds on the strengths of Pascal.

o   It is suitable for both high-level and low-level programming.

o   It possesses excellent facilities for designing and implementing large software systems.

o   It is a "small" language that can be implemented on microcomputers.

o   It is extensible through the open-endedness of its module libraries.

An increasing number of reference and expository books and articles are being published about Modula-2. The original language specification can be found in Niklaus Wirth's book <u>Programming In Modula-2</u> published by Springer Verlag (New York, 1985).

Audience. This book is a comprehensive text and reference on the Modula-2 language. It is suitable for use by professional software developers, students and hobbyists.

The book assumes the reader has some fundamental understanding of the nature of computers and computer programming.

Generality. At the time of writing there are four or five commercially obtainable implementations of the Modula-2 language. As with almost all programming languages, implementations differ in small but important respects. In the body of the book, care has been taken to remark on implementation dependencies where appropriate.

The authors have used the Logitech implementation of Modula-2 which runs on the IBM PC to test all examples appearing in the book. References and comments regarding other implementations are found in Appendix I.

Organization of the Material. The book has four parts that describe: values and data structures, actions, the system interface, and supplementary material respectively. The following four paragraphs provide a brief summary of each part.

Part I contains an introductory chapter that enables a reader to run simple Modula-2 programs. Chapter 2 begins the systematic, rigorous presentation of the language. It describes the basic types of values; Chapter 3 explains the method of declaring constants, types and variables; Chapters 4 and 5 present the static and dynamic data structuring facilities of the language. In summary, Part 1 deals with the passive elements of the language.

Part II which consists of Chapters 6 through 11, describes the ways of expressing actions in Modula-2. Following an overview in Chapter 6, Chapters 7 through 10 explain increasingly higher-level logical units namely, statements, procedures, coroutines and modules. Chapter 11 describes how to use and extend the module services that perform input-output operations.

Part III is called "The System Interface" and has but one chapter -- Chapter 12. It describes how to directly access and control the computer's resources. The tools described are therefore "low-level" and their presence is the reason Modula-2 is suitable for all varieties of programming tasks.

Part IV contains supplementary material. As well as the usual reference material found in most programming books, it contains a number of appendixes that we believe are useful to a wide audience. Specifically, Appendix D has source code listings for a number of modules developed and used frequently by the authors. Appendix E contains the source code for building a library of graphic processing services. Appendixes F and G discuss principles of software design and programming style respectively. Pascal programmers will find Appendix H particularly helpful as it summarizes the salient differences between Modula-2 and Pascal. Finally, Appendix I discusses differences in implementations of the language.

Use as a Reference. The authors believe this book to be the most complete and comprehensive book on Modula-2 yet published. The organization of the material is such that all material on a topic is found in one place. The index is extensive with numerous cross references. For example, information about reading a character of data is indexed under "input", "CHAR", and "Read". The appendixes provide extensive reference material for the serious programmer.

Use as a Text. The number of programming courses that use Modula-2 is increasing rapidly. As an aid to learning, the book has several features that greatly assist both the student and the instructor.

Perhaps of most importance is the number and quality of the examples used to illustrate how to program in Modula-2. Examples are chosen to illustrate each new idea in the simplest way. Explanations are extensive.

Each chapter begins with a series of questions to be answered and concludes with a summary of the chapter's information.

Topics are presented in a natural sequence which allows each chapter to build on the ideas developed previously. This permits the material to be studied in a systematic, orderly way.

Programming style is considered to be very important by the authors. Many guidelines are given throughout the book and a compendium of these recommendations is found in Appendix G.

The book includes several hundred exercise and programming problems. Each chapter contains questions that are pertinent to the material covered.

Software Availability. The book contains an extensive number of programs that may be of use to the reader. Of particular value is the source code for the modules listed in Appendixes D and E. The authors will be happy to provide the source code in machine readable form on a floppy disk that can be read by the MS-DOS operating system version 2.0 or higher. To obtain this diskette, send a check or money order for $10.00 payable to MFAM Limited to: Dr. John B. Moore, Department of Management Sciences, University of Waterloo, Waterloo, Ontario, Canada, N2L 3G1. Make sure to include your return address!

Acknowledgments. We would like to thank Kay Harrison and Trenny Cook for their assistance in entering the text material. Roger Watt was once again helpful in solving some of the special formatting problems not automatically taken care of by the GML word processor.

The text of the book uses Kosmos-12 font; examples appear in monowidth Elite-12 font.

We have tested and run the example programs. For any errors found -- and there are always some -- we accept responsibility and apologize.

Modula-2 is a fine language. Good luck and good programming.

John B. Moore   Waterloo Ontario.
Kenneth N. McKay   Canada

CHAPTER 1

GETTING STARTED

Questions Answered In This Chapter

1. What is the Modula-2 programming language?

2. What are the essentials needed to begin programming in Modula-2?

3. How is the material in the book organized?

This chapter provides an introduction to programming in the Modula-2 language. It provides enough information to write simple Modula-2 programs. For the reader who is already familiar with another programming language, references are given to the sections which contain details on each topic. The chapter concludes with a brief overview of the material in the rest of the book.

1.1 Modula-2

Modula-2 is one of many hundreds of programming languages. Each is a vehicle for specifying a set of instructions to be followed by a computer. Computer languages differ in many ways. Some are general purpose, some special purpose; some are high level (English like), some low level (symbolic); some free-form, some highly formatted; some have large numbers of nouns and verbs, others few; some are complex, while others are simple; some are old, others are recent inventions. As well, languages differ in many technical ways, an example being whether a language is compiled or interpreted.

Modula-2 is a very modern, general-purpose language. It has a small vocabulary and contains relatively few sentence structures. It allows a programmer to work both at a high level (ignore computer-dependent details) and/or to manipulate the inner workings of a particular machine.

Modula-2 was designed by Niklaus Wirth. Its use has grown tremendously since becoming commercially available. The main reasons for its success are:

o It is a "small" language. This means it can be implemented completely and efficiently on a wide variety of microcomputers.

o Although a high-level language, it contains facilities for low level programming. Thus it may be the only language needed to perform all programming tasks.

o It has consistent and simple rules of syntax (grammar and punctuation) and is therefore easy to learn.

o Its module concept makes it an ideal language for developing large computer applications which must be worked on by more than one person. The module concept has rigorous requirements for interfacing modules. Thus forcing clear, unambiguous communication among project personnel.

Modula-2 is not without its detractors. In the same way that we all have our favorite cars, football teams, and authors, programmers have their favorite languages. Fans of APL (a powerful, unstructured, very cryptic language), for example would not be easily convinced to switch to Modula-2.

Computer languages are constantly evolving. New ones appear; old ones disappear; changes are made in the ones which continue. Modula-2 results from thirty years of evolutionary activity. It will improve over time. It is already a fine programming language.

Modula-2 Implementations

When an architect designs a building, many small details are left to the drafters. Similarly, the designer of a programming language may not include specific details about some aspects of the language. This allows implementors of the language to accommodate peculiarities of hardware and exercise discretionary judgment. Such is the case with Modula-2.

Modula-2 has several implementations (see Appendix H) which run on a variety of machines in different software environments. Although they all support the language definition described in Wirth's book Programming In Modula-2, they differ in small but important ways. The largest variations occur in the library of routines which perform input and output operations.

The authors have acquired and used four different implementations of the language during the preparation of this book. We have used the implementation of Modula-2 developed and sold by Logitech Inc. for the examples shown in the book. Where important differences in implementations exist, we have indicated this fact. The documentation describing your implementation is therefore an important complement to the material which follows.

1.2   Example 1

Chapters 2 through 12 provide a systematic and rigorous presentation of programming in Modula-2. The purpose of this section and the next is to give you sufficient information to begin programming in Modula-2. This is done using two examples. The first example simply prints the word "Hello" on the computer screen. The second calculates several values of a numeric expression.

   We assume the reader has some minimal understanding of how computers are used to solve problems. In particular the five step problem-solving procedure is:

1. Define the problem. This includes describing the inputs and the corresponding outputs.

2. Develop an algorithm. You must determine a procedure for solving the problem. That is, how the outputs are produced from the inputs.

3. Translate the algorithm into a language the computer understands. The result is called a computer program.

4. Enter the program. This is done using a program called an editor. Each line in the program is entered via the keyboard under the editor's control The collection of lines is stored in a computer file called a source program.

5. Run the program. This involves two steps -- compilation followed by execution. During the compile phase, the statements in the source program are translated into their machine language (ones and zeros) equivalent by the compiler program. The result is called the object program. During the execute phase, the instructions in the object form of the program are executed and the output produced.

The problem is to print the word "Hello" on the computer screen. There are therefore no inputs, only the output "Hello". The algorithm has one step, namely, print the word "Hello". Shown next is a complete Modula-2 program to solve the problem. Comments follow the program.

```
MODULE PrintHello;

(* This program prints the word "Hello"
   on the standard output device
 *)

FROM InOut IMPORT WriteString, WriteLn;

BEGIN
    WriteString('Hello');
    WriteLn;
END PrintHello.
```

Comments.

1. This collection of lines is called a program module. A program module begins with a module header and ends with the module name and a period.

   The module header consists of the reserved word "MODULE" followed by the module name. In the example, the module header is:

   ```
   MODULE PrintHello;
   ```

   The semicolon, at the end of the header, separates the header from the rest of the module. Notice that the module ends with the module name followed by a period.

2. The three lines following the module header are

   ```
   (* This program prints the word "Hello"
      on the standard output device
   *)
   ```

   As you might have gathered, these lines represent a comment. In Modula-2 anecdotal information is enclosed within a matching "(*" and "*)" pair. Comments are important aids to understanding and should be included in all but the most trivial programs.

   When a comment occupies more than one line, it is a good idea to vertically align the comment delimiters as shown in the example. The presence or absence of comments has no effect on what the program does.

3. The rest of the module contains an import and a block. The example contains one import. It is

   ```
   FROM InOut IMPORT WriteString, WriteLn;
   ```

   It says "Import (bring in and make available) the procedures WriteString and WriteLn (pronounced "write line") from the library module called InOut.

   Each implementation of Modula-2 includes a library of modules containing commonly used routines. InOut is a module which is found in every implementation of Modula-2. It contains many of the basic tools necessary to perform input and output. Appendix C describes the standard library modules and their contents. Chapter 10 explains how to create your own library modules.

4. The form of an import is:

   ```
   FROM modulename IMPORT objectlist
   ```

"FROM" and "IMPORT" are <u>reserved</u> <u>words</u>. A reserved word cannot be used for any other purpose.

A semicolon separates the imports from the block.

5. In the example the <u>block</u> consists of the following four lines.

```
    BEGIN
        WriteString('Hello');
        WriteLn;
    END PrintHello.
```

Blocks usually have one or more <u>declarations</u> preceding the reserved word BEGIN. In this first example, no declarations are needed.

The four lines shown specify the actions performed by the program module and are often called the <u>body</u> of the module.

6. The program body contains the pair of statements

```
        WriteString('Hello');
        WriteLn;
```

"WriteString('Hello')" causes the five characters "Hello" to be sent to the standard output device. On most computers, this is the screen associated with the microcomputer or terminal.

The procedure "WriteLn" sends an end-of-line character to the output device. This causes any subsequent output to start on the following line. WriteLn is normally invoked after each line of output has been constructed.

A semicolon separates statements in a sequence. In the lines above the semicolon between the procedure calls to WriteString and WriteLn is necessary; the one following WriteLn is not, because "END" is not a statement -- it delimits the end of the block. No trouble arises if you do put a semicolon at the end of each statement.

Two Unanswered Questions

Case Sensitivity. Modula-2 is case sensitive. This means upper- and lowercase letters are <u>not</u> equivalent. Thus "MODULE" cannot be written as "Module"; "Writeln" is not the same as "WriteLn" and "end" is not a reserved word.

You will quickly find -- unless you are a great typist with an excellent memory -- that case sensitivity is frequently a frustration. Consequently, the authors have provided in Appendix D a program called CaseFix, which we use all the time. CaseFix recognizes all of Modula's reserved words and standard identifiers and puts them in the correct case. It further assumes the first instance of any nonstandard identifier is the correct form and converts all subsequent occurrences of that spelling to the same form! Additional details are found in the CaseFix listing.

Style. How you say something is often as important as what is said. In the field of computer programming, the form may be as important as the content as an aid to understanding. Good programs have well-defined structures, are clear, concise, and understandable as well as logically correct. These attributes constitute good programming style. Throughout this book, style guidelines are provided. Appendix F contains a compendium of the style guidelines found in the body of the book.

Aside from comments, two important style principles illustrated in the first example are:

1. Use blank lines and spaces liberally to separate program components. This helps to make the program structure visible. The lines below show the example program written without any excess blanks. It works identically to the one which used good style.

```
MODULE PrintHello;FROM InOut IMPORT WriteString,WriteLn;
BEGIN WriteString("HELLO");WriteLn END PrintHello.
```

2. Use consistent rules of vertical alignment and indentation. In a program module, vertically align the words MODULE, FROM, BEGIN and END. Indent and vertically align the statements in the module body.

1.3 Example 2

The Problem. Calculate and display values of the expression $x/(x-3)$ for $x=0,1,2,...,10$. Ignore any remainder in the division.

Analysis. We are to take each of the eleven different values of x and for each compute the value of the expression $x/(x-3)$. We note that the division is undefined when $x=3$ and therefore an appropriate message should be printed when this situation occurs. Although a brute force algorithm giving specific instructions as to what to do with each value of x could be used, a shorter and more flexible algorithm which employs a looping or iterative approach is preferable. It is shown next.

```
.1 Set x = 0
.2 While x <= 10
        .1 Display the value of x
        .2 If x = 3 then
                .1 Print "the division is undefined"
        Otherwise
                .1 Calculate y using the formula
                .2 Display the value of y
        .3 Add 1 to x
```

Following is a program module to solve the problem. The new ideas illustrated include: variable declarations, numeric processing and output, use of assignment, WHILE and IF statements. Further comments follow the program.

```
MODULE Tabulate;

(* This program tabulates values of the expression x / (x-3)
   for x = 0, x = 1, x = 2, ... , x = 10
*)

FROM InOut IMPORT WriteString, WriteLn, WriteInt;

VAR
    X : INTEGER;
    Y : INTEGER; (* the value of the expression *)

BEGIN
    X := 0;                          (* initialize the value of X *)
    WHILE X <= 10 DO
        WriteInt(X, 7);              (* display the value of x *)
        IF X = 3 THEN
            WriteString('   division is undefined ');
        ELSE
            Y := X DIV (X - 3); (* calc the expression value *)
            WriteInt(Y, 7);
            END; (* IF *)
        WriteLn;                     (* terminate the line *)
        X := X + 1;   INC(X);        (* increment X *)
        END; (* WHILE *)
END Tabulate.
```

When the program is executed, the following eleven lines of output are displayed.

```
     0        0
     1        0
     2       -2
     3    division is undefined
     4        4
     5        2
     6        2
     7        1
     8        1
     9        1
    10        1
```

Comments.

1. The program module imports the WriteInt procedure from InOut along with WriteString and WriteLn. WriteInt is used to display a single INTEGER value.

2. The block contains a declaration part as well as a body. The lines

```
VAR
    X : INTEGER;
    Y : INTEGER; (* the value of the expression *)
```

constitute the declaration part of the block and declare the identifiers X and Y to be variables which can be assigned an INTEGER value. X and Y are said to be INTEGER variables. Every variable used in a program must have its type declared in a variable declaration. A variable declaration has the form shown in the <u>syntax</u> <u>diagram</u> of Figue 1.1.

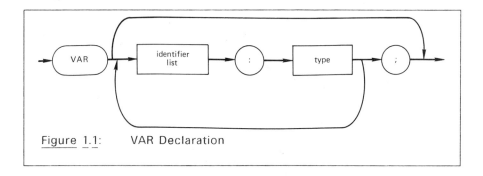

Figure 1.1:   VAR Declaration

A syntax diagram depicts valid sequences of programming language entities. That is, it defines the grammar of the language. Allowed sequences are those which can be obtained by tracing a path through the diagram. Thus a valid VAR declaration is one which contains the reserved word VAR followed by an identifier list, a colon and a type. The return arrow in the diagram means that a type can be followed by a semicolon and another list-colon-type triple. In syntax diagrams, objects enclosed in ellipses or circles must be written exactly as shown. Those without an enclosure such as "identifier list" in the example have their meanings explained elsewhere. An identifier list for instance can be described by the syntax diagram of Figure 1.2.

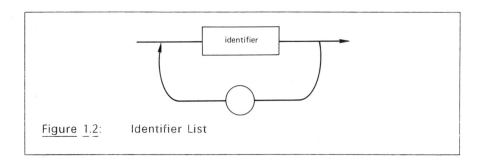

Figure 1.2:   Identifier List

The VAR syntax diagrams thus indicate that the three line declaration could be replaced by the following equivalent declaration.

```
VAR  X, Y : INTEGER
```

We recommend the form used in the example. Syntax diagrams for the complete Modula-2 language are found in Appendix B.

VAR declarations are described fully in Section 3.4.

3. The body of the module contains two assignment statements, one WHILE statement, one IF statement and four procedure calls. We consider each in turn.

a) The assignment statement "X := 0" causes the value zero to be assigned to the variable X. The pair of characters ":=" is called the <u>assignment</u> <u>operator</u> and means "is given the value of". The value assigned must be compatible with the variable appearing on the left of the assignment operation. The statement "X := 2.5" for instance is invalid because 2.5 is a REAL value and X is an INTEGER variable. An INTEGER value does not contain a decimal point.

The other assignment statement namely "Y := X DIV (X-3)" shows that the assigned value can be constructed by an expression. DIV is the division operator used with INTEGER or CARDINAL (nonnegative whole numbers) values.

Full details of the assignment statement can be found in Chapter 7. The basic types and operations which can be performed with whole numbers are described in the next chapter.

b) A WHILE statement has the form

```
WHILE condition DO
    statement sequence
END
```

The condition is evaluated prior to each execution of the statement sequence. If the condition is true, the statement sequence is executed. When the condition is false, execution continues with the statement following the WHILE statement. The condition tested is "X <= 10". The character pair "<=" means less-than-or-equal-to and it is one of the six <u>relational</u> <u>operators</u>. The other relational operators and their meanings are "<" (less than), "=" (equals), ">" (greater than), ">=" (greater-than-or-equal-to) and either "<>"" or "#" (not equal). When inserted between a pair of compatible values, a relational operator creates an expression which is either true or false.

The statement sequence which is repeatedly executed contains the following four statements.

```
WriteInt(X, 7);            (* display the value of x *)
IF X = 3 THEN
    WriteString('   division is undefined ');
ELSE
    Y := X DIV (X - 3); (* calc the expression's value *)
    WriteInt(Y, 7);
    END; (* IF *)
WriteLn;                   (* terminate the line *)
X := X + 1;                (* increment X *)
```

The WHILE statement is an example of a compound statement. A compound statement contains one or more imbedded statement sequences and with one exception (the REPEAT statement) is terminated by the reserved word "END". Complete information about the WHILE statement and the three other looping statements (LOOP, REPEAT, and FOR) is found in Sections 7.6 through 7.9.

c) The body of the WHILE loop contains the IF statement below.

```
IF X = 3 THEN
    WriteString('   division is undefined ');
ELSE
    Y := X DIV (X - 3); (* calc the expression's value *)
    WriteInt(Y, 7);
    END; (* IF *)
```

IF is also a compound statement. It contains two statement sequences -- one which is executed if the condition is true; the other if the condition is false. In either case execution subsequently continues with the statement following the END which terminates the IF statement.

The IF statement is described in detail along with the other conditional execution statement (the CASE statement) in Sections 7.4 and 7.5.

4. The WriteInt procedure called "WriteInt(X,7) displays one INTEGER value. In the example the statement "WriteInt(X,7)" causes the value of X to be displayed in the next seven characters sent to the output device. The value is right justified meaning it is moved as far to the right as possible.

The InOut module contains procedures for displaying three of the basic types of values (INTEGER, CARDINAL, and CHAR). These are described in Chapter 3. Appendix C contains a complete description of the contents of InOut.

Style. The example program illustrates recommended rules of statement indentation in compound statements. In the forms below, the start of each statement in the statement sequence should be vertically aligned.

```
BEGIN                WHILE condition DO      IF condition THEN
    statements           statements              statements
END                  END                     ELSE
                                                 statements
                                             END
```

If a compound statement contains a lengthy statement sequence, you may find it helpful to append a comment to its END indicating the type of compound statement that is being terminated as was done in the example. With proper indentation however, this is unnecessary.

Three Additional Points

1. Input statements. A value can be assigned to a variable at execution time by obtaining the value from an input device such as a keyboard. This is accomplished using one of the Read procedures which are described in Section 3.6.

2. Terminating program execution. The Modula-2 language does not have a "stop" statement. Instead program execution automatically terminates when the end of the module body is reached. If it is necessary to terminate execution at some other point, the standard procedure called HALT can be invoked. Standard procedures unlike library procedures do not need to be IMPORTed. A list of the standard procedures is found in Appendix A.

3. Quotes. A string of characters may be enclosed in either single quotes or double quotes. This permits the non-enclosing character to be part of the character string. An example is "It's" in which the single quote is one of the four characters in the string.

1.4   The Rest of This Book

A glance at the table of contents shows the book contains four major parts.

   Part I consists of Chapters 1 through 5. Aside from Chapter 1 which gives you enough information to get you going, Part I focuses on the passive elements of the language. These include: the basic types of values (Chapter 2); constant, type and variable declarations (Chapter 3); named collections of data (Chapter 4); and dynamic data structures (Chapter 5).

   Part II provides a comprehensive description of active elements in the language. The concepts are introduced in Chapter 6. Subsequently, we build toward larger and larger logical units. Specifically, the sequence is statements (Chapter 7), procedures (Chapter 8), processes (Chapter 9) and modules (Chapter 10). Chapter 11 describes the library modules used for input and output operations.

Part III is entitled "The System Interface". This chapter is of interest to those who must directly interface with the computer hardware. Chapter 12 describes memory management and low-level device handling.

Part IV contains helpful supplementary material often found in appendices. Of special interest are Appendices D and H. The former contains listings of modules developed and used by the authors. Appendix H is of particular interest to those who already know the Pascal programming language. It summarizes the major differences between Pascal and Modula-2.

1.5 Summary

1. A Modula-2 program has the following typical form.

```
MODULE name;
FROM name IMPORT list;
declarations
BEGIN
    statement sequence
END name.
```

A module body consists of BEGIN-statement sequence-END. A block comprises the declarations and body.

2. Each Modula-2 implementation comes with a number of library modules for performing common tasks such as input-output. These modules are not part of the language per se but there is a consensus among implementors as to what a standard library should contain. All input-output is performed by imported procedures.

3. Modula-2 contains a total of forty reserved words. They cannot be redefined to have another meaning. They are:

AND	ELSIF	LOOP	REPEAT
ARRAY	END	MOD	RETURN
BEGIN	EXIT	MODULE	SET
BY	EXPORT	NOT	THEN
CASE	FOR	OF	TO
CONST	FROM	OR	TYPE
DEFINITION	IF	POINTER	UNTIL
DIV	IMPLEMENTATION	PROCEDURE	VAR
DO	IMPORT	QUALIFIED	WHILE
ELSE	IN	RECORD	WITH

The reserved words used in this chapter are MODULE, FROM, IMPORT, VAR, BEGIN, WHILE, DO, IF, THEN, ELSE, END.

4. All identifiers in Modula-2 are case sensitive.

5. Modula-2 contains a number of standard procedures as distinct from library procedures. Standard procedures are part of the language and do not need to be imported. The standard procedure mentioned in this chapter is HALT. A complete list is found in Appendix A.

6. Statements are either simple or compound. Two simple statements are the assignment statement and the procedure call. The compound statements used are the WHILE statement and the IF statement. Each compound statement except REPEAT is terminated by an END.

7. The operators used were the assignment operator ":=", relational operators such as "<=" and the arithmetic operators, +, − and DIV.

8. Punctuation symbols used include: the period to terminate a module; a semicolon to separate the parts of a module and successive statements; a comma to separate items in a list.

9. Syntax diagrams concisely describe the valid sequences of constructs in a language. The complete syntax of Modula-2 is described in Appendix B.

10. Programming style is very important. Elements of good programming style include the liberal use of comments enclosed in "(*" and "*)" pairs; ample blank space; consistent indentation and alignment; and meaningful identifiers.

1.6   Exercises and Programming Problems

1. Exercise. Modify the algorithm used in the second example to process the following values of x:

   a) X = 0, 2, 4, 6, 8, 10

   b) X = −1, 4, 9 , 14, 19

   c) X = −10, −9, −8, ... , 9, 10

   d) X = 100, 99. 98, ... , 2. 1

2. Exercise. Suppose the formula used for y in the example problem is changed. Write an assignment statement to assign y each of the following expressions in x.

   a) $x^3 - x$

   b) $14(x - 7)$

c) $5x^5 + 4x^4 + 3x^3 + 2x^2 + x + 8$

3. Exercise. The following lines contain a perfectly valid Modula-2 program. Reformat them to demonstrate good programming style and predict the output when the program is run. Enter and run the program to verify your answer.

```
MODULE DUMBSTYLE;FROM InOut IMPORT WriteInt;VAR MOM,
DAD:INTEGER;BEGIN MOM:=5;DAD:=25;WHILE MOM<=
DAD DO MOM := MOM + MOM END;WriteInt(
MOM,8) END DUMBSTYLE.
```

4. Write a Modula-2 program to calculate the sum of 127 and 584.

5. Tabulate (calculate and print) the values of

$$y = 3x^2 - 2x + 7$$
$$\text{for } x = 1, 3, 5, \ldots, 21$$

6. In the Fibonacci sequence of numbers 1, 1, 2, 3, 5, 8, ..., each term after the first two is obtained by adding the values of the two previous terms. Write a program to calculate and display the first fifteen terms in the Fibonacci sequence.

7. Write a program to print your name in large letters. Use a sequence of seven 'WriteString's and 'WriteLn's. An example is shown below.

```
*****     *****     *   *     *     *
    *     *   *     *   *     *     *
    *     *   *     *   *     **    *
    *     *   *     *****     * *   *
    *     *   *     *   *     *  * *
*   *     *   *     *   *     *   **
***       *****     *   *     *    *
```

CHAPTER 2

VALUES IN MODULA-2

Questions Answered In This Chapter

1. What five basic types of values can be used in Modula-2? How are they defined and manipulated?

2. How can you define your own kinds of values? What operations can be performed with them?

3. When is it desirable to name and define a subrange of values as a distinguishable entity? How is this done?

2.1 Introduction

This chapter begins the systematic description of the Modula-2 language. The simplest object which is manipulated by statements in a program is a single value. In Modula-2 there are three kinds of essentially different values – numbers, characters and boolean (true-false) values. For reasons to be found in the next section three types of numbers are provided, CARDINAL, INTEGER and REAL. Together with the CHAR (character) and BOOLEAN types, they make up the five basic types of scalar values.

Modula-2 allows you to define your own scalar types. They are called enumerated types because you must enumerate (exhaustively list) all the values in the type. Enumerated types are described in Section 2.10.

Modula-2 also allows you to define a type which is a subrange of a type. Subranges are described in Section 2.11.

When discussing any type, four questions should be asked:

1. What are the values belonging to the type?

2. What are the operations which can be performed with values of the type?

3. How do you convert values of the type to equivalent values of another type?

4. What means are available for performing input and output operations with values of a given type?

In this chapter we answer these questions for the five basic types, enumerated types and subranges in Modula-2. The chapter concludes with brief descriptions of the other types of objects in Modula-2. These are data structures, pointers and the PROC (procedure) type.

2.2 Numbers and Numeric Processing

There are three predefined types of numbers in Modula-2: INTEGER, CARDINAL and REAL. Each is a basic type.

Before proceeding, you might ask why are there three kinds of numbers – won't one do? The basic reason is that computers store numbers with and without decimal points in two fundamentally different ways. By giving you the programmer control over which type of number to use, you can exercise some control over the number of significant digits in a number and the speed of operations.

2.3 Integers

Concepts

The types INTEGER and CARDINAL are subsets of the set of whole numbers. In particular the type INTEGER includes the values

    MinInt, MinInt+1, ..., -1,0,+1, ... MaxInt-1, MaxInt

where the values of MinInt and MaxInt represent the expressions MIN(INTEGER) and MAX(INTEGER) respectively. The functions MIN and MAX are used to obtain the smallest and largest values of a type. On many microcomputers MIN(INTEGER) is -32,768 and MAX(INTEGER) is 32767. Some implementations of the language include a LONGINT type that allows a larger range of integers to be used.

The type CARDINAL has the values

    0,1,2, ..., MaxCard

where MaxCard represents the expression MAX(CARDINAL). On most microcomputers MAX(CARDINAL) is 65,535. MIN(CARDINAL) is always zero.

MinInt, MaxInt and MaxCard are not standard Modula-2 identifiers. They can be defined as CONSTants (see Section 3.2) if you wish.

The types INTEGER and CARDINAL overlap. Values in range 0 through MaxInt are members of both the INTEGER and CARDINAL types. The word "integer" will be used when a remark applies to both INTEGER and CARDINAL values. The foregoing ideas are summarized in Figure 2.1.

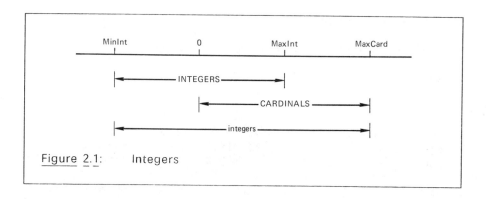

Figure 2.1:   Integers

Why do we have CARDINAL values? Each INTEGER value occupies sixteen bits (ones and zeros) of memory. Since one bit must be used for the sign, there are only fifteen bits available to represent the magnitude of the number. The largest magnitude is 32767. If you can guarantee that no negative values are needed, the sign bit can be used in representing the magnitude. This is the rationale for having CARDINAL numbers – the upper limit MaxCard is effectively twice that of MaxInt. Details of the representation of INTEGER and CARDINAL values are found in the document describing your implementation of the language.

Most operations are identical for both INTEGER and CARDINAL values, that is "integers". If there is a difference, either INTEGER or CARDINAL will be explicitly used. When writing integers, an optional sign may immediately precede the first digit. No decimal is used nor are commas used to separate groups of three digits. Examples of valid integers are:

+123   –   both INTEGER and CARDINAL

-4096   –   INTEGER only

+0   –   both INTEGER and CARDINAL

40000   –   CARDINAL only (if value is greater than MaxInt)

Invalid integers are

4,096   –   comma not permitted

-25.   –   decimal point means noninteger

-200000 –   less than MinInt

99999   –   greater than MaxCard

Operations with Integers

Five basic operations can be performed with integers:

Operation	Symbol	Example
addition	+	$-4 + 7$ $= 3$
subtraction	–	$22 - 30$ $= -8$
multiplication	*	$12321 * 3 = 36963$
division	DIV	17 DIV 3 $= 5$ (no round off)
modulus	MOD	17 MOD 3 $= 2$ (remainder)

DIV and MOD are reserved words. Note that DIV truncates any remainder. MOD is not defined for negative values. In general, for any pair of positive integers A and B

$$A = (A \text{ DIV } B) * B + (A \text{ MOD } B)$$

The priorities are those of conventional mathematics. From highest to lowest these are:

1. Function evaluation
2. Parentheses (inside to outside)
3. Multiplication and Division equal (left to right)
4. Addition and Subtraction equal (left to right)

Standard Procedures

The following predefined procedures operate on or produce an integer value. They do not need to be imported. In the following "i" denotes an INTEGER or CARDINAL and "c" denotes a CARDINAL value.

ODD(i)   returns the BOOLEAN value TRUE if i is odd; that is if (i MOD 2) equals 1. Otherwise the function value is FALSE.

ORD(c)   returns c. Some implementations permit ORD(i) where i is INTEGER. In such cases, ORD(i) is i.

DEC(i)   a procedure which executes the statement i := i – 1. Note that DEC (–MaxInt) is an error.

INC(i)   a procedure which executes the statement i := i + 1. Note that INC(MaxCard) is an error.

INC(i,n)   executes the statement i := i + n where n is a positive or negative integer. The result must be in the range of integers.

MAX(type)   returns the largest value of the type.

MIN(type)   returns the smallest value of the type.

VAL(type, c) The VAL procedure can also be used with integers. Given a type and a cardinal value c, it returns the c'th value in the given type. For example,

VAL(CARDINAL, 7) = 7

VAL(INTEGER, 7) = 7

VAL(INTEGER,-7) = -7

Standard Output of Integers

The module InOut contains the procedures WriteCard and WriteInt for displaying integer values. In particular:

WriteCard(c,n) writes the digits of the CARDINAL expression c on the standard Output file (usually the terminal's screen). "n" denotes a nonnegative integer. If n is greater than the number of digits in the integer, blanks are appended to the left so that a total of n characters is written. If n is less than or equal to the digit count, only the digits are written.

WriteInt(i,n) operates identically to WriteCard, except that "i" denotes an INTEGER expression and that a negative sign immediately precedes the first digit if the value of i is less than zero.

Note the following invalid uses of these procedures.

WriteCard(-50,6) –   negative 50 is not a CARDINAL value; use WriteInt

WriteInt(50000,6) –   50000 is not an INTEGER value; use WriteCard

The corresponding input procedures ReadCard and ReadInt are described in Section 3.5. They obtain a value from the input device and assign it to an integer variable.

2.4 REAL Numbers

Concepts

The type REAL includes numbers such as 2.34 which have values between whole numbers and/or which are written with an exponent such as 3.5E+4 which represents a value of 35000.

Constants

REAL values must contain a decimal point. Thus −2.0 is REAL whereas −2 is INTEGER and these values are represented by different bit patterns in the computer. The formal definition of a REAL constant is described by the syntax diagram of Figure 2.2.

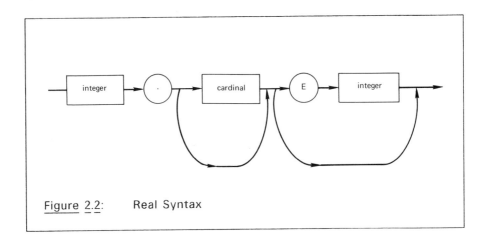

Figure 2.2:   Real Syntax

The syntax diagram shows that a REAL constant consists of an integer followed by a decimal point followed (optionally) by a fractional part and/or an exponent. Examples of valid REALs are

     −123.45   +12.E−5   0.E3

Invalid REAL constants include

     .123   –   no integer preceding the decimal point

     5.E 6   –   blank between "E" and the exponent value

Because a finite amount of memory is used to represent a REAL value (usually 16, 32 or 64 bits on a microcomputer) there are limits to both the number of significant digits in the value and the range of the exponent (power of ten) associated with the value.

   The number of significant digits of a REAL is usually 16.2 (the .2 is due to the use of the binary number system). Some implementations provide a LONGREAL type which effectively doubles the number of significant digits in the value. For those implementations subscribing to the IEEE standard, the range of exponents is between plus and minus 308. That is, the IEEE range of REAL values magnitudes is 2.23E − 308 to 1.79E + 308. Because of these limits, the REAL numbers do <u>not</u> form a continuum. Note the gap around zero in Figure 2.3. The functions MAX and MIN can be used to obtain the largest and smallest REAL values.

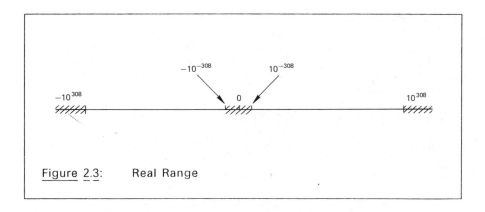

Figure 2.3:   Real Range

Because a finite number of bits represents each REAL value, some fractional values cannot be represented perfectly. For example, in the base 2 number system 1/5 is represented by the following repeating pattern of binary digits:

0.00100110011...

This sequence is terminated after a fixed number of bits which means the stored value is a very good but not a perfect representation of the value one-fifth. Hence small computational errors may be introduced when working with fractional REAL values.

The limit on the precision of a REAL value also means that 1.E20 +1 has a value of 1.E20 because only the most significant digits are kept after any operation.

Defining a REAL constant with more than sixteen digits is an error. Defining or generating an exponent outside the permitted range is likewise an error. For example,

1.E200 * 1.E200   produces an "exponent overflow" message

1.E-200 * 1.E-200   produces an "exponent underflow" message

Operations with REAL Numbers

The four basic arithmetic operations are denoted by + - * and / (for division). For example,

(2.0 * 5. - 3.) / 2. = 3.5

The slash operator must have two REAL operands. For example, 2/3, 2./3, and 2/3. are all invalid. DIV must only be used with INTEGER and CARDINAL operands.

Standard Functions

The absolute value function ABS is the only standard function which performs arithmetic with a REAL value. Because of the possibility of round-off errors, ABS should be used when comparing two REAL values for equality. For example, use

    IF (ABS(x-2.0) < 1.E-10) THEN ...

instead of

    IF (X = 2.0) THEN ...

Although not a part of the language definition, all Modula-2 implementations include a library module called MathLib0 from which the following useful functions can be IMPORTed. The contents of MathLib0 are listed in Appendix C. In all cases but the last, the result is REAL.

    sqrt(r)   –   square root

    exp(r)   –   power of e

    ln(r)   –   natural (base e) logarithm

    sin(r)   –   sine of an angle of r radians

    cos(r)   –   cosine of an angle of r radians

    arctan(r) –   primary angle (in radius) having a tangent value of r

    real(i)   –   returns the INTEGER value as a REAL number

    entier(r) –   returns the whole number part of the parameter as
                       an INTEGER

Standard Output of REAL Values

The module RealInOut contains the procedure WriteReal for displaying REAL values. The format is

    WriteReal(r,n)

where r is a REAL value and n is the number of positions to be used for displaying the value. The result is in exponent notation. For example,

    WriteReal(-1.5, 8)   produces "-1.50E+000".

To display REAL values without exponents, some implementations include a second WriteReal procedure in a module other than InOut.

2.5   Numeric Type Conversions

Integer and REAL values cannot be mixed in the same expression. 2+3. for example, is invalid. Similarly an expression such as −1+50000 is invalid because −1 is INTEGER and 50000 (if greater than MaxInt) is CARDINAL. Modula-2 provides functions for converting a value of one type to its equivalent value in another type. Details follow the diagram.

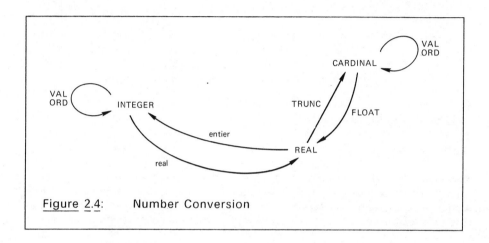

Figure 2.4:   Number Conversion

ORD(i)   produces the CARDINAL value represented by the bit pattern of the value i. For example, ORD (0) = 0, ORD(MaxInt) = MaxInt. Note that ORD(c) is the identity function.

VAL(type,c)

is the inverse of ORD. That is, it produces the c'th value of the given type. With CARDINALs, VAL operates as an identity function. For example, VAL(CARDINAL, 768) is 768. In some implementations, VAL is also an identity function when the first parameter is INTEGER. In general, VAL and ORD are related by the following identity.

```
VAL(type, ORD(value)) = value
```

where "type" is one of INTEGER, CARDINAL, CHAR, BOOLEAN or an enumerated type. (The last three types are described later in this chapter.)

FLOAT(c)   returns the REAL equivalent of the CARDINAL argument c. For example, FLOAT (3) returns 3.0.

TRUNC(r)   returns the CARDINAL value which is obtained by truncating the fractional part of the REAL value r. For example, TRUNC(5.7) = 5 but TRUNC(10.E50) is an error (no equivalent

CARDINAL value). TRUNC (–1.0) is also an error because CARDINAL's are nonnegative.

The functions "real" and "entier" are not standard procedures and must be IMPORTed from MathLib0.

real(i)   returns the REAL equivalent of an INTEGER value. For example, real(–2) is –2.0. Note that FLOAT cannot be used with negative arguments.

entier(r)   "entier" is the French word for "entire" or "whole". It returns the closest INTEGER which is less than or equal to the REAL value "r". For example, entier(–2.5) is –3 (the INTEGER). TRUNC cannot be used if the REAL value is negative.

2.6 Character Values

Concepts

Single characters belong to the type CHAR. Sequences of one or more characters are called strings in Modula-2. A full understanding of strings requires knowledge of arrays (described in Section 4.2). In this section we restrict ourself to the definition and output of string constants.

CHAR Constants

There are 256 values in the type CHAR. The values belong to the ASCII character set and include the upper- and lowercase characters, the decimal digits, and many commonly used characters such as punctuation marks and mathematical operators. The ASCII set is found in Appendix A. A CHAR value is defined by enclosing it in matching quotes – either single or double as in 'A' and "$".

Operations with CHAR

Arithmetic operations with CHAR values are of course meaningless. What does '$' + '/' mean? However, the two standard functions ORD and CHR give the position of a character within the ASCII set and the character at a given position respectively. For example, ORD ('A') is 65, meaning that 'A' occupies position 65 in the <u>collating sequence</u> of ASCII characters. The ORD values of the uppercase letters 'A' through 'Z' are 65 through 90; those of the lowercase letters are 97 through 122 and the digits '0' through '9' are 48 to 57 inclusive. The MIN and MAX functions yield the first and last CHAR values in the collating sequence. Note that ORD(MIN(CHAR)) is 0 and ORD(MAX(CHAR)) is 255.

ORD. Because the ORD values of the digits are consecutive, it is simple to convert any digit character to its equivalent CARDINAL value by subtracting ORD('0') from the ORD of digit. The following program constructs the CARDINAL value 12345 from the digits '1', '2', '3', '4', '5'.

```
MODULE DigitToInteger;

(* This program converts the digits 1 thru 5 into the
   integer 12345
*)
FROM InOut IMPORT WriteCard, WriteLn;

VAR
    Number : CARDINAL;
    Digit  : CHAR;

BEGIN
    Number := 0;
    FOR Digit := '1' TO '5' DO
        Number := 10 * Number + ORD(Digit) - ORD('0');
        END;
    WriteCard(Number,10);
    WriteLn;
END DigitToInteger.
```

CHR. The standard procedure CHR is the inverse of ORD – it returns the character occupying a given position in the collating sequence. For example, because ORD('A') is 65, it follows that CHR(65) is 'A'. More generally ORD(CHR(c))=c for any CARDINAL value c from 0 through 255. CHR is more convenient to use than VAL(CHAR,c) which is functionally equivalent.

CAP. When reading input from a keyboard, logic is often simplified if all letters are converted to uppercase. This is what the standard CAP procedure does. For example, CAP("a") is "A". If the parameter is a nonletter or an uppercase letter, the returned value is the same as the input value.

CHAR Comparisons

When two CHAR values are compared using one of the six relational operators = ,< >, <, >, <=, >=, the ORD values are used to establish the truth of the expression. For example,

  'A' < 'M'   is TRUE because ORD('A') is less than ORD('M')

  ';' > '2'   is TRUE because ORD(';') is greater than ORD('2')

Comparison of strings of characters is discussed in the next subsection.

  In summary, each CHAR value has a unique position in the collating sequence. These ORD values are used when comparing two characters.

Output

Write. The module InOut contains the procedure Write for sending a single character (ch) to the standard output device. "Write" has one argument – a single CHAR value. You can produce the desired number of preceding or trailing blanks by repeated invocations of Write(' ').

WriteLn. The procedure WriteLn is imported from InOut. It sends a special end-of-line character to the output device. This has the effect of terminating the current line so that the next item displayed starts at the beginning of the following line. InOut exports the character constant "EOL" (end-of-line). Thus if EOL is imported, Write(EOL) is equivalent to WriteLn.

2.7   String Constants

Definitions

A string constant is a sequence of one or more characters enclosed in either single or double quotes. The number of characters in the string is called the <u>string length</u>. The formal syntax is given in Figure 2.5.

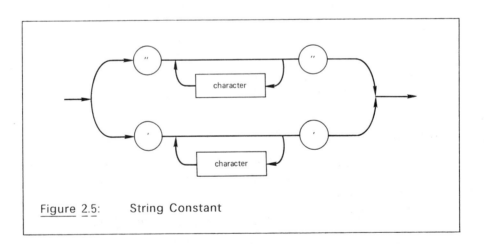

Figure 2.5:   String Constant

Some examples are:

      'This is a string constant'

      "You can't define a null string" –   the single quote is part of
                  the constant

      '"' –   the constant contains the double quote as its only character

The third example is an example of a string of length 1. Strings of length 1 are compatible with the type CHAR.

String constants are not a basic type like INTEGER or REAL. They do have an implicit type however. Specifically a string constant of length N has the type

```
ARRAY [0 .. N-1] OF CHAR
```

An array is an ordered sequence of values of the same type. Arrays are discussed fully in Chapter 4. Strings are therefore amenable to all the operations which can be done with arrays.

Operations

The Modula-2 language does not contain any operators for manipulating strings. However, a Strings module is supplied with most implementations of the language. It contains procedures for assigning, inserting, deleting, scanning, concatenating and comparing strings. Examples are found in Chapter 4.

Output

WriteString(string). The InOut module contains the procedure WriteString for sending a string to the standard output device. An example is

```
WriteString("This will be output")
```

No preceding or trailing blanks are appended to the output.

2.8   BOOLEAN Values

Concepts

The two BOOLEAN values are TRUE and FALSE. As constants, they can be used to state the presence or absence of a given condition as in:

```
LastRecord := FALSE
```

BOOLEAN values arise each time one of the relational operators is used. The expression "2 < 3" for example, has a value of TRUE.

Operations

The operators NOT, AND, & and OR require BOOLEAN operands and produce BOOLEAN values. AND and & are synonyms. In the following, 'b' denotes a BOOLEAN value.

NOT (b)   reverses the value of b. NOT (TRUE) is FALSE; NOT (FALSE) is TRUE.

b AND b   has a value of TRUE only if both operands are individually true; otherwise the result is FALSE.

b OR b   has a value of TRUE if either or both operands are individually true. The expression is FALSE only when both operands are FALSE.

Of the three logical operators, NOT has the highest priority; AND the second highest and OR the lowest. Thus, any or all pairs of parentheses in the following expression could be omitted without affecting the value of the expression. The number below each operator indicates the order of evaluation and shows that for operators of equal priority, the evaluation proceeds left to right.

```
( ( ( (NOT b) AND b) OR (NOT b) ) OR b)

        1       3        4    2        5
```

In the absence of parentheses the priority of Modula-2 operators is as summarized in the following table. Operators within the same level have equal priorities and are processed left to right. The IN operator (used to test membership in a set) is discussed in Chapter 4.

Operator Priorities – Highest to Lowest

1. Prefix Operators

   NOT, unary + , unary -

2. Multiplication Operators

   *, DIV, /, MOD, AND, &

3. Addition Operators

   +, -, OR

4. Relational Operators

   <, >, =, #, < >, <=, >=, IN

DeMorgan's Laws. Two common identities define equivalent BOOLEAN expressions. They are known as DeMorgan's Laws and are:

```
NOT (b1 AND b2) = NOT b1 OR  NOT b2
NOT (b1 OR b1)  = NOT b1 AND NOT b2
```

Conditional Evaluation. The right operand of the AND and OR operators is not evaluated if the truth of the expression can be established from the value of the left operand. In particular, the BOOLEAN expression represented by "b" in the next two expressions is not evaluated.

```
FALSE AND b
TRUE OR b
```

This makes programming easier because you can bypass evaluation of an expression which would otherwise cause an execution time error. Consider

```
WHILE (X <> 0) AND ((1000 DIV X) >= 7) DO
```

Observe that when X has a value of zero, evaluation of the right operand would cause an execution time error (division by zero). Because of conditional evaluation however, X = 0 means the left operand of AND is FALSE and hence the right operand is not evaluated.

Without conditional evaluation, the required logic could still be programmed. One approach is shown next. It employs a LOOP statement which is described in Chapter 7.

```
LOOP
     IF X = 0 THEN
         EXIT
         END;
     IF 1000 DIV X < 7 THEN
         EXIT
         END;
     .
     .
END (*LOOP*)
```

Of course, the smart reader will realize the original condition could be rewritten to avoid the potential division by zero using

```
WHILE (X <> 0) AND (1000 > (7 * X ))   DO
```

An even smarter reader will realize this is equivalent only if it can be assumed X is nonnegative!

Relational Operators. TRUE and FALSE can be compared using any of the relational operators, such as "<". This is because FALSE and TRUE are defined to have ORD values of 0 and 1 respectively. Put another way, MIN(BOOLEAN) is FALSE; MAX(BOOLEAN) is TRUE. That is:

```
ORD(FALSE) = 0  and  VAL(BOOLEAN, 0) = FALSE
ORD(TRUE)  = 1  and  VAL(BOOLEAN, 1) = TRUE
```

Although two BOOLEAN expressions can be compared using a relational operator, in general, this is not recommended. Consider for example the statement fragment

```
IF b1 < b2 THEN
```

The condition is TRUE only if b1 is FALSE and b2 is TRUE. A more meaningful expression is

```
IF (b1 = FALSE) AND (b2 = TRUE) THEN
```

It would be better to avoid the use of relational operators completely as in

```
IF NOT b1 AND b2 THEN
```

Output. The definition of Modula-2 does not include procedures such as ReadBoolean and WriteBoolean for reading and writing BOOLEAN values. Because there are only two values, TRUE and FALSE, it is a simple matter to either create an appropriate procedure (see Chapter 8) or use a statement of the following form:

```
IF b THEN
    WriteString ('TRUE')
ELSE
    WriteString ('FALSE')
    END
```

2.9 The Five Basic Types

A Summary. The previous sections describe what are called the five basic types in Modula-2. They are:

CARDINAL nonnegative integers from 0 to MaxCard

INTEGER integers from −MaxInt to +MaxInt

REAL numbers with decimal points and an optional exponent; limits are placed on the number of significant digits and the range of the exponent

CHAR single characters belonging to the ASCII character set

BOOLEAN the values TRUE and FALSE

For each type there are unambiguous rules for writing the constants belonging to the type. There are operations which can be performed with values of the type using operators and standard procedures. The standard procedures ORD and VAL can be used with each of the basic types except REAL. With the exception of BOOLEAN, there are procedures for writing a value on an output device.

The names of the basic types and their associated standard identifiers are not reserved words. You could define them to have some other meaning but this is not recommended.

2.10   Enumerated Types

Concepts. Associated with any type is a set of values or constants of the type. For example, the type CHAR has 256 values; the type CARDINAL has (MaxCard +1) values, etc. An enumerated type is one for which you choose identifiers to represent the values of the type. Thus an enumerated type has an explicitly declared set of constants each of which has a unique name.

Definition. Enumerated types should be used to make your programs more readable. This reduces the chance for logic errors and decreases debugging time. The following are declarations for three enumerated types.

```
TYPE
    WeekdayType        = (Mon,Tues,Wed,Thurs,Fri);
    SuitType           = (Clubs,Diamonds,Hearts,Spades);
    StopLightColorType = (Red,Green,Amber);
```

"TYPE" is a reserved word which must precede a sequence of type definitions. Semicolons separate successive type definitions. Each enumerated type declaration consists of the type name followed by an equal sign, followed by a list of the types values enclosed in parentheses. That is, the syntax of an enumerated type definition is as shown in Figure 2.6.

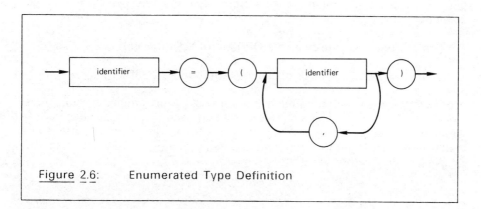

Figure 2.6:   Enumerated Type Definition

The values in the type must be unique and may not have any other use within the domain of their use.

A recommendation. Use the suffix "Type" in the enumerated type name. This does two things. First, it clearly indicates what kind of object the identifier represents. Second, it allows the name less the suffix to be used as a variable name. With the example types given, for instance, appropriate variables could be declared with

```
VAR
    Weekday        : WeekdayType;
    Suit           : SuitType;
    StopLightColor : StopLightColorType;
```

Operations. Five operations (ORD, VAL, MIN, MAX and comparison) can be performed on the values of an enumerated type. The ORD and VAL procedures have the same role as with the five basic types. For example, given the preceding definition of WeekdayType,

```
ORD(Mon) is 0 , ORD(Tues) is 1, ..., ORD(Fri) is 4
```

The first value in an enumerated type has an ORD value of 0.

The VAL procedure performs the inverse operation. For this same example, it follows that

```
VAL(WeekdayType,0) = Mon,      VAL(WeekdayType,3) = Thurs
```

The second parameter of the VAL procedure must be within the range of ORD values. VAL(WeekdayType, 26) for example, is an error.

MIN and MAX return the values having the smallest and largest ORD values respectively. For example, MIN(WeekdayType) is Mon and MAX(WeekdayType) is Fri.

Comparison. As with other types, values in an enumerated type may be compared using the relational operators. For the WeekdayType example, it follows that

```
Mon < Wed    is true because ORD(Mon) < ORD(Wed)

Thurs >= Fri    is false because ORD(Thurs) < ORD(Fri)
```

Output. Because enumerated types are of your choosing, you must create your own procedures for reading and writing values of an enumerated type. For the WeekdayType values, the following procedure could be defined. (Ignore the syntax details for now – they are described thoroughly in Chapter 7.)

```
PROCEDURE WriteWeekday (Weekday : WeekdayType);
    BEGIN
        CASE Weekday OF
            Mon   : WriteString('Monday')
          | Tues  : WriteString('Tuesday')
          | Wed   : WriteString('Wednesday')
          | Thurs : WriteString('Thursday')
          | Fri   : WriteString('Friday')
            END (*case*)
    END WriteWeekday;
```

If a particular enumerated type is used frequently, a module should be created which contains the type declaration and the procedures for processing values of the type. These objects can then be IMPORTed by other modules. Details are found in Chapter 10.

2.11   Subranges

Concepts. Frequently the value of a variable should be restricted to a subrange of values of some other type. For example, a day of the month should be in the range 1 to 31. In Modula-2, subranges can be declared as a distinct type and variables declared as belonging to that type. When this is done, the assignment of a value to a variable is allowed only if the value lies within the subrange. In this sense, the use of subranges provides automatic value checking in an assignment statement. The range check is not necessarily made when a variable obtains its value as a result of a read operation.

Definition. Shown next are declarations for the subrange types, DayOfMonthRange and UpperCaseLetterRange and for variables having these types.

```
TYPE
    DayOfMonthRange      = CARDINAL[0..31];
    UpperCaseLetterRange = CHAR['A'..'Z'];

VAR
    DayOfMonth      : DayOfMonthRange;
    UpperCaseLetter : UpperCaseLetterRange;
```

It is recommended that the suffix "Range" be used in the subrange name. This clearly identifies the purpose of the identifier and allows the name without the "Range" suffix to be used as a variable name.

Given these declarations, the assignment statements

```
DayOfMonth := 5 and UpperCaseLetter  := 'S'
```

are acceptable, whereas

```
DayOfMonth := 50 and UpperCaseLetter := 'a'
```

produce a compile time error. Range checking is not performed by all implementations when a value for a subrange variable is obtained from an input device using one of the Read procedures. Consider the following procedure calls:

ReadCard(DayOfMonth);   Read(UpperCaseLetter)

These may not <u>check the range</u> of the input values. They will however check that the input data belong to the base types CARDINAL and CHAR respectively. (The result of the check is stored in the variable Done which can be imported from InOut. If Done has a value of TRUE, the data belongs to the base type. Further details are found in Chapter 11.) Put another way, all one can guarantee after executing the preceding statements is that DayOfMonth has a CARDINAL value and UpperCaseLetter has a CHAR value. You are responsible for performing any range checks deemed necessary.

Subrange Types

Form:

name = type[lowbound .. highbound]

Rules:

1. The reference type is optional.

2. "lowbound" and "highbound" must be constants from CARDINAL, INTEGER, BOOLEAN, CHAR, an enumerated type or another subrange type. ORD(lowbound) must be less than ORD(highbound).

3. The type to which lowbound and highbound belong is called the <u>base type</u> of the subrange.

4. If the lowbound is a negative integer, the base type is assumed to be INTEGER; if it is nonnegative, the base type is CARDINAL.

5. If a value is assigned to a variable having a subrange type, the value must be within the range from the lowbound to the highbound.

6. Range checking may not be performed if the value of a subrange variable is obtained from an input device.

As with other types in Modula-2, MAX and MIN can be used to obtain the smallest and largest values in the subrange.

2.12   Other Types In Modula-2

As well as the basic types (INTEGER, CARDINAL, REAL, BOOLEAN, CHAR), enumerated types and subranges, Modula-2 allows you to define three other kinds of values. The key idea and the section where they are described is given next.

structured types: There are three predefined ways of structuring values – arrays, records and sets. They differ primarily in the homogeneity of their components and the method of referring to a component of the data structure. Data structures are described in Chapter 4.

pointer type: A pointer is a memory address. That is, a pointer indicates the location of a variable in memory. The definition and use of pointers are described in Chapter 5.

procedure types: A variable which has a procedure type may be assigned the name of a procedure at execution time. This allows you to pass the name of one procedure to a second procedure and have the second procedure use it. Procedure types are described in Chapter 8.

2.13   Exercises and Programming Problems

1. Exercise. What is the error in each of the following?

```
a) +20 * DIV * 3
b) (4 * (2 - ABS (-8))
c) 14 MOD -1
d) 8 + ABS[-6]
e) 10 DIV 3.0
```

2. Exercise. Using only the operators, +,–,*,DIV,MOD and the number 4, write INTEGER expressions which produce each of the values 1, 2, 3, ..., 20. For example, 4 DIV 4 produces 1;

3. Exercise. What is the value of each of the following expressions?

```
a) NOT FALSE AND NOT TRUE
b) (2 < 3) OR (2 <> 3)
c) (5+(7 DIV 3) > 2 MOD 6) OR FALSE
```

4. Exercise. Explain the error in each of the following

```
a) X < Y < Z
b) X < 2 OR X > 5      (assume X is REAL)
```

5. Exercise. The following expression is invalid because of operator priorities.

```
NOT 3 < 5 OR 7-2 MOD 2  <= 6 AND TRUE
```

a) Insert the minimum number of pairs of parentheses to make it an expression which can be evaluated. b) Add one additional pair of parentheses which will reverse the truth value from that in (a).

6. Exercise. Replace each of the following with a simpler expression which does not have a relational operator. (Assume X is a BOOLEAN variable.)

```
a) X < TRUE
b) X <= FALSE
c) X = FALSE
d) X >= FALSE
e) X > TRUE
f) X <> FALSE
g) X AND NOT(NOT (X))
```

7. Exercise. Write enumerated type declarations to define each of the following

a) PitchType having the values Strike and Ball

b) SpectrumType having the values Red, Orange, Yellow, Green, Blue, Indigo and Violet.

c) GradeType having the values Pass, Fail, DidNotWrite, Audit, and Credit.

8. Exercise. Write subrange declarations to declare the following types

```
a) PosIntRange      - the set of positive integers
b) LowLetterSRange  - the set of lower case letters
c) MonthLengthRange - the range of integers 1 through 31
```

9. Exercise. Given the declaration

```
TYPE
      DayType = (Mon,Tues,Wed,Thurs,Fri,Sat,Sun);
```

define subrange types WeekdayRange and WeekendRange appropriately. Explain why this couldn't be done if Sun was listed as the first day of the week.

10. Exercise. Explain the error in each of the following type declarations.

```
a) AlertnessType = ALERT,SLEEPY,DRUGGED,EXCITED
b) NonNegRange   = (0..MAXINT)
c) LetterRange   = 'a'..'z' OR 'A'..'Z'
d) PuncType      = (',','.',';',':')
e) NegRange      = -1..-MAXINT
```

11. Exercise. Can you think of any good reason for declaring a subrange type consisting of a single value as in

    TYPE
            TenRange = [10 .. 10];

12. Exercise. Given that DayType consists of the enumerated values Mon through Sun and given two variables Today and Tomorrow of type DayType, write a statement or statements which will assign Tomorrow the next day of the week following the value of Today.

13. Calculate and display the first eight values in the sequence x, $x^3/3$, $x^6/6$, $x^{10}/10$,... Observe that the exponent and the denominator in sucessive terms increase by 2,3,4,etc. Take this into account in defining the loop in the algorithm and corresponding program.

14. Calculate the sums 1^3, 1^3+2^3, $1^3+2^3+3^3$, ..., $1^3+2^3+3^3+..+9^3$. Print the square root of each sum of cubes. What general result is being illustrated?

15. One measure of the spread of a set of N values (called the variance) $X_1, X_2, X_3, ..., X_N$ is given by the formula

$$\frac{(X_1-AVG)^2 + (X_2-AVG)^2 + \ldots +(X_N-AVG)^2}{N}$$

where AVG is the average of the N values.

a) Develop an algorithm to calculate the variance of the set of values a, a+k, a+2k, .. a+(N-1)k

b) Using a = 5, k = 3, N = 10, translate the algorithm into Modula-2 and run the program.

16. Write a program to calculate the value of $12-(6-i)^2$ for values of i of 1, 2, 3, ..., 12. Twelve lines of output should be produced. The first value on each line should be the value of i, the second, the value of the expression.

17. Tabulate (calculate and display) values of x and y given by the formula

$$y = \frac{x^3 - 4x^2 + x - 3}{|x + 2|}$$

for a) x = 0., .25., .5, .75, ..., 1.75, 2.0
    b) x = -1, -3, -5, ..., -11, -13
    c) x = 10, 9, 8, ..., -9, -10

18. Read values of X and N. Print the values of X, X/2, X/4, ..., $X/2^N$.

19. Read twelve values each of which represents a number of hours. Express each value as the sum of weeks, days and hours. For example, 193 hours becomes 1 week + 1 day + 1 hour.

20. For integer values in the range 11 through 77 print the number and the remainder when the number is divided by the number obtained by leaving off the last digit. For example, for 36, 12 0 would be printed since 36 divided by 3 is 12 with 0 remainder.

21. Find the roots of the equation $x^2 - 325678x - 0.02 = 0$. Check the results by substituting the values found in the original equation. (You may get something far from zero, illustrating the potential problems of round off errors!)

22. Check balancing. The input contains a deposit-withdrawal code in position one and a dollar amount of the form XXX.XX in positions three through eight. A "1" in position one indicates a deposit and a "2" indicates a withdrawal. The dollar amount indicates the size of the deposit or withdrawal. Write a program which reads an unknown number of lines of data and for each prints either

$XXX.XX DEPOSIT, BALANCE IS NOW $XXXX.XX
                         or
$XXX.XX WITHDRAWAL, BALANCE IS NOW $XXX.XX

Assume the starting balance is zero. If the attempted withdrawal is larger than the balance, print the line "WITHDRAWAL OF $XXX.XX WOULD EXCEED BALANCE, NOT PROCESSED" .

23. The digital sum of a number is obtained by summing the values of the digits to get a new number. The process (sum of digits) is repeated until the sum has only one digit. The result is called the sum of the digits of the original value. For example:

123456789 -> 45 -> 9

Write a program to calculate the sum of the digits for several values in the input.

CHAPTER 3

IDENTIFIERS, TYPES, VARIABLES, INPUT

Questions Answered In This Chapter

1. What are the rules for defining identifiers in a Modula-2 program?

2. How are the three classes of objects -- constants, types and variables declared?

3. How are read procedures used to assign values to variables?

4. How can the standard input and output devices be changed?

3.1 Identifiers

Classes of Identifiers

An identifier is a sequence of letters and digits. The first character must be a letter. In Modula-2 the classes of identifiers are:

Standard Identifiers: There are twenty-six standard identifiers. Examples include: the five basic types INTEGER, CARDINAL, REAL, CHAR and BOOLEAN; the "built-in functions" such as ABS, TRUNC and HIGH; and the procedures NEW, DISPOSE and HALT. Standard identifiers are predeclared and can be used anywhere in a Modula-2 program. They are thus <u>pervasive</u>. Although not recommended, you can redefine the meaning of a standard identifier by including your own declaration for it. A list of the standard identifiers is found in Appendix A.

Implementation-Defined Identifiers: Each Modula-2 processor comes with a library of modules containing commonly used types, procedures and objects. An example is the InOut Module with components such as WriteString and ReadInt. Fortunately the suppliers of these libraries have agreed to provide the modules specified by Wirth in his original definition of the language. These modules are described in Appendix D. You may choose to ignore the services provided by these libraries and redefine the identifiers for some other purpose. If required, the objects in the library modules must be IMPORTed before they can be used.

User-Declared Identifiers: Each identifier appearing in a program must be declared (unless it is a reserved word or standard identifier). The kinds of objects which can be declared include constants, types, variables, procedures and modules. Two aspects of a declared object deserve special comment – its <u>existence</u> and its <u>visibility</u>. Existence refers to the lifetime of the object. This is the interval between its creation and is destruction. Visibility refers to the territory in which it is known. A complete discussion of these concepts is found in Chapter 8.

Rules for Identifiers

Identifiers

1. Syntax. An identifier must begin with a letter (upper- or lowercase) and be followed by a sequence of zero or more letters or digits. Shown below are examples of valid and invalid identifiers.

Valid	Invalid
X	9R – must being with a letter
Read	X(4) – contains a nonletter, nondigit
HelloThere	Hello There – blank is not a letter
P9999	LOOP – LOOP is a reserved word

2. Case sensitivity. Identifiers are case sensitive. This means the identifiers Mother and mother are considered different as are any of the other 64 mixtures of cases of its six component characters.

3. Length. In most Modula-2 implementations, all characters in an identifier are considered significant. Some processors may only look at the first eight or sixteen characters to determine uniqueness of identifiers.

Identifier Style

1. Use meaningful names. For example, use GrossPay and NetPay instead of X and Y.

2. Use mixed case unless your keyboard has uppercase only. For example, use Count in preference to COUNT. Experiments have shown that mixed case is more readable.

3. Use word pairs or word triples. Capitalize the first letter in each word as in "LastYearToDate."

4. Avoid names similar to the reserved words, standard identifiers and library components. For example, don't use Loop, If, Real or Halt as variable names.

5. Avoid using the same name with different cases in the same program.

3.2   Constant Declarations

Purpose. A constant declaration associates an identifier with a value. Why would you want to do this? The most important reason is that use of the name is often more meaningful than use of the value – for example, Pi instead of 3.14159. A second reason is that only one statement needs to be changed should a different value be appropriate. A third reason is that many compilers provide a cross reference listing which shows where each identifier is used in a program. Modula-2 implementations may include several constants. For example, InOut exports the end-of-line constant EOL. The ASCII module gives names for certain unprintable characters.

Modula-2 unlike many other languages allows simple expressions to appear in the constant definition. Some examples follow.

```
CONST
    MaxCard         = 65535;
    MaxInt          = 32767;
    Pi              = 3.14159;
    ReportTitle     = "Payroll Register";
    WorkDaysPerYear = 200;
    WorkWeeksPerYear = WorkDaysPerYear DIV 5;
    Set123          = {1,2,3};
    Different       = (2 <> 3);
```

These examples show that the value of a constant declaration is not
limited to scalar values but may include string, constants, sets and
expressions involving constants or constant identifiers. (Sets are
described in Chapter 4.) A diagram of the constant declaration syntax is
given in Figure 3.1.

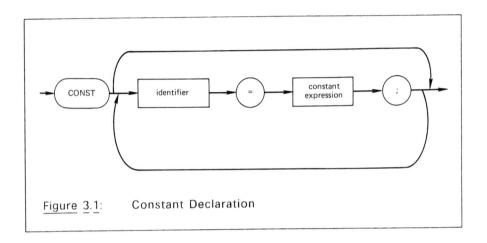

Figure 3.1:   Constant Declaration

Notes:

1. A constant expression has the same structure as an "ordinary"
   expression. Its syntax is formally defined in Appendix B. The primary
   restriction is that the establishment of the value of the constant
   expression must not require execution of the program.

2. A constant identifier may be used anywhere the constant expression is
   valid.

Examples that violate the rules are:

```
CONST
    WS      = WriteString; (* a procedure is not a value *)
    Xplus2 = X + 2;        (* invalid if X is a variable *)
    Pi     := 3.14;        (* use an equal sign, not ":=" *)
```

Constant Declaration Style

1. Use a single CONST declaration in a procedure or module and put it ahead of all other declarations. (See "Order of Statements" in Section 3.5.)

2. Use meaningful identifiers.

3. Indent and vertically align all constant identifiers and within reason vertically align the equal signs.

4. When there is a large number of identifiers, put them in alphabetic order.

3.3 Type Declarations

Types in Modula-2

A type has three attributes: a type name; a rule of membership; and either implicitly or explicitly -- a set of values belonging to the type.

    The five basic types in Modula-2 are INTEGER, CARDINAL, REAL, CHAR and BOOLEAN. These were described in chapter 2. Enumerated types and subrange types were also described. Section 3.2 provided a brief overview of the other types available in the language. The purpose of this section is to formally define the syntax of type declarations. The syntax diagram is given in Figure 3.2.

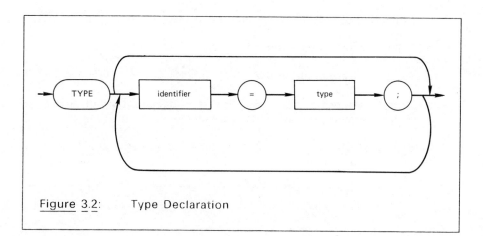

Figure 3.2:   Type Declaration

Notes:

1. The "type specification" is one of: a simple type (see Note 2) an ARRAY, RECORD or SET type (see Chapter 4); a POINTER type (Chapter 5); on a PROCEDURE or PROC type (see Chapter 8).

2. The simple types include type identifiers such as REAL, enumerated types and subrange types.

Examples. Shown next is an example of a type declaration involving the three kinds of simple types. Assume that MaxCard has been declared as a constant.

```
TYPE
    WholeNumber    = INTEGER;
    WeatherType    = (Cold, Cool, Comfortable, Warm, Hot);
    LargeCardRange = [MAX(CARDINAL)-1000 .. MAX(CARDINAL)];
```

This example shows that constant expressions are permitted. Examples of invalid type declarations are:

```
TYPE
    Bool1, Bool2 = BOOLEAN; (* each identifier must have a
                                   separate definition *)
    IN           = INTEGER; (* IN is a reserved word *)
```

Type Declaration Style

1. In general use a single TYPE declaration within a procedure or module. Put it after the CONST declaration and ahead of the VAR declaration.

2. Use meaningful type names which have the suffixes:

   o "Type" for an enumerated type

   o "Range" for a subrange identifier

   o "Array", "Record", "Set" and "Ptr" for declarations of array, record, set and pointer types respectively

3. Indent and vertically align the type identifiers and when reasonable, the equal signs.

3.4   Variables

A variable has three attributes – a name, a type and a value. The first
two attributes are provided in a variable declaration. Values are assigned
by either using an assignment statement or by executing a procedure
which performs the value assignment. The next subsection covers
variable declarations; the remaining section describes the use of the
standard input procedures. Assignment statement details are found in
Chapter 7. Figure 3.3 gives the variable declaration syntax.

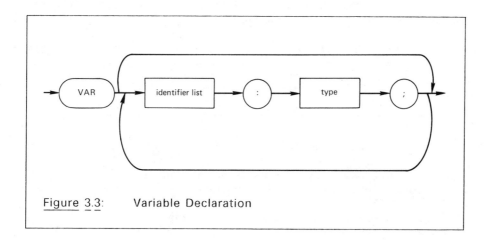

Figure 3.3:   Variable Declaration

Examples. Consider the following variable declaration.

```
VAR
    LowLimit, HighLimit : CARDINAL;
    PrimaryColor        : (Red, Green, Blue);
    Subscript           : CARDINAL[0..N-1];
```

The first example illustrates that more than one variable may appear in
the identifier list.

The second and third examples show that the type of a variable is not
limited to a type identifier but may be specified in the variable
declaration. The advantage is a saving in time because a separate type
declaration is not required. However, the practice in general is not
recommended for the following three reasons.

1. Consistency. It is important to be consistent when writing programs.
   A good rule is to name all types.

2. The constants in an enumerated type can only be declared once. For
   example, the following is invalid because the constants are twice
   declared.

```
VAR
    PrimaryColor   : (Red, Green, Blue);
    SecondaryColor : (Red, Green, Blue);
```

Even if two subrange types have identical specifications, they are considered different because the compiler only compares two identifiers to determine if two types are the same; it does not check the meaning of the identifiers.

3. When data is passed to procedures, the types of the formal procedure parameters must be specified by identifiers – the corresponding actual parameters must have the same type name.

For the foregoing reasons, the use of type identifiers in variable declarations is recommended in all but the simplest programs.

Variable Declaration Style

1. In general, use a single variable declaration in a procedure or module. Put it after the TYPE declaration.

2. Use meaningful variable names. Follow the style guidelines for identifiers in Section 3.1.

3. Indent and vertically align the identifiers and when reasonable, the colons preceding the types. A style sometimes used when there is a list of identifiers of the same type is the following format:

```
VAR
    Low      , (* low value in range *)
    High     , (* high value in range *)
    Average    (* average of the values *)
             : REAL;
```

4. If there are many variables, declare them in alphabetic order.

3.5   Order Of Declarations

There are usually no restrictions on the order of declarations in a block. Some implementations however may have ordering constraints such as the requirement that identifiers used in a TYPE declaration must have been previously declared. In general however the ordering of constant, type, variable and other declarations is not restricted. The following guidelines are used and recommended.

Order of Declarations

1. Declare constants first, followed by types, variables and procedures. This results in an identifier being defined before it is used elsewhere.

2. If a large number of identifiers fall into mutually exclusive logical groups, keep the constant, type and variable declarations for each group together.

3.6   The Read Procedures

A variable only serves a useful purpose when it is assigned a value. There are two ways of assigning a value to a variable -- by using an assignment statement or by obtaining the value from an external device such as the keyboard at execution time. The assignment statement is described in detail in Chapter 7. This section describes the use of standard procedures for reading the value of a CARDINAL, INTEGER, REAL and CHAR variable. The procedure ReadString which can be used to read a string of characters is described in Chapter 4. A general discussion of input-output in Modula-2 is found in Chapter 11.

The standard (default) input device in Modula-2 is the keyboard. This can be changed using the OpenInput procedure described later in this chapter.

ReadCard and ReadInt

The form and rules of the procedures used to obtain a CARDINAL or INTEGER value respectively are summarized next.

ReadCard, ReadInt

Forms:

```
ReadCard (c)
ReadInt  (i)
```

Rules:

1. The "c" denotes a CARDINAL variable; "i" denotes an INTEGER variable.

2. ReadCard and ReadInt must be IMPORTed from InOut.

3. The value assigned to the variable is constructed as follows:

   a) Leading blanks are ignored.

   b) Most implementations terminate the read when a character less-than-or-equal-to a blank is read. Other implementations terminate the read with the first nondigit (aside from a leading "+" or "−" in the case of INTEGER input) entered.

   c) The characters comprising the value are echoed on the standard output device.

   d) The character which terminates the read is stored in the variable termCH which is exported by InOut.

   e) The variable Done (exported by InOut) is set to TRUE if a read was successfully performed and FALSE otherwise.

   f) When the input is entered from a keyboard, a backspace character has the effect of erasing the previous character.

Examples. Suppose ReadInt(i) is executed. Let "!" denote the end-of-line character

1. "123!" is entered. Results:

   − i is assigned the value 123
   − termCH has the character "!"
   − Done is set to TRUE

2. "a!" is entered. Results:

    – i is unspecified
    – termCH is set to "!"
    – Done is set to FALSE

3. "–4A5!" is entered. Results:

    – i is unspecified
    – termCH has the value "!"
    – Done is set to FALSE

4. "!" is entered. Results are implementation dependent. For the Logitech implementation the program waits until a terminating character is entered. In other implementations:

    – i is unspecified
    – termCH is set to "!"
    – Done is set to FALSE

5. "–123!" is entered in response to ReadCard(c). Results:

    – the value of c is undefined
    – termCH is set to "!"
    – Done is set to FALSE

A good idea when entering a sequence of integer values is to use a special sentinel value such as 999 to indicate the end of the sequence. This avoids the requirement for importing and examining the variable termCH. A recommended loop structure is shown in the following program fragment:

```
ReadCard(c);
WHILE c <> 999 DO
    (* process c *);
    ReadCard(c);
    END;
```

ReadReal

The form and rules of the ReadReal procedure are as follows.

ReadReal

Form:

    ReadReal(r)

Rules:

1. The "r" denotes a REAL variable

2. ReadReal is imported from ReallnOut

3. The value assigned to the variable is constructed as follows:

   a) Leading blanks are ignored.

   b) Characters composing a valid REAL value are read sequentially and echoed on the standard output device. Examples of valid character strings are "1.", "-2.3", and "-0.12E-05".

   c) The first character following the last character in the value (often an end-of-line character) terminates the reading of further characters.

   d) If a valid REAL value is found, the variable Done (exported by ReallnOut) is set to TRUE. Otherwise Done is set to FALSE.

   e) When the input is from the keyboard, the backspace character erases the previously entered character.

Examples

Assume ReadReal(r) is executed and that "!" denotes the end-of-line character.

1. "123.45!" is entered. Results:

   - "r" is assigned the value 123.45
   - Done is set to TRUE

2. "-000.05E02!" is entered. Results:

   - "r" is assigned the value -5.
   - Done is set to TRUE

3. "123A!" is entered. Results:

   - the value of r is indeterminate
   - Done is FALSE

4. "!" is entered. Some implementations (e.g. Logitech) require that a nonterminating character be entered. If an end-of-line character is entered for example, the program waits for another character from the input device. Other implementations simply set Done to FALSE.

Note: In order to perform its task the module RealInOut imports some of the procedures in InOut. The experienced programmer may be able to take advantage of this fact when analyzing the results of a ReadReal by looking at termCH (imported from InOut) for example.

   The comment at the end of the previous subsection regarding the use of a sentinel value to flag the end of a sequence of numbers applies to reading REAL numbers as well as integers.

Read

The form and rules of the Read procedure follow.

Read

Form:

   Read (ch)

Rules:

1. The "ch" denotes a CHAR variable.

2. Read is imported from InOut.

3. The value assigned to ch is the next character obtained from the standard input device.

4. In most implementations the character read from the input device is <u>not</u> echoed on the standard output device.

5. The variable Done (exported by InOut) is set to TRUE unless: (a) input is from a device other than the keyboard, and (b) the end of the file on the input device has been reached. If both these conditions are met, Done is set to FALSE.

Note. The character is not echoed because:

o You may want to keep the character(s) hidden from view as when reading a password

o The input device may not be the keyboard. If the input device is the keyboard, each Read(ch) is normally followed by a Write(ch).

When reading characters one at a time from the keyboard, the end-of-line character generated by the "return" key often has special significance. To test for the end-of-line character, IMPORT the EOL constant from InOut and compare each character read to this value.

3.7 Changing The Standard Input and Output Devices

To save you time in specifying input and output devices at the beginning of each program, Modula-2 defines the keyboard to be the default or standard input device and the computer's screen to be the standard output device. These device assignments can be changed using the procedures OpenInput and OpenOutput which are exported by the InOut module. These device assignments revert to the defaults using the corresponding procedures CloseInput and CloseOutput. An example follows the detailed descriptions of these procedures.

OpenInput

The OpenInput procedure is used to reassign the standard input device. Modula-2 allows many sources of input data to be accessed simultaneously but only one is the standard input device.

OpenInput

Form:

> OpenInput(extension)

Rules:

1. OpenInput must be imported from InOut.

2. The "extension" denotes a <u>file</u> <u>extension</u>. File extensions are explained next.

3. When the OpenInput procedure is executed:

   a) "in>" is displayed on the screen.

   b) A character string is read from standard input device. The character string specifies the identification of the new standard input file.

   c) If the string does not contain a file extension (see next section), the "extension value" is appended to the file name in order to construct a complete file specification.

   d) An attempt is made to open the new standard input file.

   e) If the open is successful then Done is set to TRUE and all subsequent requests for data from the standard input device are directed to the new device.

   f) If the open is unsuccessful then Done is set to FALSE, and the standard input device is left unchanged.

File Extensions

Modula-2 runs on several different kinds of computers. The operating systems which run on these computers typically use different conventions for uniquely identifying computer devices and files stored on them. The file identifier often has three components -- a device identifier, a file name and a file extension. In the MS-DOS operating system an example of a file identifier is "C:JOHN.TXT" where "C:" is the device specification, "JOHN" is the file name and "TXT" is the file extension.

The parameter in the OpenInput and OpenOutput procedures is the file extension used if the file specification entered does not include a file extension. Check with the documentation describing your implementation of Modula-2 for additional information.

OpenOutput

The OpenOutput procedure is used to reassign the standard output device to another device or file. The default device is the screen associated with your microcomputer or terminal.

OpenOutput

Form:

    OpenOutput(extension)

Rules:

1. OpenOutput must be imported from InOut.

2. The "extension" denotes a default file extension. File extensions are described in the previous subsection.

3. When the procedure is executed.

   a) "out>" is displayed on the screen.

   b) A character string is read from standard input device. The character string is assumed to specify the name of the new standard output file.

   c) If the name does not contain a file extension (see next section), the "extension value" is appended to the file name in order to construct a complete file specification.

   d) An attempt is made to open the new standard output file.

   e) If the open is successful then Done is set to TRUE and all subsequent displays of data are directed to the new device.

   f) If the open is unsuccessful then Done is set to FALSE, and the standard output device is left unchanged.

CloseInput and CloseOutput

The procedures CloseInput and CloseOutput cause the standard input and output devices to be reassigned to their default values respectively. Each is IMPORTed from InOut. No parameters are required.

Standard Input–Output: An Example. The problem is to copy the data
in one file to another. The names of the source and target files are to be
obtained from the keyboard. A suitable program is shown next.
Important comments follow the program.

```
MODULE CopyFile;

(* This program copies a file character-by-character from
   a user-specified input file to a user-specified output file
*)

FROM InOut IMPORT Read, Write, ReadString, WriteString, WriteLn,
                  OpenInput, OpenOutput, CloseInput,
                  CloseOutput, Done;

VAR
    ch : CHAR;

BEGIN
    (* 1 - Open the files - OpenInput and OpenOutput
                            display 'in>' and 'out>' prompts *)
    WriteString('Enter the names of the output, input files');
    WriteLn;
    OpenOutput("OUT");
    IF NOT Done THEN
        WriteString('Output file cannot be opened');
        WriteLn;
        HALT;
        END;
    OpenInput("IN");
    IF NOT Done THEN
        CloseOutput;
        WriteString('Input file cannot be opened');
        WriteLn;
        HALT;
        END;

    (* 2 - Copy the data from the input to the output file *)
    Read(ch);
    WHILE Done DO
        Write(ch);
        Read(ch);
        END;

    (* 3 - Close the files *)
    CloseOutput;
    CloseInput;
    WriteString("Copy completed");
    WriteLn;
END CopyFile.
```

Comments.

1. OpenOutput must be executed before changing the standard input file. If OpenInput is done first, the request for the name of the new output fiile would be directed at the file containing the data to be copied! Executing OpenOutput first allows the input file name to be entered from the keyboard.

2. Note that Done is checked after OpenInput, OpenOutput and each Read. If the opens are not verified, it may be erroneously assumed that the copy has been done when in fact it hasn't.

3. The CloseOutput procedure is executed in order to print the message "Copy completed" on the screen.

3.8 Summary

1. There are three classes of identifiers in Modula-2.

   o Standard identifiers are predeclared. They are pervasive.

   o Implementation-supplied identifiers are found in the library modules. They must be imported.

   o User-defined identifiers are declared in a block for the purpose at hand.

2. Modula-2 blocks usually include declarations for constants, types and variables. (Procedure and local module declarations are described in Chapters 8 and 10 respectively.)

3. The InOut module contains procedures for reading a single CARDINAL, INTEGER or CHAR value. The ReadReal procedure must be imported from the RealInOut Module.

4. OpenInput and OpenOutput are exported by InOut. They can be used to change the standard input and output device assignments.

Exercises and Programming Problems

3.9 Exercises and Programming Problems

1. Write a program which reads ten pairs of numbers, each pair representing a distance in millimeters and centimeters. After each pair of values is read, convert the distance to an equivalent distance in meters.

2. Write a program which reads six values, each representing a weight in kilograms. After each value is read, convert it to an equivalent weight in grams and milligrams. For example, a weight of 3.56789 kilograms becomes 3567 grams and 890 milligrams. The results of this program will clearly demonstrate the errors which may result when working with fractional REAL values.

3. An approximate value of the square root of x for x in the range 0.1 through 10 is given by the formula (1+4x)/(4+x). Write a program which calculates the value of the square root of 0.5, 1.0, 1.5, ..., 9.5, 10, using both the formula and the MathLib0 function sqrt. Print the value of each result and the percentage error resulting from using the formula.

4. For values of x in the range .1 through 1 an approximate value of the logarithm of x is given by the formula

$$\log x = -.076 + .281x - \frac{.238}{x + .15}$$

Write a program which displays the values of log x using the formula and the MathLib0 function ln. Use values of x of .2, .4, .6, .8, and 1. For each print the absolute value of the difference of the two log values.

5. Write a program which reads values of A, B and C representing the lengths of three sides of a triangle. Calculate the area of the triangle using the formula

$$\text{Area}^2 = S(S - A)(S - B)(S - C)$$

where S is one-half the perimeter of the triangle. Calculate the radius of the inscribed circle (given by Area/S).

6. A series circuit consists of a resistor of R ohms, an inductance of L henries and a capacitor of C farads. If the voltage across the circuit is E volts at F cycles per second, the current in amperes flowing through the circuit is given by the formula

$$i = \frac{E}{\sqrt{R^2 + \left(\frac{2\ FL - 1}{2\ FC}\right)^2}}$$

Write a program which reads values of R, L and C and computes the current through the circuit at 60 cycles per second for values of E of 100, 200, 300, ..., 900 volts.

7. Suppose you borrow $X for a period of N months at a monthly interest rate of i (e.g. 0.01). The size of your monthly payment is given by the formula

$$iX\left(\frac{(1+i)^N}{(1+i)^N - 1}\right)$$

Write a program which reads values of X, i and N and calculates the size of the monthly payment.

8. Tabulate the values of the sine, cosine and tangent of angles of 0, 5, 10, ..., 60 (degrees). Note that the angles must be converted to radians before the MathLib0 functions can be used.

9. You are required to determine the smallest total number of bills required to pay a sum of $1579.00 using only fifties, tens and one dollar bills. Write a program to do this. No loop is required.

10. A rectangular room has a length, width and height of L, W, and H respectively. The length of the room runs in an east-west direction. An ant is located on the East wall a distance AH above the floor and AN North of the South wall. The ant's food is stuck on the West wall a distance FB below the ceiling and FS south of the North wall. Write a program which reads values of L, W, H, AH, AN, FB and FS and calculates the shortest distance the ant must travel to reach its food. Hints: The shortest distance is a straight line which will include travel along one of the ceiling, floor, South wall or North wall. (Naturally parts of the East and West walls will have to be covered as well.) To evaluate the lengths of the four paths, pretend the room is made of cardboard and "unfold" it in four different ways to see the four paths. The length of each path can be calculated easily using the Pythagorean theorem.

11. A corridor three feet wide and seven feet high makes a right-angled turn into another corridor having the same dimensions (The corner is "L" shaped.). A plumber has a long thin rigid pipe which he wants to take around the corner.

a) What is the longest length of pipe which will go around the corner?

b) What is the narrowest width of corridor which will permit an eight foot pipe to go around?

c) Do your answers to (a) and (b) change if the corner is "T" shaped?

12. The program reads one or more lines of characters from the input representing a statement, question or exclamation. Assume that the first occurrence of a period, question mark or exclamation mark denotes the end of the input. Echo each "sentence" read and print one of "statement", "question" or "exclamation" on the line following.

13. The input contains the names of several cities having one-word names of not more than ten characters. More than one name may appear in a line. Read the data and print the names, one city per line so that the last character of each name appears in print position 12. Test your program using the following four lines of input.

```
CHICAGO
DENVER PARIS
LONDON WATERLOO MOSCOW
BOMBAY  TEHRAN TOKYO
```

14. Prepare a number of lines of data, each containing a different person's height in inches and weight in pounds. Write a program that reads the lines one at a time and prints a table of the following form:

```
HEIGHT          WEIGHT

   XXX             XXX
   XXX             XXX
   etc.            etc.


AVERAGE HEIGHT IS XXX.X INCHES
AVERAGE WEIGHT IS XXX.X POUNDS
```

15. The economic order quantity (EOQ) for a product is the optimal number of units of the product to order based on the ordering cost, the demand and the cost of holding the product in inventory. In the simplest case, the EOQ is given by the formula

$$Q = \sqrt{(2KD/H)}$$

```
where: K is cost of placing an order
       D is the demand (products/unit of time)
       H is the holding cost ($/product/unit of time)
```

For example, if it costs $100 to place an order; the demand is $1600 widgets/month and the holding cost is $2.00 per widget per month, then the optimal order quantity is the square root of 2*100*1600/2 or 400. The order should be placed each D/Q units of time which, for the example above means every 1600/400 or 4 months.

Write a program which reads values for K, D and H from the input and prints a table showing the order quantity and ordering frequency for values of the demand of D, 2D, 3D, ..., 10D.

16. A ladder of length L leans against a wall. The top of the ladder is initially a distance H above the floor. The top of the ladder starts to slip down the wall. Calculate the position of the midpoint of the ladder when the top is .95H, .90H, .85H, ..., .05H above the floor. Read values of L and H from the input.

17. A man travels 24 miles northwest, 40 miles 35 degrees east of north and then 36 miles 20 degrees south of east. How far and in what direction is he from his starting point?

CHAPTER 4

STATIC DATA STRUCTURES

Questions Answered In This Chapter

1. What are the attributes of named collections of data?

2. What is the ARRAY type? How is it defined and used?

3. What are character strings? What operations are permitted with strings that are not permitted with other arrays?

4. What are RECORDs? How are they defined and used?

5. How are SETs defined and used?

This Chapter begins with an overview of data structures in general and the three types available in Modula-2 in particular. A separate section describes each the ARRAY, the RECORD, and the SET.

4.1 Collections of Data

Concepts. Thus far we have considered single or scalar values. Often it is desirable to give a name to a collection of values. In fact many programming tasks would be almost impossible to program without using aggregations of data.

Data collections have one attribute in common – they all contain one or more components. They differ in the following ways.

o Homogeneity of components. The components in an array of integers are homogeneous (they all have the same type). In a payroll record on the other hand, components such as name and salary have different types (are heterogeneous).

o Order of components. In some collections the order in which components are stated is not significant. For example, the set of colors {red, yellow, green} may be considered identical to the set {yellow, green, red}. On the other hand the point with coordinates (2,5) is not the same as the point (5,2).

o Referencing a component. In some cases it may be necessary to reference an individual component. The two common ways are by its position (if the components are ordered) or by its name. In other cases it may be sufficient to simply know if a value is present or absent.

o Extensibility. Some collections may be open ended in the sense that there is no theoretical limit to the number of components in the collection. An example is a library because items may be added indefinitely to the collection. On the other hand there is a limit on the number of characters in a single print line.

o Structure of components. Some data collections such as sets in Modula-2 restrict the components to be scalars. Others such as records permit components to have a structure. For example, one component of an employee record may be a birthdate which itself has three components - year, month and day.

The three structures described in this chapter are all static - meaning that all their properties are specified at the time they are declared. Furthermore, the entire structure must reside in memory at one time. This characteristic is not true for files that typically reside on an external device. Often in the case of files, only one component resides in memory at one time.

A summary of the attributes of the data structures available in Modula-2 is found in the following table. Dynamic structures are described in Chapter 5.

	ARRAY	RECORD	SET	file	dynamic structures
Homogeneous components	yes	no	yes	yes	yes
Ordered	yes	no	no	yes	no components
Component reference	position	name	test for membrshp	position	by pointers
Extendable	no	no	no	yes	yes

As can be seen from the table there is a variety of attributes and capabilities. In most cases the choice of which structure to use is made by matching the requirements of the problem with those in the table.

This chapter describes the three static (nonextensible) structures - ARRAYs, RECORDs and SETs. Methods of processing files are described in Chapter 11; dynamic structures are described in Chapter 5.

4.2 Arrays

An array is a named, ordered collection of components of the same type. The properties of an array are the number of components, the component type, and component position references. These are determined by the array type specification. Consider the following example:

```
TYPE
     MarkArray = ARRAY [0..19] OF CARDINAL;
VAR
     Mark : MarkArray;
```

Consider the TYPE declaration. It defines the type MarkArray which includes all arrays of twenty CARDINAL components each in which the component positions are identified by the numbers 0,1,2,...,19. The words ARRAY and OF are reserved words. How many "values" are in the type MarkArray? Put another way, how many ordered sequences of twenty CARDINAL values are there? Since there are MaxCard + 1 CARDINALs (don't forget zero!), there are (MaxCard + 1) choices for the first component and for each of these there are (MaxCard + 1) choices for the second component and for each of these there are (MaxCard +1) choices for the third component, etc. In other words (MaxCard + 1)^{20} "values" can be assigned to a variable of the type MarkArray.

Some vocabulary: in the example, CARDINAL is called the component type. The subrange [0..19] is called the index type. The index type specifies two items of information about the array. First, the number of values in the index type determines the number of components in the array. Second, the values of the index type are the component positions. In the example, the component positions are position 0, position 1, position 2, ..., position 19, because the index type is the subrange [0..19]. Consider now the variable declaration:

```
VAR
     Mark : MarkArray;
```

This declares Mark to have the type MarkArray. Thus at any time the value of Mark will be one of the (MaxCard +1)^{20} sequences of 20 CARDINAL values. The components in an array can be processed independently. You can think of the components as being the twenty CARDINAL variables Mark[0], Mark[1], ..., Mark[19]. That is to refer to a component of an array, the component position (index value) or subscript is enclosed in brackets and appended to the array name.

When choosing a name for an array type such as MarkArray, append the suffix "Array" to a meaningful identifier. As with other variable declarations, either or both of the index type and the component type may be defined in the array declaration. An example is

```
VAR
     InitialCount : ARRAY ['A'..'Z'] OF [0..100];
```

Such an array may be appropriate for counting the number of people's surnames beginning with each letter of the alphabet. This array has twenty-six components. The fifth component is InitialCount['E'] and its value (which must be in the subrange [0..100]) represents the number of people having surnames beginning with 'E'.

Two Dimensional Arrays

Frequently it helps to visualize a collection of values as forming a table or matrix having rows and columns. Suppose a house-to-house census obtains the following data:

	PreSchool	SchoolChildren	Adults
House 1	0	2	2
House 2	0	0	2
House 3	1	0	1
House 4	2	3	3
House 5	0	1	1

An appropriate declaration for this matrix with 5 rows and 3 columns is

```
TYPE
    HouseRange = [1..5];
    PeopleType = (PreSchool, SchoolChildren, Adults);
VAR
    Survey : ARRAY HouseRange, PeopleType OF CARDINAL;
```

In a matrix, a pair of values is required to uniquely identify a component – the row position and the column position.

As can be seen from the variable declaration, the row selector is a value in the type HouseRange and the column selector must be a value in PeopleType. The components in the third row are Survey[3,PreSchool], Survey[3,SchoolChildren], and Survey[3,Adults].

A matrix or table is a two-dimensional array because it has two index types. Its components are often called doubly-subscripted variables. Array types may have three, four, or more dimensions. For example, to store the temperature at the location (x,y,z) at time T requires a four dimensional array. When choosing the name for a two-dimensional array type, append "table" or "matrix" to a meaningful name.

The rules of array type declarations are summarized in Figure 4.1.

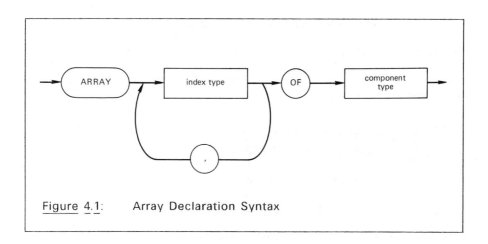

Figure 4.1:   Array Declaration Syntax

Notes.

1. The index type(s) must be one of CARDINAL, INTEGER, CHAR, BOOLEAN, an enumerated type or a subrange type. In particular, REAL is not a valid index type.

2. The component type may be any type (including another array type).

The rules for component references are given in Figure 4.2.

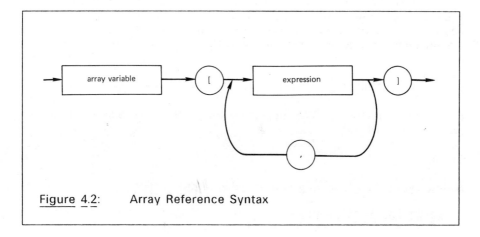

Figure 4.2:   Array Reference Syntax

Notes.

1. Each index value may be an expression which results in a value belonging to (compatible with) the corresponding index type.

2. An index value is often called a subscript.

Operations with Arrays

The only operation that can be performed with an entire array is assignment. For example, given

```
VAR
    A, B : ARRAY[0..9] OF REAL;
    C    : ARRAY[0..9] OF REAL;
```

The assignment statement "A := B" is valid and is equivalent to

```
A[0]:=B[0]; A[1]:=B[1]; ... ; A[9]:=B[9]
```

Note however that "A:=0" is invalid because the source and target have different types. Note also that "A:=C" is invalid because although we can see the types are identical, the compiler considers the types of two variables to be identical only if they have the same type identifier.

Two arrays cannot be compared using a relational operator as in "A<B". Because of the common requirement to compare two strings of characters, most implementations include a "Strings" module that contains procedures for performing comparisons and other string operations. Similarly, input and output operations must (except for strings) be done on a component-by-component basis.

HIGH. The standard procedure HIGH returns the largest index value in a one-dimensional array. In the Mark array, for example, HIGH(Mark) is 19 because the largest index type is the subrange [0..19]. If an index type has the subrange 3..7, the value returned by HIGH is 7. For a two dimensional array such as that declared by:

```
VAR
    X : ARRAY [2 .. 5],['A' .. 'Z'] OF CHAR
```

the value of HIGH(X) is the upper bound of the first dimension of the array. That is, HIGH(X) is 5.

Strings

String Types. The following type is called a string type.

```
ARRAY [0..N-1] OF CHAR
```

That is, a string type is an array of N characters. N is called the length of the string. A string constant such as "Monday" is implicitly defined as having the type "ARRAY[0..5] OF CHAR".

Special Properties. Strings are special for three reasons. First, a shorter string can be assigned to a longer string. Second, the procedures

ReadString and WriteString are supplied with all implementations of Modula-2. Third, most implementations of Modula-2 have a module called Strings which contains a number of useful procedures for manipulating strings. Further details follow.

Consider the following declarations.

```
TYPE
    DayNameString = ARRAY [0..7] OF CHAR;
VAR
    Day1, Day2 : DayNameString;
```

Thus Day1 and Day2 are arrays of eight characters each. Their components have subscripts 0, 1, 2, ..., 7. Consider the following assignment statements:

```
Day1 := "Saturday";
Day2 := "Monday";
```

Because the string constant "Saturday" has an implicit type of "ARRAY [0..7] OF CHAR", the eight components of "Saturday" are assigned one-for-one to the eight components of Day1.

In the assignment Day2 := "Monday", a string constant of length 6 is assigned to a string of length 8. When this happens, the first excess position is assigned the character which has an ORD value of 0. CHR(0) is called the nul character. Thus following the assignment, the first six components of Day2 will collectively contain the characters "Monday"; and Day2[6] will contain CHR(0).

A string which has the nul character as its first component is called an empty string and has a "length" of zero. Note that the word "length" may have two interpretations. It may mean the number of components in a string array. Alternatively, it may mean the number of characters preceding the first nul character. Unfortunately both usages of "length" are natural. We will try to avoid ambiguity.

Input-Output of Strings. The procedure WriteString sends the value of a string variables to the standard output device. WriteString displays all characters up to the first nul character or, if none is present, all characters in the string. Thus, with respect to the array Day2, the output consists of six characters, not eight, because the seventh component is a nul character.

When a string variable is passed to the procedure WriteString, the logic is equivalent to the following. Assume the procedure invocation is "WriteString (Data)" and that index has the type CARDINAL.

```
Index := 0;
WHILE (Index <= HIGH(Data) AND
       (Data[Index] <> CHR(0)) DO
    Write(Data[Index]);
    Index := Index + 1;
    END;
```

Note the benefit of conditional evaluation in the expression following "WHILE". If the string does not contain a nul character, index will attain the value HIGH(Data)+1 which means Data[index] would be invalid. However, conditional evaluation means Data[index] never gets evaluated because the expression "index <= HIGH(Data)" is FALSE.

The ReadString procedure performs three steps:

.1 Skip all leading blanks.
.2 Store all subsequent characters in the target string.
.3 (If necessary) put a nul character in the string.

Details follow.

The following logic is equivalent to "ReadString(Data)". The fragment has been written to maximize clarity; improvements in efficiency could be made. Recall that EOL is the CHAR constant EXPORTed by InOut and represents the character stored when the Enter key is pressed. The variable termCH also exported by InOut always contains the last character read.

```
CONST
    MaxInputSize = 8;

VAR
    ch          : CHAR;
    Index       : CARDINAL;
    InputBuffer : ARRAY [0..MaxInputSize-1] OF CHAR;

BEGIN
    WriteString('Enter readstring example: ');
    (* skip and echo leading blanks *)
    Read(ch);
    WHILE ch = ' ' DO
        Write(ch);
        Read(ch);
        END;
    (* load until full or non-alphanumeric *)
    Index := 0;
    LOOP
        IF ORD(ch) <= ORD(' ') THEN
            InputBuffer[Index] := CHR(0);
            EXIT;
            END;
        InputBuffer[Index] := ch;
```

```
        Write(ch);
        IF Index = MaxInputSize-1 THEN
            (* flush rest *)
            WHILE ch > ' ' DO
                Read(ch);
                END;
            EXIT;
            END;
        Index := Index+1;
        Read(ch);
        END;
    WriteLn;
    WriteString(InputBuffer);
    WriteLn;
END;
```

The Strings Module

A Strings module is provided with most Modula-2 implementations. The procedures described next are those found in the Logitech implementation of Modula-2 for the IBM Personal Computer. They are meant to illustrate the kinds of string processing procedures which have a high utility. If the ones given are not present in your implementation, you can create a module containing them using the techniques described in Chapter 10. The list which follows summarizes the functions performed by the Strings procedures.

Length(str): returns the number of characters in str preceding the first nul char. For example, Length('ABC') is 3.

Assign(str1, str2): assigns the variable str1 to the variable str2. Equivalent to "str2:=str1" if HIGH(str2) >= HIGH(str1); truncates excess characters if HIGH(str2) < HIGH(str1). For example, if the variable "str1" has the value "ABCDE" and HIGH(str2) is 2 then "Assign(str1,str2) results in str2 having the value 'ABC'.

Insert(str1, str2, index): causes str1 to be inserted in str2 starting with subscript index. For example, if str2 was 'ABCDE' then after "insert('XYZ', str2, 3)", str2 has the value 'ABCXYZDE'.

Delete(str, index, length): deletes "length" characters from str starting with component index. For example, if str was 'ABCDE' with HIGH(str)=4, then, following "Delete(str, 2, 1)", str has the value 'ABDEnul'.

Pos(str1, str2): returns the index of the component in str2 at which str1 begins. If the value of str1 is not found, in str2, the procedure returns HIGH(str2)+1. For example, Pos('CD', 'ABCDE') is 2 and Pos('CF', 'ABCDE') is 5.

Copy(str1, index, length, str2): Starting at index in str1, replaces str2
with length characters obtained from str1. For example, assuming str1
has the value 'ABCDE', Copy(str1, 2, 1, str2) means str2 has a value 'C'.

Concat(str1, str2, str3): str3 will contain the characters in str1 followed
by those in str2. For example, 'Concat('AB', 'XY', str) causes str to be
'ABXY'.

CompareStr(str1, str2): performs a dictionary comparison of str1 and
str2 and returns: −1 if str1 comes before str2; 0 if they are identical; +1
if str1 follows str2. For example, "Compare('AAA', 'ABC')" is −1;
"Compare ('a', 'A') is +1; and "Compare('ABC', 'ABC ') is −1 because the
nul character implicitly terminates a string and ORD(nul) < ORD(' ').

4.3 Records

Concepts

A record is a named collection of usually different types of components.
Each component has a unique name. A component of a record is called
a field. The following is the declaration of a record type and variable
suitable for storing the information about a date.

```
TYPE
    DateRec = RECORD
        Year  : [1985..1999];
        Month : [1..12];
        Day   : [1..31];
        END;
```

The type DateRec has three fields with the field name Year, Month and
Day. Each has a different (subrange) type. How many values are in the
type DateRec? Because there are 15 possible Year values, 12 Month
values and 31 valid Day values, the type DateRec defines 15 x 12 x 31
different triples of values. Any variable with the type DateRec, will have
one of those triples as its value.

   Consider now the variable Date. It has three components, Date.Year,
Date.Month and Date.Day. A field is designated by appending a period
and the field name to the record variable name.

   The form and rules of a simple record declaration are given in Figure
4.3. The most general form is given in the section called "Record
Variants".

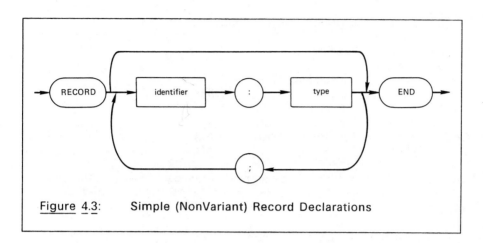

Figure 4.3:   Simple (NonVariant) Record Declarations

Notes.

1. RECORD and END are reserved words.

2. The field names must be unique within the record type but can be the same as other identifiers declared "outside" the record.

3. If several fields in a record have the same type, they may be put in a list preceding the field type.

Record Declaration·Style

1. Use the suffix "Rec" or "Record" in a record type identifier.

2. Indent and vertically align the field names, "END". Where reasonable align the colons in the field declarations.

3. If more than one field has the same type, define the field type separately and put each field name on a separate line (see BirthDate and HiredDate in the following example).

The following example illustrates the preceding guidelines and shows that fields may be structures as well as simple variables. Note the vertical alignment.

```
String20 = ARRAY [0..19] OF CHAR;

PersonRec = RECORD
    Surname    : String20;
    Given      : String20;
    Address    : ARRAY [1..55] OF String20;
    BirthDate  : DateRec;
    HiredDate  : DateRec;
    Sex        : (Male,Female,Other);
    END;
```

Note that the type PersonRec defines six fields. Three of the fields – Surname, Given and Address are arrays; BirthDate and HiredDate have record types and Sex has an enumerated type.

Consider now the following variable declaration.

```
VAR
    John : PersonRec;
```

The following are examples of component references.

John.Surname   –   Surname field; a string of twenty characters

John.Surname[0]   –   first character in John's surname

John.Address   –   Address field; an array of five twenty character strings

John.Address [2]   –   second line of John's address; a twenty character string

John.Address [2][19] –   last character in the second line of John's address. Note that "John.Address[2]" is an array and the [19] selects a component of that array.

John.BirthDate   –   a record having three fields

John.BirthDate.Year   –   the year of John's birth. Note that "John.BirthDate" is a record and the Year field is selected by appending the period and field name to the record.

The foregoing example illustrates that components of structures can be structures. Structures may be nested to the depth permitted by the Modula-2 implementation (often eight levels). The component at any level is selected by appending a sequence of subscript or field selectors to the outermost structure. Consider

Data[i].Fld1.Fld2[j].Fld3

Proceeding right to left this component reference tells us that Fld3 is a field belonging to the j'th element of the array Fld2 which itself is a field within the record Fld1 where Fld1 is a field in the i'th component of the array Data. Although legitimate, the use of such highly nested structures is not recommended for two reasons. First, writing the sequence of component selectors to reference an inner component is time consuming and prone to error. Second, although we can easily visualize one- or two-dimensional structures, getting a mental picture of the sixth level of a hierarchy such as in this example is difficult.

The WITH Statement : A convenience

The WITH statement allows you to use a field name without preceding it with the record name. This saves time and may reduce the probability of making spelling or syntax errors. Compiler efficiency may also be improved. One example will suffice. Consider the declaration

```
VAR
     Date : DateRec;
     John : PersonRec;
     Accident : RECORD
          Code    : CARDINAL;
          Officer : ARRAY [0..19] OF CHAR;
          Time    : RECORD
               Hours   : [0..23];
               Minutes : [0..59];
               END;
          END;
```

Accident has three fields, Accident.Code, Accident.Officer and Accident.Time. If in a long sequence of statements there are many references to these fields, the three field names may be used without the record qualifier by enclosing those statements within a WITH statement as follows:

```
WITH Accident DO
     .
     Code :=_____;
     Read (Officer [i]);
     .
     WriteCard (Time.Hours,10);
     .
     END
```

Consider

```
WITH Accident.Time DO
     (* statement sequence *)
     END
```

Within the statement sequence, the fields Accident.Time.Hours and
Accident.Time.Minutes may be written as Hours and Minutes. Finally the
comments in the structure below specify the permitted field references.

```
WITH Accident DO
    (* references to Code, Officer, Time *)
    WITH Time DO
        (* references to Code, Officer, Hours, Minutes *)
        END;
    (* references to Code, Officer, Time *)
    END
```

Remember that the WITH statement applies to a single record variable
and not all instances of a record type.

Record Variants

This subsection may be omitted on first reading.

This subsection describes how to define and use record types which have
two or more alternative structures. For example the vehicle descriptors
for a car, truck and bus are different; payroll information for wage earners
and salaried employees is not identical; the data describing a football
running play is distinct from that describing a passing play.

Suppose a record structure is required to store appropriate
information for a variety of geometric figures among which are: a line
(requires a length descriptor only); a rectangle (requires length and
width); a triangle (requires the lengths of the three sides). The type of
figure is indicated by a code. Specifically let 1, 2 and 3 be the codes for
a line, rectangle and triangle. The name of the figure is required for all
types. A suitable record type is declared as follows:

```
FigureRec = RECORD
    Name   : ARRAY [0..9] OF CHAR;
    CASE Code : CARDINAL OF
        1 : Length    : REAL;                  (* Line *)

      | 2 : RecLength : REAL;                  (* Rectangle *)
            Width     : REAL;

      | 3 : Side      : ARRAY [1..3] OF REAL; (* Triangle *)

      ELSE  Radius    : REAL;                  (* Circle *)
      END;
    END;
```

Comments.

1. The Name field and the Code field belong to all records of the type FigureRec. The remaining fields depend on the value stored in the Code field.

2. If Code has a value of 1, the record has one additional REAL field called Length; If Code has a value of 2, FigureRec has a RecLength and Width field in addition to Name and Code; if Code is three, there is a field called Side which is an array of three REAL values; if Code is other than 1, 2 or 3, the record has a Radius field as well as the Name and Code fields.

3. The vertical bar following the definition of the Code 1 field Length is called a <u>case</u> <u>separator</u> and is used to separate case declarations. Similarly, the second vertical bar separates the Code = 2 and Code = 3 field definitions.

The syntax and rules of a record variant are given in Figure 4.4. A variant declaration may be used in a record type definition in place of a field declaration.

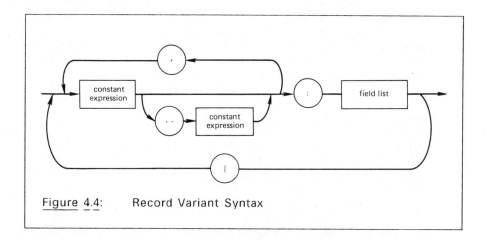

Figure 4.4:   Record Variant Syntax

Notes.

1. CASE, OF, ELSE and END are reserved words.

2. The tagfield if present is a component of every record.

3. The tagfield type must be specified by a type identifier and must designate CARDINAL, INTEGER, BOOLEAN, CHAR, an enumerated type or a subrange of one of these.

4. ELSE followed by a field list is optional. If not present and the value of the tagfield is not found in a variant definition, an execution error occurs.

5. The vertical bar is called the case separator symbol. It separates the cases. A null case is not allowed.

6. A fieldlist is a list of field names and/or record variants separated by semicolons.

7. The case selector list specifies the tagfield values which are associated with a variant. The list may contain a list of one or more constants and/or subranges of the tagfield type. Either constants or constant expressions may be used in defining this list. For example, consider the case selector list "0, 100..1000, 10000..MaxCard". It specifies that if the tagfield value is either 0, or in the ranges 100 to 1000 or 10000 to MaxCard, then include the fields in the field list.

Record Variant Style

1. Even though optional, use a tagfield. Without it there is nothing in a record to indicate which variant is being used, hence knowledge of which fields are present would have to be determined by other means. As an example, suppose a date is one field in a record. If the date value is in the future with respect to the current date, it could mean a future reservation; if in the past it would contain fields describing some past event. Much better would be to use an enumerated tagfield with the value Future and Past.

2. Indent and align the start of each case selector list. If one or more of these lists are lengthy, indent the start of the field list on the line below the case selector list.

3. If the case logic is extensive, insert a blank line between cases.

4. Vertically align the case separator characters, ELSE (if used) and END.

These guidelines are illustrated by the following variant declaration:

```
TYPE
    DemoRec = RECORD

        Field1 : CARDINAL;

        Field2 : BOOLEAN;

        CASE IntTag : INTEGER OF
            -10,0,5      :
                Field3A : CARDINAL;
                Field3b : REAL;

          | 1..4,6..99   :
                Field4A   : ARRAY [0..1] OF CHAR;
                CASE OK   : BOOLEAN OF
                     TRUE  :
                         Field4B1 : REAL;
                   | FALSE :
                         Field4B2 : CHAR;
                     END;

          | -MaxInt,
            +MaxInt    :
                Field5 : RECORD
                    X  : REAL;
                    Y  : REAL;
                    END;

        ELSE
                Field6 : ARRAY [0..1] OF CHAR;
        END;

        Field7 : REAL;
        END;
```

4.4 Sets

Definition

A set is an unordered collection of values chosen from the same
reference set. The reference set is called the base type of the set. The
values in a particular set are called the members of the set. For example,
suppose an elevator stops at floors 1, 2 and 3 of a building. We require
a variable to represent the floors at which people may be waiting. There
are eight possibilities ranging from no one waiting to people waiting at
all three floors. A suitable set type and variable declaration follow:

```
TYPE
    WaitingSet = SET OF [1..3];
VAR
    Waiting : WaitingSet;
```

The type WaitingSet has eight "values" or subsets. They are

        WaitingSet{ }   WaitingSet{1,2}
        WaitingSet{1}   WaitingSet{2,3}
        WaitingSet{2}   WaitingSet{1,3}
        WaitingSet{3}   WaitingSet{1,2,3}

The character sequence "{}" denotes the <u>empty</u> <u>set</u>. Because the values
in a set are unordered and because a member may be listed more than
once, the following sets, among others, are equivalent.

        WaitingSet{1,2}, WaitingSet{2,1}, WaitingSet{1,2,2,1,1,2}

The form and rules of set type declarations are summarized in Figure 4.5.

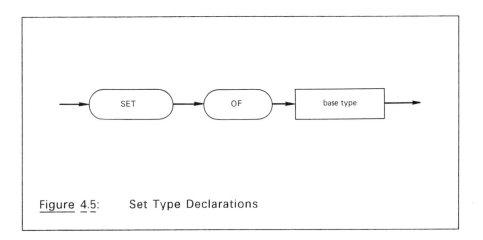

Figure 4.5:   Set Type Declarations

Notes.

1. The base type must be a subrange or an enumerated type.

2. Each implementation of Modula-2 specifies a limit on the number of
   values in the base type. (A frequently found limit is 16. However, some
   implementations use 256.)

3. Suppose there are n values in the base type. Since each value may be
   present or absent in any given set, the set type defines 2^n values.

A set constant is specified using the syntax and rules given in Figure 4.6.

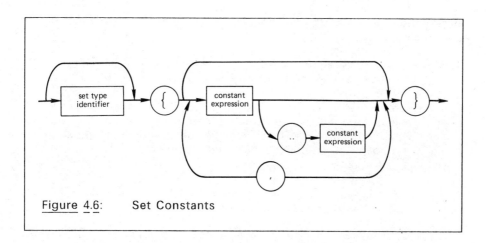

Figure 4.6:   Set Constants

Notes.

1. The constants must belong to the base type.

2. Subranges may be used to specify a contiguous sequence of values to be included in the set. Given an appropriate set type for example, an element list could be written as {2, 5..8, 0..1}.

3. Note that variables cannot be used directly to define set elements. How to do this is described in the subsection "Operations With Sets".

The Type BITSET

Modula-2 includes one predefined set type called BITSET. Its base type is the subrange of CARDINALs 0..WordSize-1 where WordSize is a constant specifying the number of bits (ones and zeros) in the unit of memory called a word. On many microcomputers, the value of WordSize is 16 meaning there are 2^{16} set values in BITSET. BITSET is the default set when specifying a set constant. That is {3,5..8,12} is equivalent to BITSET{3,5..8,12} BITSETs are further discussed in Chapter 12.

Operations With Sets

Arithmetic Operations. The symbols +,-,*,and / are respectively the union, difference, intersection and symmetric set difference operators. They have the same priorities as when used with numbers. Assume A and B are sets belonging to the same set type.

Union: A + B is the set containing elements of A or B or both. For example, {1,2,3} + {3,4,5} is {1,2,3,4,5}

Difference: A - B is the set formed by removing from A the elements found in B. For example, {1,2,3} - {3,4,5} is the set {1,2}.

Intersection: A * B is the set containing elements in both A and B. For example, {1,2,3} * {3,4,5} is the set {3}.

Symmetric Set Difference: A / B is the set containing elements in A or B but not both. For example, {1,2,3} / {3,4,5} is the set {1,2,4,5}.

Comparison Operations: The relational operators =, < >, ,=, >= but not < or > may be used to compare two sets belonging to the same set type. Equal and not equal have obvious meanings. The operators <= and >= mean "is contained in" and "contains" respectively. For example,

> {2,3} <= {1,2,3,4,5}   is true because both members of {1,2} are members of {1,2,3,4,5}

> {3,4,5} >= {3,4}   is true because every member of {3,4} belongs to {3,4,5}

Note that for any set X, {} <= X is true and {} >= X is false unless X is also the empty set.

Membership Testing: The operator IN is used to determine if a value belongs to a set. For example, 2 IN {1,2,3} is TRUE because 2 belongs to {1,2,3}. An expression involving IN has the form

> value IN set

where value must belong to the base type of the set. Value may be a variable or expression. IN has the same priority as the relational operators.

Inclusion and Exclusion: Modula-2 has two standard procedures called INCL and EXCL for adding and removing a number from a set variable. In the following, assume s is a member of BITSET.

INCL(s,x)   includes the value x in the set s. For example, if set S is {1,3}, INCL(S,2) yields the set S = {1,2,3}. INCL (s,x) is equivalent to {x} + s.

EXCL(s,x)   removes the value x from the set s. For example, if set S is {1,2,3}, EXCL(S,3) yields the set S = {1,2,}. EXCL(s,x) is equivalent to the set difference s - {x}.

InputOutput: There are no standard procedures for reading or writing sets. Suppose the following declarations have been made.

```
TYPE
    DigitSet = SET OF [0 .. 9];
VAR
    Digits : DigitSet;
```

Suppose further that Digits has been given a value. The following fragment could be used to display which digits belong to Digits.

```
FOR value := 0 TO 9 DO
    IF value IN Digits THEN
        WriteCard(value,5);
        END;
    END;
```

Three Useful Techniques

The illustrations in this subsection assume the following declarations have been made.

```
TYPE
    OneToTenRange = [1..10];
VAR
    S : SET OF OneToTenRange;
```

1. Complement. The complement of a set S is the set containing members of the base set not in S. For example, the complement of S is OneToTenRange{1..10} – S.

2. Cardinality. The cardinality of a set is the number of elements in the set. It can be obtained by counting the number of values in the base set belonging to the set of interest. Assuming the appropriate declarations have been made the following statement sequence obtains the cardinality of the example set S.

```
Count := 0;
FOR value := 1 TO 10 DO
    IF value IN S THEN
        Count := Count + 1;
        END;
    END;
```

3. Proper subsets. The operators < and > are not permitted with set operands. However, for two sets A and B, the following BOOLEAN expression is equivalent to A < B

```
(A <= B) AND (A <> B)
```

Power Sets:An Application

Given a base type, its powerset consists of all possible sets chosen from values in the base set. For example, the powerset of base set BOOLEAN consists of the four sets.

```
BOOLEAN{},BOOLEAN{TRUE},BOOLEAN{FALSE},BOOLEAN{TRUE,FALSE}
```

If there are N values in the base type, there are 2^N sets in the powerset.

There are several algorithms for generating all the sets in a powerset. One is the following. It operates by starting with the empty set and generating successive sets until the empty set is again reached. The heart of the algorithm is the following logic which transforms one set into another. To "flip a value" means to remove the member if it is present and to add it if it is absent.

If the cardinality is even then
   .1"flip" the lowest value in the base set
Else
    .1 Find the lowest value in the current set
    .2 If this low value is less than the largest value
        in the base set then
        .1"flip" the successor of the low value
      Else
        .1"flip" the high value (results in the empty set).

Next we give a complete Modula-2 program to generate the sixteen sets in the powerset of the base type "1 .. 4". Good programming practices would dictate the use of procedures to flip a member, generate the next set and print the members in a set. Procedures are discussed in Chapter 8.

```
MODULE PowerSet;

(* This program displays all sixteen subsets of the
   digits 1 through 4
*)

FROM InOut IMPORT WriteCard, WriteLn;

CONST
    LowValue  = 1;
    HighValue = 4;

TYPE
    DigitRange = [LowValue .. HighValue];
    DigitSet   = SET OF DigitRange;

VAR
    NextSet : DigitSet;       (* the next subset to be generated *)
    Even    : BOOLEAN;        (* show odd-even count in NextSet *)
    Digit   : DigitRange;           (* lowest value in the set *)

BEGIN
    Even    := TRUE;
    NextSet := DigitSet{};            (* start with the empty set *)
    REPEAT
        (* 1. calculate the next subset *)
        IF Even THEN                     (* flip the low value *)
            IF LowValue IN NextSet THEN
                EXCL(NextSet,LowValue)
```

```
                    ELSE
                        INCL(NextSet,LowValue)
                        END;
            ELSE                          (* find lowest value in set *)
                    Digit := LowValue;
                    WHILE NOT(Digit IN NextSet) DO
                        INC(Digit);
                        END;
                    IF Digit = HighValue THEN        (* flip it out *)
                        EXCL(NextSet,HighValue);
                    ELSE                  (* flip successor of Digit *)
                        INC(Digit);
                        IF Digit IN NextSet THEN
                            EXCL(NextSet, Digit);
                        ELSE
                            INCL(NextSet, Digit);
                            END;
                        END;
                    END;

            (* 2. change cardinality *)
            Even := NOT(Even);

            (* 3. Write the values in NextSet *)
            FOR Digit := LowValue TO HighValue DO
                IF Digit IN NextSet THEN
                    WriteCard(Digit,2);
                    END;
                END;
            WriteLn;
            UNTIL NextSet = DigitSet{};
END PowerSet.
```

The output produced by the program is as follows:

```
 1
 1 2
 2
 2 3
 1 2 3
 1 3
 3
 3 4
 1 3 4
 1 2 3 4
 2 3 4
 2 4
 1 2 4
 1 4
 4
```

4.5 Summary

1. Modula-2 has three predefined static data structures – arrays, records and sets which make the programming of many problems much easier.

2. An array is an ordered collection of homogeneous components. An array type declaration has the form

```
ARRAY index-type OF component-type
```

Individual components are selected by appending a subscript of the form [index1, index2, ...] to the array variable name. The assignment of one array to another of the same type is permitted but all other all-array operations must be done on a component-by-component basis.

3. A record is an unordered collection of named, heterogeneous components. A record type declaration has the form

```
RECORD fieldlist END
```

A single record type may have different collections of fields. A record component (field) is selected by appending a period and the field name to the record variable name. The assignment of one record to another of the same type is permitted but all other full-record operations must be done on a field-by-field basis.

4. A set is an unordered collection of scalar values chosen from a base type. A set constant is specified by a construct of the following form

```
set-type{element list}
```

BITSET is the default set type and is a predefined identifier with a base type of [0..15] (the 15 is implementation dependent). Arithmetic operations and comparisons of sets are permitted. The IN operator is used to test for the presence or absence of a value in a set.

4.6 Exercises and Programming Problems

1. Exercise. Is there any purpose in defining an array with one element as opposed to a simple variable? For example:

```
VAR
     Next : ARRAY [1..1] OF CHAR;
```

2. Exercise. Given the type

```
TYPE
     WeatherType = (Hot, Cold, Nice);
```

You want to keep track of how many days in a month are of each type. Which of the following would you recommend and why?

```
ARRAY [1..31] OF WeatherType     or
ARRAY WeatherType OF [1..31]
```

3. Exercise. Suppose elements of the array BAC declared by

```
BAC : ARRAY [1..5] OF INTEGER;
```

have been assigned values using the following FOR statement:

```
FOR N := 1 TO 5 DO
    BAC[6 - N] := N;
    END;
```

What is the value of the following?

a) BAC[2]* 3 DIV BAC[3]
b) BAC[4]MOD 3 + 3 MOD BAC[4]
c) BAC[3]-BAC[2] < BAC[1] DIV 4
d) BAC[BAC[BAC[BAC[1]]]]

4. Exercise. For each of the following, define an array then write a FOR statement to assign the values shown to the elements of the array.

a) 2, 5, 8, 11, 14, 17
b) 1, 3, 7, 15, 31, 63
c) TRUE, FALSE, TRUE, FALSE, TRUE, FALSE
d) 1, 0, -1, 1, 0, -1

5. Exercise. In processing a true-false test of N questions suggest a use for the following arrays.

```
ONE : ARRAY BOOLEAN OF [1..N];
TWO : ARRAY [1..N] OF BOOLEAN;
```

6. Exercise. Suppose a two-dimensional array has been declared as follows.

```
Data : ARRAY [0..2],[0..3] OF INTEGER;
```

Suppose the values assigned to the elements are as shown below:

```
2   5   -7   3
4   8   22   7
5   9   -8   3
```

a) How many rows and columns are there?
b) What is the element in position [2,1]?
c) What are the subscript pairs of the prime numbers?
d) What is the sum of the elements in the third row?
   The second column?

7. Exercise.   Write   appropriate   record   declarations   for   each   of   the
following: a) A student record containing a name, address, sex and an
array of 10 marks. b) A complex number containing a real and an
imaginary component which are REAL numbers. c) A piece of art
containing descriptors for its: author, date, period (Middle Ages,
Renaissance, Modern), size (a pair of integers), owner's name, coloured
or black and white (boolean value).

8. Exercise. Given the follwoing declarations, write statements to perform
the assignments requested.

```
    TYPE
        DateRec = RECORD
            Year  : [1900..2000];
            Month : [1..12];
            Day   : [1..31];
            END;

        PersonRec = RECORD
            Name             : ARRAY [1..20] OF CHAR;
            BirthDate        : DateRec;
            EmploymentDate : RECORD
                Hired : DateRec;
                Fired : DateRec;
                END;
            END;(*PersonRec*)
    VAR
        Date     : DateRec;
        Employee : ARRAY (Tom,John,Ann,Sue) OF PersonRec;
        Person   : PersonRec;
```

a) Assign Date to Tom's birthdate.
b) Assign Sue's record to Ann's record.
c) Make John's fired date equal to his hired date.
d) Assign the year of Ann's birthdate to the year of Tom's hired date.

9. Exercise. Sometimes when choosing a data structure to store the data
associated with a particular problem, one has a choice between an
array of records and a record of arrays. What factors should be
considered in making this choice?

10. Read five INTEGER values from a single input line and store them in
an array of variables called K. On four successive lines print the
values; the subscripts of the variables which have positive values,
negative values, and zero values.

11. Read a set of ten INTEGER values from a single line. Print all pairs of values which add up to twelve.

12. Read ten INTEGER values each of which represents some person's age. Determine which two persons are: closest in age; farthest apart in age.

13. Read four lines of data each of which contains seven REAL values representing daily temperatures (one line per week). For each week, calculate the average temperature and the maximum and minimum temperatures. Calculate the average, high and low temperatures for the four week period. Display your results as shown below.

```
                Temperatures
          M   T   W   TH   F   S   S    Avg  Hi  Lo
Week 1   XX  XX  XX  XX   XX  XX  XX    XX.X XX. XX.
Week 2   XX  XX  XX  XX   XX  XX  XX    XX.X XX. XX.
Week 3   XX  XX  XX  XX   XX  XX  XX    XX.X XX. XX.
Week 4   XX  XX  XX  XX   XX  XX  XX    XX.X XX. XX.

                                       ----  --  --
          Four week statistics         XX.X XX. XX.
```

14. Add statements to the program for the previous problem so that the average, high and low temperatures for each day of the week are calculated.

15. Read an unknown number (less than fifty) of INTEGER values one at a time. Stop when any value occurs for the second time. Print the message "The value XX was the XX and XX value in the sequence".

16. A programming project. Suppose a fifty-by-fifty matrix contains elements having values of zero or one. Suppose less than 20 percent of the elements have a value of one and all the rest are zeros. Design any scheme you like for reducing the memory required to store the array values. Make sure your technique will work for an arbitrary set of values and does not depend on the array values having a particular pattern.

17. Binary Search. Suppose you have a vector X of 100 REAL values ordered such that $X[I] <= X[I + 1]$ for $I = 1, 99$. A value of Y is read and you want to determine if the value of Y is already stored in X. Naturally you could use the brute force method of comparing Y with X[1], Y with X[2], etc. looking for a match. A more efficient way is to compare Y with the middle element of X, X[50] and if $Y < X[50]$ search X[1] through X[49]; if equal the search is over; if $Y > X[50]$ search X[51] through X[100]. If not equal, continue with the same technique (compare Y to the middle element of the elements remaining). By repeatedly dividing any remaining interval in two, either a match will be found or all possibilities will have been exhausted. This method is known as a binary search.

Write a program which reads a value of N, then N more values and stores them in a vector X. Assume N is 25 or less. Read ten more values and for each determine if it matches one of the N values previously read using a procedure called BinarySearch. Second, modify the procedure so that it is recursive. That is BinarySearch calls itself to search a subarray. Do you think this is a good use of recursion? What are its advantages and disadvantages?

18. The game of Tic-Tac-Toe is well known. Suppose the elements of a three-by-three matrix called Board contain values of -1, 1, or 0 where: -1 indicates Player One has chosen the square; +1 indicates Player Two has chosen the square; and 0 indicates neither player has chosen the square. Write a program that reads values for Board and prints one of "Player one wins", "Player two wins", or "Undecided".

19. Input consists of ten pairs of numbers representing the coordinates of 10 points. Store the coordinate of each point in a record having three fields -- Point.X, Point.Y, Point.Length where Length is the square root of $x^2 + y^2$. After the data has been read, read a value for N and print the coordinates of the point having the Nth largest Length value.

20. Write a program to count the number of occurrences of each letter of the alphabet in a sentence contained on a single input line.

CHAPTER 5

DYNAMIC DATA STRUCTURES

Questions Answered In This Chapter

1. What are dynamic data structures?

2. What is the POINTER type? How is it used in creating dynamic data structures?

3. What are stacks, queues, lists and trees? How can they be defined and used?

Note: This chapter may be omitted on first reading.

5.1   Concepts

A dynamic data structure is one that can change during the lifetime of a program. Both the number of components and the relationships among them may change under program control. Using dynamic variables, it is possible to create and destroy variables as needed. An example of a dynamic structure is the waiting line at a supermarket checkout. Components (people) join and leave the queue, and their positions in the line change over time.

Although arrays can often be used to emulate the properties of dynamic data structures such as queues, arrays have one major limitation – the number of components is fixed. This may mean insufficient components are available or that a large amount of memory is unused. Dynamic structures on the other hand are extendable. Only sufficient components to do the job are created.

The basic building tools of dynamic data structures are pointer variables (having the type POINTER) and the procedures NEW (create a variable) and DISPOSE (destroy a variable). NEW and DISPOSE are not standard procedures. They are implemented using the standard procedures ALLOCATE and DEALLOCATE. We have chosen to use NEW and DISPOSE in the examples which follow because these identifiers more clearly indicate the purpose of the statement.

This chapter describes the concepts and mechanics of building and using dynamic data structures. Appendix D contains a description of the modules ListHandler and TreeHandler which EXPORT several of the most commonly used structure types and the procedures for manipulating them.

5.2   Pointers and NIL

Bytes and Addresses. Each variable occupies a contiguous portion of the computer's memory. Memory is measured in bytes. A <u>byte</u> contains eight bits (ones or zeros) and thus a byte has 2^8 or 256 different possible patterns. Bytes are numbered consecutively starting from zero. The byte number is called the <u>address</u> of the byte. If a variable occupies more than one byte of memory, the address of the variable is the address of the leftmost byte used to store the value.

A <u>pointer</u> <u>variable</u> contains the address of a variable. For example, a variable which can point to (contain the address of) an INTEGER variable can be defined by

```
VAR
      Int : POINTER TO INTEGER;
```

What values can be assigned to Int? The values in the type 'POINTER TO INTEGER' are addresses of possible locations of INTEGER variables in the computer's memory. Knowledge of the range of these addresses is not necessary to use pointers successfully.

The predefined identifier NIL means "no address." Thus the assignment statement Int := NIL means Int is not pointing anywhere.

5.3   Variable Creation and Destruction: An Example

The procedure NEW creates a variable of a given type and assigns its address to a pointer variable. The following program creates at execution time a single CARDINAL variable, reads and print its value and then destroys it.

```
MODULE PointerExample;

(* This program creates a CARDINAL variable at execution time;
   uses it, then destroys it
*)

FROM InOut   IMPORT ReadCard, WriteCard, WriteLn;
FROM Storage IMPORT ALLOCATE, DEALLOCATE;

TYPE
    CardPtr = POINTER TO CARDINAL;

VAR
    CardVar : CardPtr;

BEGIN
    NEW(CardVar);            (* create a CARDINAL variable and
                                put its address in CardVar *)
    ReadCard(CardVar^);      (* Read a value *)
    WriteCard(CardVar^,8);   (* Display the value *)
    WriteLn;
    DISPOSE(CardVar);        (* destroy the variable *)
END PointerExample.
```

Comments.

1. The procedures NEW and DISPOSE make use of the lower level procedures ALLOCATE and DEALLOCATE respectively, which are contained in the Storage module. ALLOCATE and DEALLOCATE must be IMPORTed whenever NEW and DISPOSE are used.

2. The type declaration

```
    CardPtr = POINTER TO CARDINAL
```

means that variables of the type CardPtr will have addresses of CARDINAL variables. Because of the declaration

```
    VAR
        CardVar : CardPtr;
```

CardVar may be assigned the address of a CARDINAL.

3. The statement "NEW(CardVar)" does two things. First, it makes use of ALLOCATE to reserve an area of memory sufficient to contain a CARDINAL value. (The amount of memory needed is known because CardVar is a pointer to a CARDINAL variable). Second, the address of the newly reserved area of memory is assigned to CardVar.

4. Consider the expression "CardVar^". Given a pointer, the variable pointed at is designated by appending the hat or caret symbol "^" to

the pointer variable. Thus CardVar^ is the variable pointed at (addressed by) CardVar. The caret is called the <u>dereferencing</u> <u>operator</u>.

5. The statement "DISPOSE(CardVar)" releases the area of memory occupied by the variable whose address is in CardVar. Subsequent use of CardVar^ is recognized by most implementations of Modula-2 as an execution error. DISPOSE invokes the DEALLOCATE procedure to perform its function.

The following box summarizes the rules of pointer declarations.

Pointer Type Declarations

Form:

typename = POINTER TO referencetype

Rules:

1. POINTER is a reserved word.

2. The reference type may be any type including a pointer type.

3. NIL belongs to every pointer type.

Three ideas summarize the use of pointer variables.

1. A pointer variable (one having a POINTER type) may be assigned a value in one of two ways.

   a) An assignment statement may be used to assign it a value of NIL or the value of another variable of the same (pointer) type. (A value of the type ADDRESS -- described in Chapter 12 -- is also assignment compatible with pointers.)

   b) Executing "NEW(ptrvar)" creates a variable of the reference type associated with the parameter variable and assigns the address of the newly created variable to the parameter. (The assignment is actually performed by ALLOCATE which is invoked by NEW.)

2. A variable created by NEW(ptrvar) may only be accessed by appending the dereferencing operator "^" to a pointer variable containing the variable address.

3. DISPOSE(ptrvar) releases the memory allocated to the variable addressed by pointer variable.

Pointer Style

1. Pointer types. Use the suffix "Ptr" in the name of a pointer type.

2. Pointer variables. Use names appropriate to the objects (variables) being created.

The following four sections describe the two most common dynamic data structures - linked lists and trees.

5.4   Linked Lists

Concepts. A linked list is a collection of variables linked by pointers to form a chain. The essential features of a linked list are illustrated in Figure 5.1.

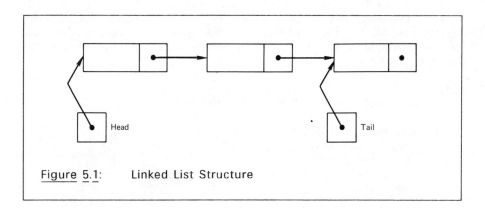

Figure 5.1:   Linked List Structure

Notes:

1. The rectangular boxes in Figure 5.1 are the elements in the list or nodes of the structure.

2. The square shapes denote pointer variables; the arrows represent the values of these variables.

3. The pointer called Head points to the first element in the list. The pointer called Tail points to the last element in the list.

Operations with Linked lists. Two operations can change the structure of a linked list - insertion of an element and removal of an element.

Other processing requirements in addition to insertion and removal of elements include:

o Creation of an empty list.

o Creation of a new element.

o Counting the number of elements in a list.

o Finding an element with a given value.

o Determining if sufficient memory is available to create a new element.

These operations are normally performed by procedures exported by a service module such as ListHandler found in Appendix D. Knowledge of procedures (Chapter 8) and Modules (Chapter 10) is necessary to fully understand these routines. In this chapter we shall focus on the logic involved with the preceding operations.

Element Creation. As shown in the Figure 5.1 a list element has two parts – the data associated with the element and a pointer to the next element in the list. Furthermore, some component of the data usually uniquely identifies the element. It is called the component key. A very natural vehicle for representing list elements is a record with the following structure and its associated pointer type. Assume the key has the type CARDINAL.

```
TYPE
    ElementRecPtr = POINTER TO ElementRec;

    ElementRec    = RECORD
        Next : ElementRecPtr;
        Key  : CARDINAL;
        (* other field declarations go here *)
        END;
```

5.5 Stacks

A stack is a linked list in which elements are added to and removed from only one end. Because stacks are frequently depicted vertically, the end used for insertion and deletion is often called the top of the stack. Stacks are also known as push-down lists. The verbs push and pop mean insertion and deletion of the top element respectively.

The structure and vocabulary of a three-element stack are shown in Figure 5.2.

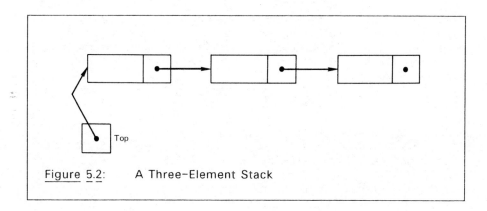

Figure 5.2:   A Three-Element Stack

An Example. The input stream consists of a sequence of signed integer values entered one at a time from the keyboard. A zero terminates the input stream. A positive value means push the value onto a stack; any negative value means pop the top element. The output is a sequence of messages of the type "xxx pushed" or "xxx popped". A sample input stream is

    +245   +75   -1   +300   -1   -1   +25   0

With this input, the required output is:

    245 pushed
     75 pushed
    245 pulled
    300 pushed
      etc.

The algorithm is straightforward. The names in parentheses below are names of commonly used routines for processing stacks.

    .1 Create an empty stack
    .2 Loop
         .1 Read a value
         .2 If the value is 0 then
              .1 Exit
           Else if value is > 0 then
              .1 Create an element (Create)
              .2 Push the value onto the stack (Push)
           Else
              .1 If stack not empty then
                   .1 Pop the top element (Pop)
                   .2 Display the popped value
                Otherwise
                   .1 Print error message "Stack underflow"

"Stack underflow" occurs when an attempt is made to pop a stack containing no elements. Always check for this condition prior to performing a pop. Shown next is a complete (except for the module body) Modula-2 program for solving the problem. The missing components are subsequently provided.

```
MODULE  StackExample;

(* This program illustrates stack processing *)

FROM InOut   IMPORT WriteString, termCH, EOL,
                    WriteLn, WriteInt, ReadInt;

FROM Storage IMPORT ALLOCATE, DEALLOCATE;

TYPE
    ElementRecPtr = POINTER TO ElementRec;

    ElementRec = RECORD
        Next : ElementRecPtr;
        Data : INTEGER;
        END;

VAR
    Temp  : ElementRecPtr;
    Top   : ElementRecPtr;
    Value : INTEGER;

BEGIN (* Stack Example *)
   (* module-body is described below *)
END  StackExample.
```

The program statements (the module body) to perform each step in the algorithm follow:

```
(* Create empty stack *)
Top := NIL;

(* Main processing loop *)
LOOP
    WriteString(' Enter an Integer, 0 to stop: ');
    ReadInt(Value);
    WriteLn;
    IF Value = 0 THEN
        EXIT;
        END;
    IF Value > 0 THEN
        (* create the element - see below *)
        IF Top = NIL THEN
            Top := Temp;
        ELSE
            (* push the element - see below *)
            END;
        WriteInt(Temp^.Data,8);WriteString(' pushed');
        WriteLn;
    ELSE
        (* pop the element from the stack *)
        IF Top <> NIL THEN
            (* stack is not empty *)
            (* perform pop - see below *)
            WriteInt(Temp^.Data,8);WriteString(' pulled');
            WriteLn;
            (* release the element *)
            DISPOSE(Temp);
        ELSE
            WriteString(' stack underflow ');
            WriteLn;
            END;
        END;
    END;
```

Create an element. Element creation involves two steps – the use of NEW to obtain a new variable and the assignment of values to fields in the newly created record. The statements are

```
NEW(Temp);              (* put address of variable in Temp *)
Temp^.Next := NIL;      (* pointer to next record *)
Temp^.Data := Value;    (* store data in new element *)
```

Push. Adding an element to a stack requires that the new element point to the current top element and Top to point to the new element. The statements are therefore:

```
Temp^.Next := Top;      (* new points to current top *)
Top        := Temp;     (* top now points to new *)
```

Make sure you understand why the order of these statements could not
be reversed.

Pop. Removing the top element means returning a pointer to the top
element and changing Top to point to the second element in the stack.
The statements are

```
Temp        := Top;        (* return pointer to top *)
Top         := Top^.Next;  (* set top to next element *)
Temp^.Next  := NIL;        (* good housekeeping *)
```

The IF statement ahead of the pop instructions checks for an empty stack
before changing the Top pointer.

5.6 Queues

Concepts and Vocabulary

A queue is a linked list in which elements are added at one end called
the back of the queue and removed from the other end – the front of the
queue. A queue is also called a FIFO (first-in-first-out) list. In keeping
with the vocabulary associated with waiting lines, we shall use the verbs
arrive and départ to denote the insertion and removal of an element from
a queue respectively.

The structure of a three element queue is depicted in Figure 5.3.

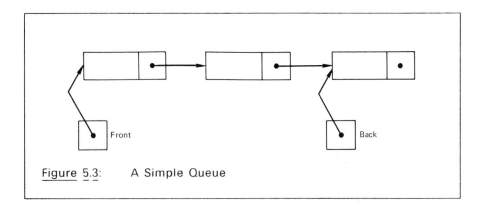

Figure 5.3:   A Simple Queue

An Example. The input stream consists of a sequence of positive and
negative integers entered one at a time from the keyboard. A zero
denotes the end of the input stream. A positive value denotes the
identification number of a person joining the queue; a negative number,
regardless of its value, means the element at the front of the queue
departs. The output is to consist of a series of lines of the form "xxx
arrived" and "xxx departed."

For example, the input +150 −1 +200 +5 +3 −1 0 should produce the lines:

```
150 arrived
150 departed
200 arrived
  5 arrived
  3 arrived
200 departed
```

The algorithm is straightforward. A complete set of procedures for processing queues is found in the ListHandler module described in Appendix D.

```
.1 Create an empty queue (Create)
.2 Loop
       .1 Read the next value
       .2 If the value is zero then
              .1 Exit
           Else if value > 0 then
              .1 Create a queue element (CreateElement)
              .2 Add the element to the back of the queue
           Otherwise
              .1 If queue not empty then (NotEmpty)
                     .1 Remove the front element
                  Otherwise
                     .1 Print error message "queue underflow"
```

A queue underflow condition arises when an attempt is made to remove an element from an empty queue. Always check for this condition prior to removing an element from the queue.

The following program solves the problem. The statement groups corresponding to the main steps in the algorithm follow the mainline.

```
MODULE QueueExample;

(* This program demonstrates simple queue processing *)

FROM InOut    IMPORT WriteString, termCH, EOL,
                     WriteLn, WriteInt, ReadInt;

FROM Storage IMPORT ALLOCATE, DEALLOCATE;

TYPE
    ElementRecPtr = POINTER TO ElementRec;

    ElementRec = RECORD
        Next : ElementRecPtr;
        Data : INTEGER;
        END;
```

```
VAR
    Temp  : ElementRecPtr;
    Front : ElementRecPtr;
    Back  : ElementRecPtr;
    Value : INTEGER;

BEGIN
    (* Create an empty Q *)
    Front := NIL;
    Back  := NIL;

    (* Main loop goes forever until zero entered *)
    LOOP
        WriteString(' Enter an Integer, 0 to stop: ');
        ReadInt(Value);
        WriteLn;
        IF Value = 0 THEN
            EXIT;
            END;
        IF Value > 0 THEN
            (* create the element - see below *)
            (* Insert the temp element - see below *)
            WriteInt(Temp^.Data,8);WriteString(' arrived');
            WriteLn;
        ELSE
            (* Remove the first element - if nonempty *)
            IF Front <> NIL THEN
                Temp  := Front;
                Front := Front^.Next;
                WriteInt(Temp^.Data,8);
                WriteString(' departed');WriteLn;
                (* release the element *)
                DISPOSE(Temp);
            ELSE
                WriteString(' queue underflow ');
                WriteLn;
                END;
            END;
        END;
END QueueExample.
```

Create an Element. Element creation involves two steps – the use of NEW to obtain a new variable and the assignment of values to fields in the newly created record. The statements to create an element are:

```
(* Create a Q element *)
NEW(Temp);              (* put address of variable in Temp *)
Temp^.Next := NIL;  (* pointer to next record *)
Temp^.Data := Value (* assign data value(s) *)
```

Join. The logic to append an element to the back of a queue is straightforward. A special case occurs when the queue is empty.

```
(* Insert the element at the back of the queue *)
IF Front = NIL THEN (* Q is empty *)
    Front := Temp;
    Back  := Temp;
ELSE
    Back^.Next := Temp;
    Back       := Temp;
    END;
```

Depart. Removing the front element in the queue involves returning a pointer to the top element and changing Front to point to the second element.

```
(* Remove the front element; return address in Temp *)
Temp  := Front;
Front := Front^.Next (* change Front *)
```

5.7 Doubly Linked Lists

Previously we considered singly linked lists of which stacks and queues are special cases. One limitation with these lists is that we can only move in the direction of the pointers. In cases where it is necessary to move in either direction easily, it is helpful to have each element point to the preceding as well as the succeeding node. A special case is a circular list in which the pointers in each direction form a loop.

Elements in a doubly linked list must have at least three fields. An example declaration is

```
TYPE
    ElementRecPtr = POINTER TO ElementRec;

    ElementRec    = RECORD
        Previous : ElementRecPtr;
        Next     : CARDINAL;
        (* Data field declarations go here *)
        END;
```

It is clear that logic for creating elements and adding and removing elements requires updating two pointers in each element rather than one. As such the logic is slightly more complex.

The ListHandler Module

The ListHandler module described in Appendix D contains the following procedures for processing doubly linked lists. The names of the procedures are self-explanatory. Details are found in Appendix D.

CopyElement   CreateList   CreateElement
CreateList   InsertAfter   InsertBefore
InsertList   RemoveElement   RemoveList

5.8   Trees

Concepts

A tree is a collection of linked elements or <u>nodes</u> in which the pointers
from one node to another result in a hierarchy of the type shown in
Figure 5.4..

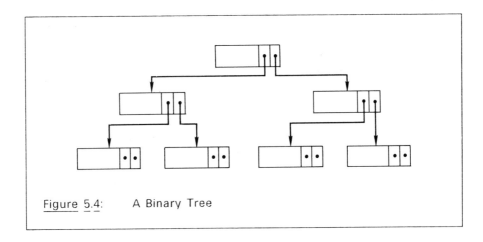

Figure 5.4:   A Binary Tree

A tree such as this in which each node has two pointers is called a
<u>binary tree</u>. The vocabulary associated with trees is used in describing
this structure. In particular, although upside down, the node at the top is
called the <u>root</u> node. The nodes at the bottom are called the <u>leaf nodes</u>.
Each node, other than the leaf nodes are <u>parent nodes</u> and (with
apologies to the ladies), each parent may have two offspring called the
<u>left son</u> and <u>right son</u>.

Binary trees have many useful applications including storing ordered
lists and information retrieval. Examples are given later in this section.

Most applications of trees require each node to have a unique value.
A field that serves to distinguish one node from another is called the
record <u>key</u>. We shall use the following declaration of a node record. The
type of the key field can be changed to fit the problem to be solved.

```
TYPE
    NodeRecPtr = POINTER TO NodeRec;

    NodeRec     = RECORD
        LeftSon  : NodeRecPtr;
        RightSon : NodeRecPtr;
        Key      : CARDINAL;
        (* other fields declared here *)
        END;
```

The following four subsections deal with four commonly performed tree-processing activities:

o Displaying the contents of a tree.

o Finding a node with a given key value.

o Inserting a node.

o Deleting a node.

The module TreeHandler described in Appendix D contains a family of procedures for performing these and other tree-processing functions. In this chapter we concentrate on the logic involved.

Displaying the Contents Of A Tree

Consider the binary tree in Figure 5.5 in which only the key values are shown.

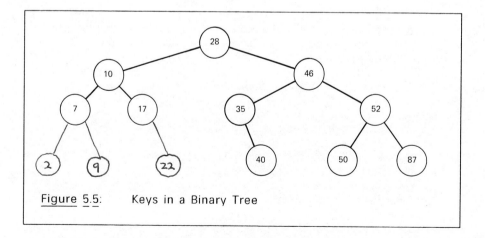

Figure 5.5:   Keys in a Binary Tree

In order to display all the key values in a tree, a rule for what-node-to-visit-when is needed. Note that every node is the root of the subtree below it. Thus each node has a left subtree and a right subtree either or both of which may be empty. There are three systematic sequencing rules which differ only in the order of visiting the root and its left and right subtrees. Specifically the orderings are:

Preorder (root first)
>root, left subtree, right subtree. For the example tree, the keys in preorder are 28, 10, 7, 2, 9, 17, 22, 46, 52, 50, 87.
>
>   ^
>   35 40

Inorder (root between)
>left subtree, root, right subtree. The example keys in inorder are 2, 7, 9, 10, 17, 22, 28, 46, 50, 52, 87.

Postorder (root last)
>left subtree, right subtree, root. For the example, postorder sequence results in 2, 9, 7, 22, 17, 10, 50, 87, 52, 46, 28.

The prefix "pre-", "in-", or "post-" indicates when the root is visited with respect to its two subtrees. Thus preorder means root first; inorder means root in between; postorder means root after the two subtrees.

Observe that the inorder sequences results in the nodes being visited in the order of increasing key values. Is this a coincidence? No. If the node keys are such that the root key value is between the left son and right son key values, then visiting the nodes in inorder will result in an ascending sequence of key values. This is the principle that is exploited in using a binary tree to store an ordered list. That is, assuming keys are unique, each node partitions the nodes in the tree below into two groups; those with key values less than the root key will be in the left subtree; those with key values greater than the root key will be in the right subtree.

Shown next is a slight modification of the procedure InOrder which is exported from the module TreeHandler described in Appendix D. It assumes the key type is CARDINAL.

```
PROCEDURE InOrder(    Root : NodeRecPtr);

    BEGIN
        IF Root <> NIL THEN
            InOrder(Root^.LeftSon);
            WriteCard(Root^.Key,10);
            InOrder(Root^.RightSon);
            END;
    END InOrder;
```

This is an example of a recursive procedure. A recursive procedure invokes itself to perform its task. The procedures for preorder and postorder traversals simply make the statement that displays the root key first and third respectively.

Finding A Value in a Tree

If the keys of the nodes of a tree in inorder sequence have ascending values then it is very easy and efficient to determine if a given value is present in a tree. The next procedure returns a pointer to the node containing a given key value. If the key value is not found, a value of NIL is returned. The second "NodeRecPtr" in the procedure header specifies the type of value returned by the procedure. Like many tree-processing procedures, it is recursive.

```
PROCEDURE FindNode(     Root        : NodeRecPtr;
                        SearchKey : CARDINAL) : NodeRecPtr;

    BEGIN
        IF Root = NIL THEN
            RETURN NIL;
        ELSIF SearchKey = Root^.Key THEN
            RETURN Root;
        ELSIF SearchKey < Root^.Key THEN
            RETURN FindNode(Root^.LeftSon,SearchKey);
        ELSE
            RETURN FindNode(Root^.RightSon,SearchKey);
            END;
    END FindNode;
```

Building A Binary Tree

To build a tree in which the left and right subtree keys are less than and greater than the root key respectively is not difficult. Because subsequent inorder traversal of such a tree produces an ascending sequence of key values, this is a common method of sorting (arranging in sequence) a collection of records. The algorithm is:

    .1 Create an empty tree
    .2 While data exists
        .1 Create a node record
        .2 Insert the node in the tree
    .3 Traverse the tree in inorder sequence

Suppose an undefined number of CARDINAL values are to be sorted and listed. The values are entered one at a time from the keyboard. The mainline of the program is given next. The statements to create a node and insert it in the tree follow.

```
MODULE TreeSort;

FROM InOut   IMPORT WriteCard, WriteString, ReadCard, termCH,
                    EOL, WriteLn;

FROM Storage IMPORT ALLOCATE, DEALLOCATE;

TYPE
    NodeRecPtr = POINTER TO NodeRec;

    NodeRec    = RECORD
        LeftSon  : NodeRecPtr;
        RightSon : NodeRecPtr;
        Key      : CARDINAL;
        END;

VAR
    Root  : NodeRecPtr;
    Temp  : NodeRecPtr;
    Temp1 : NodeRecPtr;
    Value : CARDINAL;

(* procedure InOrder goes here *)

(* procedure InsertNode goes here *)

BEGIN
    Root := NIL;
    LOOP
        (* obtain data from keyboard *)
        WriteString(' Enter a value: ');
        ReadCard(Value); WriteLn;

        (* allocate a node and initialize fields *)
        NEW (Temp);
        Temp^.LeftSon  := NIL;
        Temp^.RightSon := NIL;
        Temp^.Key      := Value;

        (* insert node in tree *)
        InsertNode(Root,Temp);

        (* stop once carriage return given *)
        IF termCH = EOL THEN EXIT END;
        END;
    (* print tree *)
    InOrder(Root);

END TreeSort.
```

The InOrder procedure is that shown previously. It is inserted immediately after the VAR satement.

The statements to create a node are:

```
NEW (Temp);
Temp^.LeftSon  := NIL;
Temp^.RightSon := NIL;
Temp^.Key      := Value;
```

Node Insertion.

When inserting the node Temp, a decision must be made as to what to do if two keys have the same value. The next procedure puts the new node in the right subtree thus preserving the original order of the input values when the tree is traversed.

```
PROCEDURE InsertNode(VAR Root : NodeRecPtr;
                         Temp : NodeRecPtr);

    BEGIN
        IF Root = NIL THEN
            Root := Temp;
        ELSIF Temp^.Key < Root^.Key THEN
            IF Root^.LeftSon = NIL THEN
                Root^.LeftSon := Temp;
            ELSE
                InsertNode(Root^.LeftSon,Temp);
                END;
        ELSE
            IF Root^.RightSon = NIL THEN
                Root^.RightSon := Temp;
            ELSE
                InsertNode(Root^.RightSon,Temp);
                END;
            END;
    END InsertNode;
```

Like many tree-processing procedures, this procedure is recursive. As with all recursive procedures, it can be converted to a nonrecursive procedure. Recursive procedures are described in Chapter 8.

Node Deletion

Removal of a node from a tree reduces to one of three cases:

1. Removal of a leaf node. This is easy; replace the pointer to the node by NIL.

2. The node to be deleted has only one subtree. Simply replace the pointer to the outgoing node with the pointer to the subtree.

3. The node being deleted has two sons. This case is discussed next.

When the node being removed has two sons it can be replaced by either its left son or right son. Suppose the left son takes his dad's place. Who becomes the father of the orphaned right son? We must maintain the property that all keys in every left subtree are less than the parent key and all keys in every right subtree are greater than the parent key. Thus the new father of the orphaned right subtree should be the node in the left subtree with the largest key. For example, consider the following:.

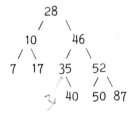

Suppose we delete the 46 node and the 35 node moves up to take its place. We then have two trees. The tree with root 52 is the orphan.

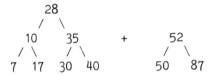

Since the 52 subtree has keys that are all greater than any in the 35 subtree it should become the right son of the highest key in the revised tree. In the example the highest key in the 35 tree is 40. Thus the 52 tree should be the right son of the 40 node. The resulting tree is therefore.

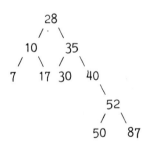

The algorithm for deleting a node that has two sons is:

    1. Replace the father with the left subtree.
    2. Make the orphaned right subtree the right
          son of the highest node in the left subtree.

A procedure that implements this logic follows:

```
PROCEDURE DeleteNode(VAR Outgoing : NodeRecPtr);

    VAR
        Temp : NodeRecPtr;

    BEGIN
        IF Outgoing <> NIL THEN
            IF Outgoing^.LeftSon = NIL THEN
                Temp      := Outgoing;
                Outgoing := Outgoing^.RightSon;
            ELSIF Outgoing^.RightSon = NIL THEN
                Temp      := Outgoing;
                Outgoing := Outgoing^.LeftSon;
            ELSE
                Temp := Outgoing^.LeftSon;
                WHILE Temp^.RightSon <> NIL DO
                    Temp := Temp^.RightSon;
                    END;
                Temp^.RightSon := Outgoing^.RightSon;
                Temp           := Outgoing;
                Outgoing       := Outgoing^.LeftSon;
                END;
            DISPOSE(Temp);
            END;
    END DeleteNode;
```

Analysis of Tree Search and Insertion

Does the shape of the tree make any difference in the performance of routines that build or examine nodes in the tree? Most definitely. Suppose the input data happens to have ascending values prior to building the tree. What shape will the tree have? With a little thought you will realize that every node including the root will only have a right son. Hence the result is simply a linked list. The power of the tree structure to efficiently sort and find particular values depends to what extent the tree is balanced. A perfectly balanced tree is one in which for every node the difference between the number of nodes in the left subtree and the right subtree is at most one.

The efficiency of a balanced tree results from the fact that you do not need to go very far down the tree to either add, locate or find a replacement node.

Since in general the order of input values cannot be controlled when building a tree, several algorithms exist for balancing a tree after it has been created. Algorithms also exist for maintaining balance when adding or deleting nodes. These can be found in a reference such as Chapter 4 of Niklaus Wirth's book Algorithms + Data Structures = Programs (Prentice Hall, 1976).

5.9 Summary

1. Pointer variables are used when creating variables at execution-time and linking together variables (usually records) to form various data structures.

2. The value of a pointer variable is a memory address of a variable of a given type. Pointer variables can be assigned the value of another pointer variable or the value NIL. Pointers can only be tested for equality.

3. Variables of the same type can be linked together by defining a record having two or more fields. Some fields contain data; others are pointers to other records of the same type.

4. One of the most commonly used data structures is a linked list. Stacks and queues are particular kinds of linked lists.

5. A tree is a suitable vehicle for storing data having a hierarchical structure. A binary tree is an efficient way to create, maintain and retrieve data having a natural ordering.

5.10   Exercises and Programming Problems

1. The input consists of the surnames of a number of individuals. Read the names and put each one in a record that is appended to the end of a linked list. After the last name has been read, point the last record to the record containing the first name thus forming a ring. Assuming clockwise to mean the original order of the data, print the name of: the second person clockwise from the first person; the fifth person counterclockwise from the last person.

2. Draw a circle. Write the letters of the alphabet and a blank around the outside of the circle in a clockwise direction. Write a program that reads a value of N and then a sentence. (a) Translate the sentence into a coded message by replacing each symbol in the sentence by the symbol that is N positions clockwise around the circle. Print the coded message. (b) Print the original message by decoding the message produced in part (a). Use a ring of records to store the letters. Make use of the logic developed for Problem 1.

3. The first line of input consists of a number of people's names. Read the names, storing them in a binary tree. Print the names in reverse alphabetical order. The second input line also contains several names. For each name found, print a message of the type: "Charlie not found" or "Charlie exists".

CHAPTER 6

ACTIONS IN MODULA-2: AN OVERVIEW

Questions Answered In This Chapter

1. What are the ways in which actions can be specified in Modula-2?

2. What are the kinds of statements available?

3. What are procedures and processes? How do they differ?

4. In what sense is a module the highest level of logical abstraction?

This chapter is a brief introduction to and overview of the material in the next four chapters.

6.1   Introduction

Part I of this book focused on the passive elements of the Modula-2 language. It described the types of values and data structures that can be defined and processed in Modula-2 programs. Part II describes the ways of expressing the actions that manipulate the data.

Modula-2 has four levels of expressing logic that increase in the degree of abstraction (scope of purpose Figure 6.1). Beginning with the least abstract, they are: statements, procedures, processes and modules. A separate section describes the essential features of each.

6.2   Statements

A Modula-2 statement is the least abstract (most specific) expression of logic. There are ten statements in the language. Statements may be classified in different ways. One useful classification is based on purpose. It is:

Assignment
- assignment statement

Conditional execution
- IF
- CASE

Iteration
- LOOP
- WHILE
- REPEAT
- FOR

Procedure
- Procedure Call/Function evaluation

Control
- EXIT and RETURN

Convenience
- WITH

Each statement can also be classified as simple or compound. The
simple statements are the assignment statement and the procedure call.
All other statements are compound and, with the exception of REPEAT,
use END to terminate the statement.

Statements are described in Chapter 7. Syntax diagrams for all
statements are found in Appendix B.

6.3 Procedures

A procedure is a named collection of declarations and statements. Each
procedure should have a single-mindedness. That is, it should perform a
well-defined task that you can express in a single simple sentence. An
example is "This procedure sorts an array of N INTEGER values".

Procedures are the basic building blocks of a program. Once the
purpose of a program has been clearly stated, the method of achieving
that purpose -- the algorithm -- is expressed as a sequence of logical
steps. Typically each of these steps is implemented as a separate
procedure.

With few exceptions, procedures must either receive values, return
values or both. As a general rule you should only pass those values to a
procedure that it needs to perform its task. Communication with
procedures is accomplished in one of two ways. A procedure can access
variables declared in its enclosing environment. Alternatively, variables
called formal parameters can serve as the means of transferring values to
and from the procedure.

Objects declared within a procedure are local to the procedure, meaning they are not "visible" outside the procedure. This means no ambiguity arises when a local object has the same identifier as one in its enclosing environment. This further implies that procedures may be written and tested independently of the programs that may subsequently use them.

Procedures lead a very transient life. A procedure is "created" each time it is called. When a procedure finishes executing, the values of its parameters and local variables are "lost" and not available should the procedure be called again.

Modula-2 distinguishes between function and nonfunction procedures. A function procedure is used when the purpose of the procedure is to return a value of a given type. A nonfunction procedure is more like a step in an algorithm. To illustrate the difference, shown next are two procedures that calculate the square of a REAL value. "Square" is a function procedure; CalculateSquare is a nonfunction procedure.

```
PROCEDURE Square (    X : REAL) : REAL;
    BEGIN
        RETURN X * X;
    END Square;

PROCEDURE CalculateSquare (    X        : REAL;
                            VAR SquareOfX : REAL);
    BEGIN
        SquareOfX : = X * X;
    END CalculateSquare;
```

As can be seen, a function procedure RETURNs the result. In a nonfunction procedure, the result is returned via a "VAR parameter".

Modula-2 contains many standard procedures. They are listed in Appendix A. Their names are recognized by the compiler provided the identifier has not been declared for some other user-defined purpose.

All Modula-2 implementations also contain procedures which are exported by modules supplied with the Modula-2 system. In fact, all input-output operations are performed by these library procedures. Using the techniques described in Chapter 11 you can create additional library modules that export services in the form of procedures.

Full details of procedures are found in Chapter 8.

6.4 Processes

A Modula-2 process or coroutine has a procedure and a workspace. A process is more general than a procedure in two important respects.

1. A process may be interrupted and subsequently resume execution from the point of the interruption. (A procedure on the other hand must execute "from the top" each time it is activated.)

2. Two or more processes may execute concurrently (simultaneously).

Interruptability. The first factor is significant primarily because it permits a program to continue execution while waiting for a input or output operation to complete. When the operation is completed, the executing process may be interrupted in order to perform any end-o -operation processing and then it can resume. The workspace associated with the process is the reason a process can resume execution following an interruption. The workspace is used to save sufficient status information to allow the interrupted process to resume.

Concurrency. Permitting two or more processes to execute concurrently is significant for two reasons. First, it allows Modula-2 to be used to write software that has more than one user sharing computer resources. Second, some programming logic can be more easily designed and expressed using concurrent processes.

Since computers have only one set of circuits for processing instructions, true concurrency is not possible and in fact Modula-2 processes are more accurately called coroutines. Nonetheless, the Modula-2 parallel processes execute <u>as</u> <u>if</u> they were running concurrently.

The communication among Modula-2 processes is accomplished in one of two ways. Processes can access shared variables or alternatively they can send and await signals in order to synchronize their actions.

The tools necessary to perform concurrent processing in Modula-2 are exported by the library module called Processes. Processes are described in Chapter 9.

6.5   Modules.

Concepts and Types

A module is the highest (most abstract) form of logical expression in Modula-2. It is the top level of the pyramid in the diagram below.

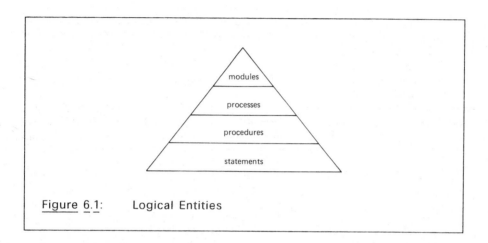

Figure 6.1:   Logical Entities

A module is a self-contained entity. A module is what is processed by the compiler and as such is called a compilation unit. Like processes and procedures, modules should have a well-defined purpose.

Program Modules. In Modula-2, there are four kinds of modules. In Part I of this book, all examples had a single program module. All Modula-2 programs have one and only one program module. However, a program module may access and use the services provided by the other three kinds of modules. The following three paragraphs summarize the role of definition, implementation and local modules.

Definition Modules. A definition module defines a set of services (procedures, variables, types and constants) that can be used by other modules. The definition module does not actually supply the services but simply defines the identifiers to be exported.

Implementation Modules. An implementation module provides the services named by its corresponding definition module. Every implementation module must have a matching definition module. Separating the provision of a set of services into definition and implementation parts has several advantages. Two of the most important are:

1. The definition of the services that are provided is separated from how they are implemented. This means that purpose is separated from how

that purpose is operationalized. Because implementation modules are compiled on their own, improvements can be made in representation or method without changing the nature of the service provided.

2. Definition modules are public whereas implementation modules are private. This allows implementation details to be hidden from a user's view either because they are not important or for proprietray reasons. For example, the source code for the InOut definition module is usually listed in each implementation's documentation (and in Appendix C). The code that implements ReadInt, WriteSpring, etc., however is not published.

Local Modules. For reasons given next Modula-2 allows a module to be declared within another module. The reasons have to do with the life-time and visibility of identifiers. These attributes are different for modules and procedures. In some instances, it may be desirable (but not necessary) to use a local module instead of a procedure. Because a local module is imbedded within a block, it cannot be compiled separately.

Module Libraries. A module library is simply a collection of compiled definition and implementation modules. The library therefore acts as a resource center that exports services to its clients.

6.6 Summary

1. A module is the entity processed by a Modula-2 compiler. It is a self-contained entity which may contain processes, procedures and statements.

2. Imports and exports are used to transfer goods and services between modules.

3. There are four types of modules -- program modules, definition modules, implementation modules and local modules.

4. Definition-implementation module pairs export services to client modules and collectively comprise the module library.

Modules are described in Chapter 10.

6.7 Exercises and Programming Problems

1. Exercise. What are the four entities used to express logic in Modula-2? What is the purpose of each?

2. Exercise. What are the primary differences between procedures and processes? Is the use of a procedure ever required? Explain.

CHAPTER 7

STATEMENTS

Questions Answered In This Chapter

1. What is the syntax of Modula-2 statements?

2. How are comments inserted in a statement sequence?

3. What are the syntactic and semantic rules for the three major groups of statements; assignment, conditional execution and iterative statements.

This chapter contains a detailed description of each action statement available in Modula-2. The nonaction or declarative statements were described in Chapters 2 through 5.

7.1 Statement Syntax

A statement denotes an action to be performed. Four statements (assignment, procedure call, RETURN and EXIT) are simple or elementary statements because they do not contain other statements. All other statements such as, WHILE, LOOP and IF are composite or structured statements because they contain other statements. Each structured statement except REPEAT ends with the reserved word END. (REPEAT terminates with "UNTIL".)

A semicolon separates statements in a statement sequence. Hence a semicolon is called a statement separator. It does not terminate a statement but separates statement pairs.

An empty statement contains no symbols. It is found between two successive semicolons or more subtly in situations such as the following WHILE statement, which contains two empty statements.

```
WHILE X <> 20 DO;
    X := X + 1;
    END
```

The first empty statement is located between the reserved word DO and the first semicolon. The second is between the second semicolon and the reserved word END. Neither is harmful. Most compilers ignore empty statements.

In fact, some programmers make a practice of putting a semicolon before and after each END as in the next example.

```
WHILE X < 100 DO
    X := X + 1;
    END;
```

The reason is that should a statement be inserted ahead of or following the END, no additional punctuation is needed in the original source statements. Examples in the book often use this style. Do any problems arise if a semicolon is used as a statement terminator instead of a statement separator? With one exception, no. The exception is that a semicolon cannot immediately follow the reserved word "RECORD".

7.2 Comments

Syntax

Anecdotal comments can be inserted between any pair of identifiers or values in a program. A comment (possibly blank) is enclosed between the character pairs "(*" and "*)". Comments may span multiple lines. Comments may also be nested. This makes it easy to "comment out" parts of a program. Shown next is a pair of nested comments.

```
x := x + 1; (* start of comment here
y := 2 * x;    continued (*inner comment*) *)
```

Note that "y := 2 * x;" is part of the comment. Comments are ignored by the compiler.

Style

1. Common sense should be used when inserting comments. The following comment has little value.

```
x := x + 1; (* add 1 to x *)
```

2. Long comments. Put a box around comments that are particularly important as follows:

```
(****** ------> ***)
(*                *)
(* comments here  *)
(*                *)
(***---------->****)
```

Alternatively, use the following style

```
(*
    first comment line
    second comment line

    last comment line
*)
```

This makes it easy to find the end of the comment.

3. Each procedure and module heading should be followed by a comment describing the purpose of the unit. Other information may include the author, the date, and the meaning of objects imported, exported or passed to and from the procedure or module. Because examples in the book are chosen to illustrate programming features of the language rather than provide production code that can be used in applications, this guideline is not always followed in the expository sections of the text. In the appendixes however extensive comments are provided.

4. When declaring a list of variables of the same type, the following format is sometimes used.

```
VAR
    var1, (* purpose of var1 *)
    var2, (* purpose of var2 *)
        .
    varN  (* purpose of varN *)
        : type;
```

If a program contains a large number of variables, it is preferable to order variables alphabetically. In this case, each variable declaration should appear on a separate line.

5. Some programmers like to align the beginning of all comments at a particular position on an input line.

6. In long structured statements, follow the END with a comment containing the reserved word that began the statement. This helps to find the end of the statement if indentations become ragged. Note that proper indentation is sufficient to match the beginning and end of a compound statement.

7. Develop your own style of commenting and use it consistently.

7.3 The Assignment Statement

The form, vocabulary and rules of the assignment statement are summarized next. The assignment statement is a simple statement.

The Assignment Statement

Purpose: To assign a value to a variable.

Form: target variable := source expression

Vocabulary: The variable that is assigned the value is called the target. The expression is called the source.

Algorithm: The target variable is evaluated (address and type determined); The source expression is evaluated; the source value is assigned to the target variable.

Rules:

1. The target and source must be assignment compatible. This means that the types must satisfy one of the following criteria.

   a) They are compatible types. That is

      o They are the same (they have the same type identifier or one is defined equal to the other as in the following example).

      ```
      TYPE
          WholeNumber = INTEGER;
      ```

      o One is a subrange of the other.

      o They are both subranges of the same base type.

   b) One is INTEGER, the other CARDINAL.

   c) Either or both are subranges with a base type INTEGER or CARDINAL.

2. A string expression (see Chapter 4) can be assigned to a string variable having an equal or greater length.

3. Data structures (arrays, records and sets) are assignment compatible only if they are declared with the same type identifier.

4. Assignment of Procedure types is described in Chapter 8.

Given the following declarations, are X and Y assignment compatible?

```
VAR
    X : ARRAY [0..10] OF REAL;
    Y : ARRAY [0..10] OF REAL;
```

The answer is no! The rule states they must have the same type identifier − not that their type specifications are equivalent. However, the next X and Y declarations are compatible because the types are declared to be equal.

```
TYPE
    XType = ARRAY [0..10] OF REAL;
    YType = XType;
VAR
    X : XType;
    Y : YType;
```

Assignment Style

1. A program is more visually pleasing if the assignment operators in a sequence of assignment statements are vertically aligned.

2. If there is a long sequence of simple assignments, arrange them in a tabular format as follows:

```
XIndex1 := 0; YIndex1 := 0; ZIndex1 := 0;
XCount  := 0; YCount  := 0; ZCount  := 0;
```

7.4   The IF Statement

There are two Modula-2 statements that allow you to selectively execute a sequence of statements. They are the IF statement and the CASE statement. The form, vocabulary and rules of the IF statement are summarized next.

The IF Statement

Purpose: To execute a sequence of statements only if a specified condition is true.

Form:

```
IF condition THEN
    statement sequence
ELSIF condition THEN
    statement sequence
ELSIF condition THEN
    statement sequence

ELSE
    statement sequence
    END
```

Vocabulary:

1. IF, THEN, ELSIF, ELSE and END are reserved words.

2. "IF condition THEN" is called the IF clause.

3. The lines beginning with "ELSIF" are called ELSIF clauses.

Algorithm:

1. Each condition is evaluated in sequence until one is found that has a value of true. The statement sequence immediately following the clause containing the true condition is executed. Execution subsequently continues with the statement following the END.

2. If all conditions are false, the statement sequence following ELSE (if present) is executed.

Rules:

1. All conditions must be BOOLEAN expressions.

2. The ELSIF clauses and their associated statement sequences are optional.

3. ELSE and the statement sequence following it are optional.

4. END is required.

IF Style

1. Indentation. Vertically align the IF, each ELSIF and ELSE. Indent each statement sequence and END. Append the comment (*IF*) to END if the statement is long and complex.

2. When the IF statement specifies a single, simple action to be performed when a condition is true, you <u>may</u> want to use the following form:

   ```
   IF X THEN statement END
   ```

3. Although empty statement sequences following IF, ELSIF and ELSE are permitted, it is not good programming style. For example, replace

   ```
   IF x = 0 THEN
   ELSE
       WriteString ('x nonzero')
       END
   ```

   with

   ```
   IF x <> 0 THEN
       WriteString ('x nonzero')
       END
   ```

4. Omit the ELSE clause if nothing is to be done when the preceding condition(s) is false. For example, the following fragments both illustrate poor style.

   ```
   IF x = y THEN           IF x = y THEN
       (* statements *)         (* statements *)
   ELSE                    ELSIF TRUE THEN
       END                      END
   ```

7.5 The CASE Statement

Example

The CASE statement allows you to select one of several statement sequences rather than one of two as in the IF statement. The restriction is that the selection must be based on the value of an expression. An example follows. Assume that Number is a CARDINAL variable.

```
CASE Number DIV 10 OF
      0    : WriteString ('Number divides by 10');
    | 1    : WriteString ('Number ends in a 1');
    | 2..4 : WriteString ('Number ends in 2,3 or 4');
    | 5,6  : WriteString ('Number ends in 5 or 6');
    ELSE     WriteString ('Number ends with 7,8,9');
    END;
```

This CASE statement logic determines the ending digit of Number and prints an appropriate message.

The expression "Number DIV 10" is called the <u>case expression</u>. The value of the case expression determines which statement sequence (if any) is executed. In the example, there are four explicitly defined cases and an "otherwise" case defined by the ELSE. Each explicitly defined case has the form

   case-label-list : statement sequence

The case-label-list consists of a list of values and/or subranges of the type of the case expression. In this example, "0, 2..5, 9, 7..8" would be a valid case label-list. The statement sequence associated with a particular case-label-list is executed if the value of the case expression is contained in the case-label-list. Cases are separated from each other by the <u>case separator symbol</u> which is the vertical bar "|". That is, a case separator is used between the end of a statement sequence and the next case-label-list. Some programmers prefer to put the case separator symbol to the left of the second and subsequent case-label-lists. Further style guidelines follow the formal description of the rules.

Note that an IF statement can be replaced by an equivalent CASE statement as follows:

```
IF condition THEN        CASE condition OF
    x := x + 1               TRUE  : x := x + 1
ELSE                       | FALSE : x := x - 1
    x := x - 1             END; (* CASE*)
    END;
```

The form, vocabulary and rules of the CASE statement follow

The CASE Statement

Purpose: To execute a statement sequence corresponding to the value of a single expression.

Form:

   CASE case-expression OF
       case-label-list : statement sequence

```
    | case-label-list : statement sequence
    |
    | case-label-list : statement sequence
  ELSE
                     statement sequence
  END
```

where a case-label-list is a sequence of one or more labels separated by commas. A label is either a constant expression or a range of constants defined by

```
  constant-expn .. constant-expn
```

Vocabulary:

1. CASE, OF and ELSE are reserved words.
2. "CASE expn OF" is called the CASE clause.
3. The vertical bar "|" is the case separator symbol.
4. The construct "case-label-list:statement sequence" is called a case.

Algorithm:

1. Evaluate the case-expression.

2. Sequentially compare the expression value to values in each case-label-list. If a match is found, execute the corresponding statement sequence. Continue execution with the statement following END.

3. If no match is found, execute the statement sequence immediately following ELSE (if present).

Rules:

1. The type of the case-expression must be INTEGER, CARDINAL, BOOLEAN, CHAR, an enumerated type or a subrange of one of these.

2. Values in the case-label-lists must be compatible with the type of the expression.

3. ELSE and the statement sequence following it are optional. If ELSE is omitted and the value of the expression is not found in any case-label-list, an execution time error occurs.

4. A value may appear in only one case-label-list.

CASE Style

1. Consistent vertical alignment of the components of the CASE statement makes the structure more visible. In particular, align the case label separators, ELSE and END. Align the colons delimiting the end of each case-label-list. If a case-label-list is lengthy, start the associated statement sequence on the line below the case-label-list.

2. Use CASE when the value of the expression is limited to a relatively small number of known, discrete values. If the values are widely dispersed or may vary from one run to another, use an IF statement with ELSIF clauses to separate the cases.

3. When the case logic is lengthy, insert a blank line between cases.

7.6 Loops, LOOP and EXIT

Introduction

Repetition of a statement sequence occurs in almost all programs. After all, if no statements were repeated, the time required to enter, list and execute a program to solve a numeric problem would likely exceed the time to solve it on a calculator.

In Modula-2 there are four structured statements that are used to define a program loop. In all loops there is a loop invariant. A loop invariant is a condition that must be true in order to begin another execution of the loop.

The four loop control statements and the most salient features of each are summarized next.

LOOP: the most general mechanism; repetitions continue until an EXIT statement is executed or the program terminates execution; LOOP can replace any of the other loop statements.

WHILE: requires a given condition to be true prior to each execution of a statement sequence; WHILE can replace the REPEAT and FOR loop logic.

REPEAT: executes a statement sequence and then requires a condition to be true in order to exit; otherwise the statement sequence is repeated. The REPEAT statement can be used to define the logic of a FOR statement.

FOR: executes a statement sequence once for successive values of a variable. The range of values may be specified in either ascending or descending order. The FOR statement generally specifies repetitions that can be controlled by a counter. It is also frequently used when processing components in an array.

The remainder of this section describes the LOOP and EXIT statements.

The form, vocabulary and rules of the LOOP and EXIT statements follow.

LOOP and EXIT

Purpose: To repeatedly execute a sequence of statements until EXITed.

Form:

```
LOOP
      statement sequence
    END
```

Vocabulary: LOOP and EXIT are reserved words.

Algorithm:

1. The statement sequence is executed over and over.

2. The first EXIT statement executed causes execution to continue with the statement following the LOOP statement.

LOOP Style

1. Indent and vertically align the start of each statement in the statement sequence with END.

2. If a single condition terminates loop execution and this condition can be tested either at the beginning or end of the statement sequence, use a WHILE or REPEAT statement respectively. Use LOOP when one of several conditions can cause loop termination or when the exit condition cannot be evaluated until the middle of the loop. More generally, use LOOP when it will simplify the programming logic.

7.7 WHILE

Characteristics

The WHILE statement provides the second most general form of loop control. Because the test to determine whether to execute a statement sequence is made prior to the beginning of the sequence, WHILE permits the possibility of not executing the sequence at all.

Each nontrivial WHILE statement has two characteristics. First, prior to the WHILE statement, statements are executed that allow the while-condition to be evaluated. Second, the statement sequence must contain a statement that eventually causes the while-condition to be false.

The following shows a simple WHILE loop and the equivalent logic expressed using a LOOP statement.

```
WHILE condition DO          LOOP
    statement sequence          IF condition THEN
    END                             EXIT
                                ELSE
                                    statement sequence
                                END (* IF *)
                            END (* LOOP *)
```

The form, vocabulary and rules of the WHILE statement are given next.

The WHILE Statement

Purpose: To repeatedly execute a sequence of statements as long as a condition is true.

Form:

```
WHILE condition DO
     statement sequence
     END
```

Vocabulary:

1. WHILE and DO are reserved words.

2. "WHILE condition DO" is called the <u>WHILE clause</u>.

3. The statement sequence is called the body of the WHILE statement.

Algorithm:

1. Evaluate the condition.
2. If the expression is true then
   .1 Execute the statement sequence
   .2 Go to step 1.

Rules:

1. The condition must be a BOOLEAN expression.

2. Variables appearing in the condition express should be assigned a value prior to entering the WHILE statement.

3. To avoid endless executions of the statement sequence, some statement in the sequence must cause the condition to become false.

WHILE Style

1. Vertically align and indent the statement sequence and END. If the statement is lengthy or complex, follow the END with the comment (* WHILE *).

2. A WHILE statement should be used when it may be necessary to skip all executions of a statement sequence.

7.8 REPEAT-UNTIL

Characteristics

The REPEAT statement executes a statement sequence repeatedly until a specified condition is true. It differs from a WHILE loop in two important ways. First, the test to continue repetitions is made <u>after</u> the statement sequence has been executed. Thus the sequence is executed at least once. Second, if the condition tested is true, the loop is exited rather than repeated.

The REPEAT statement is the only structured statement that does not terminate with the END symbol. Instead it uses "UNTIL condition". An example and the equivalent LOOP statement follow:

```
REPEAT                        LOOP
    statement sequence            statement sequence;
    UNTIL condition               IF condition THEN
                                      EXIT
                                  END (* IF *)
                              END (* LOOP *)
```

The form, vocabulary and rules of the REPEAT statement are given next.

The REPEAT-UNTIL Statement

Purpose: To repeatedly execute a sequence of statements until a condition is true.

Form:

```
REPEAT
     statement sequence
     UNTIL condition
```

Vocabulary:

1. REPEAT and UNTIL are reserved words.

2. The statement sequence is called the body of the REPEAT statement.

3. "UNTIL condition" is called the UNTIL clause.

Algorithm:

1. Execute the statement sequence.
2. Evaluate the condition.
3. If the condition is false then go to step1.

Rules:

1. The condition must be a BOOLEAN expression.

2. To avoid endless executions of the statement sequence some statement in the statement sequence must eventually cause the condition to become true.

REPEAT Style

1. Indent and vertically align the statement sequence and UNTIL.

2. Use a REPEAT statement when the statement sequence must be executed once or when it is natural to check for loop repetition at the end of the sequence.

7.9 FOR

Example

The FOR statement is ideally suited for situations in which:

1. The number of repetitions of a statement sequence is controlled by a counter, or

2. When the statement sequence is to be executed once for each value in a uniformly spaced sequence of ascending or descending discrete values such as, 1, 3, 5, 7, 9 or Z, Y, X, W, ..., B, A

Suppose the value of the expression $x^2 - 3x$ is to be printed for x = 0, 5, 10, ..., 50. Given appropriate declarations the following FOR statement below accomplishes the result.

```
FOR X := 0 TO 50 BY 5 DO
    WriteCard (x*x - 3*x, 10)
    END
```

The FOR clause (the first line of the example) contains information necessary to define and control the number of repetitions of the statement sequence that follows. In English, the line

```
FOR X := 0 TO 50 BY 5 DO
```

says "execute the statement sequence once for each value of x starting at zero and going up to 50 in steps of 5". In this example, the statement sequence would be executed eleven times.

The objects in a FOR clause have names. In particular there is the:

Control-variable
> The variable that assumes a different value during each execution of the statement sequence. In the example X is the control-variable.

Initial-value
> The value assigned to the control value prior to the first execution of the statement sequence. In the example 0 is the initial-value.

Test-value
> The value to which the control value is compared. If the control-variable exceeds the test-value, the statement sequence is not executed and execution proceeds with the statement following the END. In the example, the test-value is 50.

Step-value

> The value by which the control-variable is changed after each execution of the statement sequence. "BY step-value" is optional. If omitted, the default value is 1. In the example, the step-value is 5.

Four Additional Points.

1. The statement sequence is not executed if the initial-value exceeds the test-value (assuming a positive step-value). For example, the statement sequence following this FOR clause will not be executed.

```
FOR Count := 5 TO 0 BY 1 DO
```

2. It is not necessary that the control-variable exactly match the test-value prior to the last execution of the statement sequence. Repetitions terminate when the control-variable exceeds the test-value (if the step-value is a positive) or when the control-variable is less than the test-value (if the step-value is negative).

3. In most implementations the step-value must be INTEGER or CARDINAL even if the control-variable is not an integer. For example, the following fragment prints the letters 'Z', 'Y', 'X', 'W', ..., 'B', 'A'.

```
FOR Letter := 'Z' to 'A' BY -1 DO
    Write(Letter)
    END
```

4. When a FOR loop terminates execution, the value of the control variable is indeterminate. This means its value outside the FOR loop cannot be predicted with certainty.

Assuming a positive step-value, the following FOR and LOOP statements are equivalent.

```
FOR var := initial TO test BY step DO
    statement sequence
    END


var := initial;
LOOP
    IF var > test THEN
        EXIT
    ELSE
        statement sequence
        END;
    var := var + step
    END (* LOOP *)
```

In the LOOP example the statement "var := var + step" could be replaced by the procedure call "INC(var,step)". Similarly the call "DEC(var,step)" could be used if the increment is negative. We recommend using the addition and subtraction operators to improve readability. If the step-value is negative, the DEC operator is applied "step" times.

The form, vocabulary and rules of the FOR statement are summarized next.

The FOR Statement

Purpose: To execute a statement sequence once for each value of a control variable that is given an initial-value and is changed by a constant amount after each interation until a limiting value is exceeded.

Form:

```
FOR control-var := initial TO test BY step-value DO
    statement sequence
    END
```

Vocabulary:

1. FOR, TO, BY and DO are reserved words.

2. The line "FOR ...   DO" is called the FOR clause.

Algorithm:

```
    .1 Set control-variable = initial-value.
    .2 Repeat
        .1 Execute the statement sequence.
        .2 Add the step-value to the control-variable
                until control-variable exceeds the test-value.
```

Rules:

1. The control-variable cannot be:

   a) A component of a structured variable (see Chapter 4). Specifically, it cannot be a component of an array, record, or a variable designated by a pointer.

   b) IMPORTed.

   c) A formal parameter of a procedure (see Chapter 8).

2. Initial and test must be compatible with the control-variable. (Types T1 and T2 are compatible if T1 = T2 or if one is a subrange of the other or both are subranges of the same base type.)

3. The step-value must be INTEGER or CARDINAL.

4. "BY step-value" is optional. If omitted, "BY 1" is assumed.

5. The values of the control-variable, initial, test and step-values must not be changed by statements in the statement sequence.

6. Following execution of the FOR statement, the value of the control-variable is undefined.

FOR Style

1. Indent and vertically align the statement sequence with END.

2. Use the FOR statement to express simple loops that can be controlled by a counter.

7.10   The Other Statements in Modula-2

For the reasons given, detailed descriptions of the three remaining statements in Modula-2 are found elsewhere in this book. They are: the procedure call; RETURN; and the WITH statement.

The WITH statement is described in detail in Chapter 4 (Data Structures) because it applies only to RECORD structures.

Procedure calls such as "ReadCard(c)" require knowledge of procedure declarations in order to understand the details of parameter list requirements. This topic is discussed in detail in Chapter 8.

There are two key ideas in a procedure call. First, it is invoked by an expression of the form

procedure-name (actual-parameter-list)

The number, order and type of the parameters must match those found in the procedure declaration. Second, some procedures, such as ABS, return a value that replaces the invoking expression; others, such as WriteString, perform one or more operations. In the latter case execution resumes with the statement following the procedure call.

The standard procedure HALT deserves special attention. It terminates further execution of all statements.

7.11   Summary

1. Statements are the tools for expressing the operations to be performed by a program. There are two kinds of statements in Modula-2, simple and compound. A compound statement contains other simple or compound statements.

2. The assignment statement is a simple statement. The target variable and the value of the expression must be assignment compatible.

3. There are two conditional execution statements in Modula-2. The IF statement executes one of two statement sequences depending on the truth of an expression. The CASE statement selects one of several statement sequences based on the value of a discrete-valued expression.

4. There are four statements available for controlling the number of executions of a statement sequence. In order of flexibility, they are: LOOP, WHILE, REPEAT, and FOR.

5. Procedure invocation statements are discussed in detail in Chapter 8.

7.12   Exercises and Programming Problems

1. Exercise. Can a WHILE loop always be used to produce the equivalent logic of a FOR loop even if the body of the loop changes the values of variables used to define the initial and final values?

2. Exercise. Can a REPEAT-UNTIL loop always be written that will duplicate the logic of a FOR loop?

3. Exercise. Assuming N to be an INTEGER variable the program fragment below prints the values 2,4,6,...,10 using a FOR-loop.

```
FOR N :=1 TO 5 DO
    WriteInt(2*N,8);
    END;
```

Use a similar approach in a FOR loop to generate the following sequences of values:

a) -21, -18, -15, ..., 0
b) 1, 8, 27, 64, 125
c) 1, 0, 1, 0, 1, 0, 1, 0 (use the MOD operator)
d) 9.25, 9.00, 8.75, 8.5, ..., 6.75
e) 14, 5, 0, 5, 14

4. Exercise. Nested FOR-loops can be used to generate particular sequences of values. For example, assuming M and N to be INTEGER variables the output of

```
FOR M := 1 TO 3 DO
    FOR N := 3 TO M BY -1 DO
        WriteInt(N,8);
    END;
END;
```

is the sequence 3,2,1,3,2,3. For each of the following, write a pair of nested FOR–loops to produce the sequence of values shown.

  a) 0, 1, 2, 0, 1, 2, 0, 1, 2, 0, 1, 2
  b) 400, 300, 200, 100, 40, 30, 20, 10, 4, 3, 2, 1
  c) 1, 2, 3, 4, 5, 6, 7, 1, 3, 5, 7, 1, 4, 7
  d) 90; 81, 80; 72, 71, 70; ...; 9, 8, 7, .., 1, 0

5. If an equation can be written in the form x–F(x)=0, then, subject to certain conditions, a root of the equation can be found by obtaining increasingly accurate approximations of the root. If x_1 is some initial estimate of the root, then x_2 , x_3 , ... will be better estimates where x_n =F(x_{n-1}). Suppose F(x) has the form A/(x+B) and the initial estimate is called C. Write a program that reads values of A, B and C. Calculate increasingly accurate estimates of the root until the change in two estimates is less than 0.0001. Print every tenth estimate as well as the final estimate. Test your program using first the function 12.3/(x+5.4) and second the function 3.99/(x–4). In each case use 2.0 as your initial estimate of the root.

6. A fraction of the form

$$
\cfrac{a}{b + \cfrac{a}{b + \cfrac{a}{b + \cdots}}}
$$

is called a continued fraction. Its value may be approximated to any desired accuracy by evaluating

A_0/B_0, A_1/B_1, A_2/B_2, ... where
A_0 = 0, A_1 = a, and A_n = aA_{n-2} + bA_{n-1} for n = 2, 3, ...
B_0 = 1, B_1 = b, and B_n = aB_{n-2} + bB_{n-1} for n = 2, 3, ...

Write a program that reads several pairs of values of "a" and "b" and for each, calculates A_{10} /B_{10} . Test your program on at least the following two cases. (a) a=1, b=1; (b) a=1, b=2.

7. Suppose a cyclist takes 15 seconds to uniformly reduce his speed from 35 kph (kilometers per hour) to 10 kph. Write a program which can be used to determine how long it would take him to stop at this rate of deceleration for various initial speeds. Read the speeds one-at-a-time

from the keyboard. Use a negative number as a sentinel to terminate processing. Recall that acceleration equals the difference between the initial and final velocities divided by the time to effect the change.

8. Suppose three ranges of INTEGER values are called A, B and C. Suppose also that a value for an INTEGER variable N has been obtained. For each of the following ranges of A, B, C write one or more IF statements to determine the interval or intervals in which N lies. If it does not appear in any, write 'NONE'.

	A	B	C
a)	0 to 15	16 to 25	26 to 50
b)	0 to 15	16 to 25	0 to 25
c)	0 to 15	5 to 20	10 to 25
d)	less than 0	< >4	< >2
e)	1 to 100	20 to 80	50 to 60

9. Write a program that reads an INTEGER value and determines the number of nonzero digits in the number. Hint: Divide the number by 10, 100, 1000, etc., and add one to a counter if the quotient is nonzero.

10. Read a pair of INTEGER values M and N. Read a value of K. Determine if the last K digits in each number are the same. The output should appear as "Last __ digits of ___ and ___ are equal (unequal)".

11. Read the lengths of the sides of a triangle. Print "0" if the lengths do not form a triangle; "1" if the sides are all unequal; "2" if the triangle is isosceles; "3" if the triangle is equilateral.

12. Read an unknown number of INTEGER values recorded one value per line. Print the largest and smallest value of those that are read as well as each value that is read.

13. Temperatures in Fahrenheit (F) may be converted to Celsius (C) and vice-versa using the formulas:

$$F = \frac{9}{5} C + 32 \qquad\qquad C = \frac{5}{9} (F - 32)$$

Write a program that reads ten pairs of values. The second value of each pair is a temperature in degrees. The first value is a "1" if conversion from Celsius to Fahrenheit is required, a "2" if conversion from Fahrenheit to Celsius is required. Print ten lines of the form "___ degrees F (C) equals ___ degrees C (F)".

14. The value of the cube root of a number may be calculated by starting with two estimates -- one high (H) and one low (L). A better estimate is then (H+L)/2. A check can be made of the new estimate to see if it is high or low. If high, it can be used as the new H value, if

low, as the new L value. The process can then be repeated until any desired accuracy is obtained. Write a program that uses 3 and 4 as initial estimates of the cube root of 50. Use the procedure given until the estimate differs from the previous value by less than 0.01. Print the high and low estimates before each new estimate is calculated.

15. Read any four nonnegative INTEGER values. Call them I1, I2, I3, and I4. Replace them with the four values |I1−I2|, |I2−I3|, |I3−I4|, and |I4−I1|. If they are all equal, print the four values. If at least two of them are different, continue the process using the replacement values as the starting values. Continue until all four differences are equal. Print the values of I1, I2, I3 and I4 at each stage of the calculations.

16. The day of the week for any date consisting of a year (Y), month (M) and day (D) can be found using the following formula.

$$weekday = K \bmod 7 + 1$$

$$where \quad K = D + 2M + \frac{3M+3}{5} + Y + \frac{Y}{4} + \frac{Y}{100} + 1$$

All divisions in the formula are INTEGER (DIV) divisions. When using the formula, January and February of a year are considered as months 13 and 14 of the previous year. For example, Jan. 26, 1985 should be considered as the 26th day of the 13th month of 1984. In the formula, a value of 1 for the weekday represents Monday, 2 Tuesday, etc. Read several dates including your own birthday and print the day of the week for each. Stop when the year has a negative value.

17. Read the X-Y coordinates of three points. Determine if the third point and the origin lie on the same side of the line that goes through the first two points. Print "YES" if they do and "NO" if they don't. Print the coordinates of the three points.

18. Consider any four digit number. Let K1, K2, K3 and K4 be the values of the four digits in the number. Form a new number by adding the squares of the digit values. Repeat the process (find the digits, square and add) each time obtaining a new number. Write a program that reads a four-digit number and generates new numbers until either a value of one is found or until a value of twenty is found for the second time. One of these events will occur regardless of the number you start with.

19. Find the x that produces the largest value of y using the formula y=Ax+B when x is in the interval beween C and D. Read the values of A, B, C and D from the input.

20. Find the value of x that produces the largest value of y using the formula y=Ax^2+Bx+C when x is in the interval between D and E. Read the values of A, B, C, D and E from the input. Test your program using at least the following three sets of values.

a) A = -1, B = 0, C = 9, D = -4, E = 4
b) A = +1, B = -4, C = 1, D = 2, E = 8
c) A = -1, B = 6, C = -2, D = -1, E = 2

21. An airline operates planes which have first-class and economy seats.
If a customer approaches a ticket clerk, the clerk asks which type of
seat is wanted. If that type is available, a ticket is issued for that type.
If not available, the customer is asked if the alternate type of seat
would be acceptable (provided one is available). If it is acceptable, a
ticket of the alternate type is issued. If it is not acceptable, no ticket is
issued. Write a program that will print one of the messages "Issue first
class", "Issue economy", or "Dont issue ticket" based on the preceding
rules. Input to the program consists of four INTEGER values. The
variables to which these four values will be assigned have
(respectively) the following meanings:

$$\text{WantsFirst} = \begin{cases} 1 \text{ if customer wants first-class} \\ 2 \text{ if customer wants economy} \end{cases}$$

$$\text{Alternate} = \begin{cases} 1 \text{ if customer will take alternate type} \\ 0 \text{ if customer won't take alternate type} \end{cases}$$

$$\text{FirstAvail} = \begin{cases} 1 \text{ if first-class seat is available} \\ 0 \text{ if first-class seat is not available} \end{cases}$$

$$\text{EconoAvail} = \begin{cases} 1 \text{ if economy seat is available} \\ 0 \text{ if economy seat is not available} \end{cases}$$

For example, an input line containing "2 1 0 1" means: the customer
wants an economy seat; he will take the alternate type; no first class
seat is available; an economy seat is available. Therefore, the message
"Issue economy ticket" should be printed.

Test your program by reading sixteen different lines of data -- one
for each of the sixteen possible combinations of the four values. Print
an appropriate message after each line of data.

22. Write a program to print all integers in the range 100 to 500 that
have the property that the digits in the number are different. Print the
results four numbers per line.

23. A decision table is a method of describing rules for making decisions
in a tabular form. The following is a simple decision table for deciding
whether or not to get up in the morning.

		1	2	3	4	5
		R U L E S				
Conditions	Went to bed late	Y	Y	N	N	N
	Have a morning class				Y	N
	Test today	Y	N		Y	N
Actions	Get up	X		X	X	
	Stay in bed		X			X

The five decision rules in the table show which of two actions to take depending on three yes-no conditions. The yes-no conditions are: Did you go to bed late?; Do you have a morning class?; Do you have a test today?. The five decision rules are defined by the entries in the five columns of the table. Consider Rule (column) 1. It says that if you went to bed late and if you have a test today, then you should get up. In this rule, the action you take is independent of whether or not you have a morning class (There is no entry in Rule 1 for the second condition). Rule 5 says for example that if all three conditions are negative, then sleep

Suppose five input lines have been prepared each of which contains three numbers. The first value is a 1 (meaning went to bed early) or a 0 (did not go to bed early); the second is a 1 (morning class) or a 0 (no morning class); the third is 1 (test today) or 0 (no test today). Write a program that reads the data and for each set prints messages describing the conditions that are represented and the action to be taken.

24. Write a program to reflect the logic described by the following decision table. Choose a suitable form for representing the conditions as data values. After reading each input line and echoing the conditions, output a line of the form 'Commission rate is __ percent' or 'Case should be investigated'.

Sales Commission Table	1	2	3	4	5
	R U L E S				
Units sold < 100	Y		N	N	E
Units sold 100-199		Y	N	N	L
Units sold 200-299			Y	Y	S
With company more than 2 yrs			Y	N	E
Commission is 2% sales	X				
Commission is 3% of sales		X			
Commission is 4% of sales				X	
Commission is 5% of sales			X		
Investigate					X

25. On the island of Ho, there are two races -- the Good Guys who always tell the truth, and the Bad Guys who always lie. On my last visit to the island, I met three villagers named Tom, Dick and Zack. I asked each of them one question. Their answers are shown in parentheses.

    Q: Tell me Tom, is Dick a Good Guy? (yes)
    Q: Dick, do Tom and Zack belong to the same race? (no)
    Q: Zack, what about Dick, is he a Good Guy? (yes)

    Write a program to determine the races of the three villagers. To solve this problem, generate the eight possible combinations of race-to-people assignments using three FOR-loops. Check each combination to see if they would answer the questions in the manner described. This can be done using as few as three IF statements. Remember that the computer cannot think or reason and you must find the implications of each answer under the assumption that the speaker was first, a Good Guy, and second, a Bad Guy. The results of this analysis will permit you to construct the appropriate IF statements.

26. Three bags are labelled "cookies", "brownies" and "cookies and brownies". Although one bag contains cookies; one contains brownies and one contains a mixture, none of the labels are correct. Write a program that selects one item from one of the bags and determines the correct matchup of labels and contents. The program should output a line of the form "By sampling one item from the _____ bag, it can be determined that:" followed by three lines of the form: "The _____ bag contains _____".

27. If x_0 is an initial estimate of the value of $1/\sqrt{(z)}$, successively better estimates are given by x_1, x_2, etc. where $x_n=0.5x_{n-1}(3-zx^2_{n-1})$, $n=1,2,...$. Use this procedure in a program to calculate the fifth estimate of $1/\sqrt{(2)}$. Use 0.4 as your initial estimate. Print each estimate.

28. The probability that no two people in a group of N people have the same birthday is given by the formula

$$P_n = P_{n-1}\left(1 - \frac{n-1}{365}\right) \qquad \text{where } P_0 = 1$$

    Use this formula in a program that determines the smallest number of people such that the probability of no matching birthdays is less than one-half. Assume the result occurs for N less than fifty. Use a FOR statement in generating the values of P_1, P_2, ... Compare each value to one-half to determine if it is necessary to exit from the FOR-loop.

29. At a party of N married couples, the men pull a woman's name out of a hat to see who their next dancing partner will be. The chance that no man draws his partner's name can be obtained from the following relationship.

$$P_n = \frac{n-1}{n} P_{n-1} + \frac{1}{n} P_{n-1} \qquad \text{where } P_1 = 0, \text{ and } P_2 = 0.5$$

Read a value of N and calculate the probability that no man draws his wife's name for groups of people of 1, 2, 3, ..., N.

30. Read a value of N. Assume N is ten or less. Print out all triples of positive integer values that add up to N. Print out all triples of nonnegative integer values that add up to N.

31. Suppose the sales tax is 7 percent rounded to the nearest cent. A restaurant owner serving meals costing him between one and nine dollars (without tax) wants to price his items so that with the tax added, the total is a multiple of five cents. Print a table with two items per line showing for each the item price, tax and total that satisfy this criterion.

32. Write a program to eliminate the vowels in an input stream containing several lines of characters. That is, echo the input, ignoring vowels. Start a new line of output when an end-of-line character is detected.

33. The input consists of a single line of text. Count the number of letters, digits and other characters in the line.

34. Assume that a word is any successive sequence of non-blank characters and that a single blank separates each pair of words. Write a program that reads several lines of text, echoing each character as it is read and that prints a count of:

    - the number of words
    - the length of the longest word
    - the length of the shortest word
    - the number of words ending in 's'
    - the average length of the words

Improve the generality of the program by recognizing the common punctuation marks as denoting the end of a word.

35. Write a program that will echo an input file and that translates all lowercase letters to uppercase.

36. Write a program that counts the number of times the word "the" appears in an input file. Test your program using the following two lines:

    the problem of fat theodore goethe is the!
    accurate pronunciation of the word 'the'!

37. The input contains the names of several individuals, one individual per line each having two given names or initials preceding the surname. Extra blanks may precede the first name or separate any pair of names. Read the data and output the names one per line replacing each given name with the initial. Sample input and output are shown:

```
John Bruce Moore          -> J. B. Moore
Julian P. Huxley          -> J. P. Huxley
R. R. Reagan              -> R. R. Reagan
Z. Adolph Shickelgruber   -> Z. A. Shickelgruber
```

38. Suppose the input contains several names and ages of people as in the following two lines of input.

```
Ruth 25, Jeremiah 17, Archie 20,
Veronica 14, Tom 28
```

A comma immediately follows each age except that of the last person. Write a program to read the input and print a table as shown below following which the average age of the people is displayed.

```
Ruth            25
Jeremiah        17
Archie          20
Veronica        14
Tom             28
       Average  20.8
```

39. Write a program that reads a set of twenty-five INTEGER values of varying magnitudes and prints them using as few lines as possible. Do not print any symbols to the right of print position thirty.

40. An Armstrong number of N digits is one for which the sum of the Nth powers of the digits equals the original number. For example, 153 is an Armstrong number because $1^3 + 5^3 + 3^3 = 153$. Write a program to find all two- and three-digit Armstrong numbers.

41. A number is balanced if the largest digit in the number equals one-half the sum of the digits in the number. For example, 123 is balanced because (1+2+3)/2 = 3. Find all balanced numbers between 1 and 1000.

42. Suppose a ball dropped from a height H rebounds to a height of .9H. (a) Write a program that determines the number of bounces which the ball must make before its maximum height is 0.1E-10. (b) Add logic to the program for part (a) to determine the total length of time the ball is in the air.

43. Suppose A and B are arrays of eight INTEGER values each. Read the two sets of values using FOR-loops. Print those values that are in: both A and B; either A or B or both; A but not B; B but not A; either A or B but not both. Test your program using the following sets of values.

$$A = (2, 5, 8, 4, 7, 1, 6, 10)$$
$$B = (9, 8, 4, 10, 3, 5, 12, 11)$$

44. Start with any four-digit INTEGER value in which at least two of the digits have different values. Form the largest and smallest possible numbers from the digits. Subtract them to give a new number. Compare the number to 6174. If equal, stop. If not, repeat the entire process until the number 6174 is obtained. (It will show up in at most seven steps regardless of the number you start with!) For example, if you start with 1998 you get successively: 8082 (from 9981 - 1899); 8532 (from 8820 - 0288); 6174 (from 8532 - 2358). Print your starting value and each number obtained during the procedure.

45. Write a program that reads an INTEGER value and finds all of its divisors. For example, the divisors of 6 are 1, 2, 3, and 6. Store the divisors in an array called Vector. For each element of Vector, determine how many divisors it has. (For the example, these would be 1, 2, 2, and 4. Store these values in a vector called NumDivisors. Find the sum of cubes of the elements of NumDivisors and compare this with the square of the sum of the elements of NumDivisors. They will be equal! This is a general procedure for finding sets of numbers having this property. Write a program that reads several values and generates the set of values associated with each input number according to the preceding rules.

46. The input data contains twenty INTEGER values each of which is zero or some positive value. Read the values and store them in a vector called Data. Print the values in Data. Create a new set of values called Dense from the elements of Data as follows. If there are N consecutive zero values in Data, store a value of -N in the next element of Dense. If an element of Data is positive, store its value in the next element of Dense. (See the following example.) Print the values in Dense. Finally use the elements of Dense to generate the original set of values by reversing the logic used to create Dense. Store the re-created set of values in Copy and print its values. For example:

```
Data   2 3 0 0 0 0 1 5 7 0 0 8 4 0 9 6 0 0 3 0
Dense  2 3 -4 1 5 7 -2 8 4 0 9 6 -2 3 0
Copy   2 3 0 0 0 0 1 5 7 0 0 8 4 0 9 6 0 0 3 0
```

47. Most credit cards have an account number in which the last digit is called the "check digit". Its value depends on the values of the other digits. When the account number is read from a card, the last digit is compared with what it should be based on the other digits in the number. Suppose an account number has ten digits (including the check digit). One method of calculating the check digit is as follows. Find the sum of the 2nd, 4th, 6th and 8th digits (beginning from the left). Call this total Sum1. Form a number consisting of the 1st, 3rd, 5th, 7th and 9th digits. Multiply this value by two and add the digits in the result. Call this total Sum2. Add Sum1 and Sum2 and subtract the last digit from ten to obtain the check digit. For example, to see if the number 2520764263 is valid: we have Sum1=5+0+6+2=13; now 2*22746 = 45492 and therefore Sum2=4+5+4+9+2 = 24; thus Sum1 + Sum2 = 37 and so the check digit should be 10−7=3. Thus the account number is valid. Write a program that reads an unknown number of ten digit account numbers and determines which are valid (the check digit agrees with that calculated according to the preceding rules). When testing your program use at least two valid account numbers. Note that to obtain Sum2 you will need to extract the individual digits in a number. This can be done by repeatedly dividing the number by ten and using the remainder as the value of the next digit.

CHAPTER 8

PROCEDURES

Questions Answered In This Chapter

1. Why should program logic be partitioned into procedures? How is this done?

2. In what ways are procedures independent of the environments in which they are used? In what sense do they share that environment?

3. What are the similarities and differences of function and nonfunction procedures?

4. How are recursive procedures defined and used?

5. Variables may have a procedure type. What does this mean and how are such variables used?

The previous chapter described the statements in the Modula-2 language. Statements are the fundamental building blocks expressing actions to be performed. A higher level of logic is the procedure - an organized collection of declarations and statements that performs a well defined task.

   This section describes how to construct procedures and transfer values to them and from them.

8.1   Introduction

There are many reasons for creating a named collection of statements and supporting declarations. Among the more important are:

o By isolating a logical task in a procedure the parts of the program are more independent. Hence the detection and correction of logic errors is easier.

o The program structure is more visible.

o Procedures can be tested and debugged separately.

o The same procedure can be invoked from many locations in a program.

o A library of procedures can be developed that serves as a toolbox of resources to be called (no pun intended) as needed.

Before describing how to define and use procedures, let us briefly review two groups of procedures already described in some detail.

Standard Procedures

Modula-2 contains a number of standard procedures that are supplied with every implementation of the language. These include routines such as ABS, INC and DEC which perform arithmetic-type operations; type conversions such as FLOAT and TRUNC and several others. The standard procedures, unlike procedures such as Read and WriteString do not need to be IMPORTed from a library module. That is, the standard procedures are <u>pervasive</u> or ubiquitous – they exist everywhere.

The standard Module-2 procedures were described in Chapter 3. A complete listing is in Appendix A.

Library Procedures

Each Modula-2 implementation contains several "standard" modules that EXPORT a number of procedures. For example, the module InOut exports the procedures Read, WriteLn, the constant EOL and other objects.

Chapter 11 describes how to create modules that export objects for use by other modules.

8.2 An Example

Consider the following problem. Read three integer values; sort them in ascending order and print the sorted sequence. Three procedures – one to perform each step in the algorithm – will be used. The Print procedure illustrates how to pass values to a procedure; the Read procedure shows how to return values from a procedure; the Sort procedure shows how to nest procedures one within the other. The program aside from the procedure declarations is shown next.

```
MODULE ThreeInARow;

FROM InOut IMPORT WriteCard, ReadCard, WriteString, WriteLn;

VAR
    X : CARDINAL;
    Y : CARDINAL;
    Z : CARDINAL;

    (* procedure declarations here *)

BEGIN
    Read(X,Y,Z);
    Sort(X,Y,Z);
    Print(X,Y,Z);
END ThreeInARow.
```

Observe that identifiers in the IMPORT list do not appear explicitly in the module body but are obviously used by the procedures. This illustrates the important rule that procedures do not IMPORT (or EXPORT) identifiers – that is the prerogative of modules.

The Print Procedure. Now to the procedures. The simplest is the Print procedure. It is passed three CARDINAL values and prints them. Here it is.

```
PROCEDURE Print(    A : CARDINAL;
                    B : CARDINAL;
                    C : CARDINAL);

    (* Print the values of A, B and C *)

    BEGIN
        WriteString('The three sorted values are: ');
        WriteCard(A,8);
        WriteCard(B,8);
        WriteCard(C,8);
        WriteLn;
    END Print;
```

Comments.

1. The procedure declaration begins with a <u>procedure</u> <u>header</u> which has the following form.

    PROCEDURE name (formal-parameter-list)

PROCEDURE is a reserved word. The procedure name may be any identifier that is different from other identifiers declared in the enclosing module or procedure. In the example, the enclosing module is ThreeInARow.

The formal-parameter-list is a declaration of variables representing values which are passed to the procedure. In the Print procedure the formal parameter list is:

```
(    A : CARDINAL;
     B : CARDINAL;
     C : CARDINAL);
```

It specifies that three CARDINAL values will be passed to the procedure. The identifiers A, B, C, are surrogates for (represent) the actual values which are not known until the procedure is executed. The recommended style of declaring the formal parameters is that shown in which each parameter declaration appears on a separate line with the variable names and types aligned.

2. The body of the procedure contains no surprises. It consists of four procedure calls.

The Read Procedure. Unlike Print which is simply passed values, Read must return values to the environment from which it was invoked. Here it is:

```
PROCEDURE Read(VAR A : CARDINAL;
               VAR B : CARDINAL;
               VAR C : CARDINAL);
   BEGIN
      WriteString('Enter first positive integer:  ');
      ReadCard(A); WriteLn;
      WriteString('Enter second positive integer: ');
      ReadCard(B); WriteLn;
      WriteString('Enter third positive integer:  ');
      ReadCard(C); WriteLn;
   END Read;
```

Comments. The new idea in this procedure is the use of "VAR" in the formal parameter-list. VAR indicates the variables which follow are VAR formal parameters. A VAR formal parameter occupies the same memory locations as its corresponding actual parameter. Thus changes in a VAR parameter are changes in the actual parameter.

Since Read is invoked by the procedure call "Read(X,Y,Z)" this means the formal parameter A shares the same memory as X; likewise the pairs B and Y and C and Z occupy the same memory locations. Thus changes in A are changes in X; changes in B are changes in Y; changes in C are changes in Z. It is therefore perhaps somewhat of a misnomer to say the procedure "returns" three values because in fact each actual parameter changes when its corresponding VAR parameter changes.

If formal parameters preceded by VAR are called <u>VAR</u> <u>parameters,</u> what are formal parameters that are not preceded by VAR such as those in Print? They are called <u>value</u> <u>parameters</u>.

Value parameters differ from VAR parameters in two important ways. First, value parameters occupy memory locations distinct from those of the corresponding actual parameter expressions. Second, prior to executing the called procedure, each value parameter is assigned the value of its corresponding actual parameter. However, when the procedure finishes executing, the values of the value parameters are <u>not</u> assigned to the corresponding actual parameters.

Style. When declaring a formal parameter list, each paramter should appear on a separate line. Vertically align each instance of "VAR". Leave four blank spaces before the start of each value parameter identifier. Some programmers like to put all VAR parameters either before or after the value parameter declarations.

Sort. The Sort procedure is passed three values and returns those same three values in a (possibly) different order. What algorithm should be used to sort the three values? A series of IF statements could be used. However we shall use the method of examining each pair and exchanging their positions if not in the right order. When applied to a general sequence of values, this technique is called a bubble sort. Specifically the algorithm has three steps.

   .1 If x > y then
       .1 swap x and y
  .2 If y > z then
       .1 swap y and z
  .3 If x > y then
       .1 swap x and y

Note that swap is used three times. It is thus logical to make Swap a separate procedure. Furthermore, since it is only used within Sort, it should be declared within Sort. Nested procedures should be framed by comments or asterisks to highlight their presence and scope. The Sort procedure is given next.

```
PROCEDURE Sort(VAR A : CARDINAL;
               VAR B : CARDINAL;
               VAR C : CARDINAL);

   (* ********************************* *)
   PROCEDURE Swap(VAR X : CARDINAL;
                  VAR Y : CARDINAL);
      VAR
         Temp : CARDINAL;

      BEGIN
         Temp := X;
         X    := Y;
         Y    := Temp;
      END Swap;
   (* ********************************* *)

   BEGIN
      IF A > B THEN Swap(A,B) END;
      IF B > C THEN Swap(B,C) END;
      IF A > B THEN Swap(A,B) END;
   END Sort;
```

Comments.

1. Sort has three VAR parameters. The formal parameters A, B and C are aliases for the actual parameters X, Y, Z.

2. The procedure Swap is declared within Sort. As with CONST, TYPE and VAR declarations, procedure declarations must precede the body of the procedure or module in which they are declared.

3. The formal parameters of Swap are X and Y. Recall that these same identifiers are declared as CARDINAL variables in the program module. No ambiguity results because the formal parameters and other identifiers declared within a procedure are local to the declaring procedure – their meaning is that in the procedure in which they are declared. The variable Temp declared in Swap is an example of a variable that is local to Swap.

Ignoring the statements specifying actions to be performed the overall structure of the ThreeInARow program follows. The formal-parameter-lists are written on single lines in order to make the overall structure more visible. The fragment also illustrates the recommended rules of indentation.

```
MODULE ThreeInARow;

FROM InOut IMPORT WriteCard, ReadCard, WriteString, WriteLn;

VAR
    X : CARDINAL;
    Y : CARDINAL;
    Z : CARDINAL;

PROCEDURE Read(VAR A, B, C : CARDINAL);
    BEGIN
        (* statement sequence *)
    END Read;

PROCEDURE Sort(VAR A, B, C : CARDINAL);

    (* ********************************* *)
    PROCEDURE Swap(VAR X : CARDINAL;
                  VAR Y : CARDINAL);
        BEGIN
            (* statement sequence *)
        END Swap;
    (* ********************************* *)

    BEGIN (* Sort *)
        (* statement sequence *)
    END Sort;

PROCEDURE Print( A, B, C : CARDINAL):
    BEGIN
        (* statement sequence *)
    END Print;

BEGIN (* ThreeInARow *)
    Read(X,Y,Z);
    Sort(X,Y,Z);
    Print(X,Y,Z);
END ThreeInARow.
```

This concludes the discussion of the example. A summary of the rules and ideas illustrated is found in Section 8.8.

8.3 Scope: Life and Visibility

This section describes the lifetime and visibility of objects declared within procedures. To state the "scope" of an object means to describe both its lifetime and visibility.

Lifetime. The lifetime of a constant, type, variable or procedure begins at the time when memory is reserved to store the object and ends when that memory is released for other uses. The lifetime of objects declared within procedures is defined by the following statement.

> An object declared within a procedure is created at the time its declaring procedure is called. It ceases to exist when the procedure body terminates execution.

This statement has two important implications. On the plus side, memory is used efficiently because the memory needed for constants, variables and internally declared procedures is not reserved until the procedure is invoked. On the negative side, there is a certain amount of overhead required to allocate and deallocate memory. Furthermore, the rule means procedures cannot keep the value of a variable from one invocation to the next. Thus to save a value created by a procedure, it must be assigned to a variable declared outside the procedure.

The lifetime of objects declared in modules is different. Complete details are given in Chapter 10. The key difference is that a module's objects are created when its enclosing procedure or module is invoked rather than when the module itself is invoked.

Visibility. The visibility of a declared object refers to the collection of statements that can reference the declared object. More precisely, if an identifier is visible at a given point in a program, it means the compiler knows what it represents. There are two visibility rules.

1. The standard identifiers are visible everywhere in a program. They are pervasive. The standard identifiers are listed in Appendix A.

2. Each object or formal parameter of a procedure is visible everywhere inside the procedure except in any nested procedure which contains a declaration for the same identifier. An object is unknown outside its declaring procedure.

There is a simpler way to state the second rule. Imagine each procedure to be a box made of one-way glass so that you can see out but you can't see in. That is, you can see and use identifiers declared in outer enclosing procedures but not in internally defined procedures. The following structure illustrates the "you-can-see-out-but-you-can't-see-in" rule.

```
PROCEDURE A (...)

    PROCEDURE B(...)
       END B;

    PROCEDURE C(...)
       END C;

    END A;
```

Comments.

1. The standard identifiers such as ORD are visible in A, B and C.

2. Identifiers declared in the procedure or module which encloses A are visible in A, B and C.

3. Identifiers declared in A are visible in B and C.

4. Identifiers declared in B are visible only in B.

5. Identifiers declared in C are visible only in C.

Local and Global. The words local and global refer to the visibility of an identifier from a given procedure. The local identifiers of a procedure are its formal parameters and those declared within the declaration part of the procedure. A procedure's global identifiers are those declared in all enclosing procedures. For example, in the preceding diagram, the formal parameters and identifiers declared in procedure A are global with respect to procedure B. On the other hand, identifiers declared in C are neither local nor global with respect to B because C does not enclose B. As far as B is concerned, the local identifiers of C do not exist.

Global variables provide an alternative means of giving a procedure access to needed values. That is, instead of passing values through a parameter list, the called procedure may access its global variables directly. This may be convenient but the weakness becomes apparent when you take the idea to the extreme. That is, suppose all variables were declared in the program module declarations. Two of the more significant complications are:

o all identifiers would need to be unique

o all variables would be accessible to every procedure. This permits procedures to change any value – perhaps inadvertently and without realizing the consequences. These "side effects" make detection and correction of errors extremely difficult.

As a general rule, use global constants and types but limit use of global variables. Use VAR parameters to save and return values calculated by procedures.

The visibility rule for procedures does not allow you to selectively control the visibility of particular identifiers. Modules however, via IMPORT and EXPORT statements provide explicit control of visibility in both the inside-to-outside and outside-to-inside directions.

8.4 Open Array Parameters

An Example. This section describes and illustrates how to define formal parameter arrays for which the number of elements in the parameter array is not known at the time the procedure is written.

Suppose a procedure is required to reverse the values in any array of CHAR values. The algorithm is simple – swap the first and last elements; then the second and second last; third and third last, etc. The following procedure does the job. It contains the open array parameter "ARRAY OF CHAR" and employs the standard procedure HIGH to return the index of the highest element of an array parameter.

```
PROCEDURE Reverse(VAR X : ARRAY OF CHAR);

    VAR
        Temp     : CHAR;
        Index    : CARDINAL;
        MaxIndex : CARDINAL;

    BEGIN
        MaxIndex := HIGH(X);
        FOR Index := 0 TO MaxIndex DIV 2 DO
            Temp         := X[Index];
            X[Index]     := X[MaxIndex - Index];
            X[MaxIndex - Index] := Temp;
            END;
    END Reverse;
```

Comments.

1. The formal parameter X is an open array parameter. The form of an open array declaration is

    ARRAY OF type

2. At execution time an open array is equivalent to

    ARRAY [0..n] OF type

where n is one less than the number of elements in the actual array. The value of n can be obtained using the standard procedure HIGH.

The rules of open array parameters follow.

Open Array Parameters

Form:

ARRAY OF type

Rules:

1. Open array declarations are restricted to formal parameters.

2. The type must be the same as the component type of the actual parameter or be "ARRAY OF WORD". (The standard type WORD is described in Chapter 12.)

3. Although open arrays are one-dimensional, multidimensioned arrays can be passed to open arrays provided that the higher dimensions are found in the component type identifier. An example is given following the rules.

4. Open array variables must be processed component by component. Some implementations allow an open array to be the source or target in an assignment statement.

5. Open arrays can be passed as actual parameters to other procedures.

A Multidimensional Open Array. Suppose a matrix having two rows and three columns is to be passed to an open array parameter. The declaration of the passed array must specify the row vectors as a separate named type as follows:

```
TYPE
    RowVector = ARRAY [0 .. 2] OF REAL;
VAR
    Matrix : ARRAY [0 .. 1] OF RowVector;
```

Suppose further that Matrix is passed to a procedure called Analyze. The procedure header of Analyze will be:

```
PROCEDURE Analyze(    Table : ARRAY OF RowVector);
```

Within the procedure, HIGH(Table) will have a value of 1 since 1 is the highest index of Matrix.

Open arrays are indispensable in developing procedures that can process arrays of varying numbers of components. Open arrays are sometimes called <u>conformant arrays</u>. The most general open array is defined by ARRAY OF WORD. The WORD type is described in Chapter 12.

The standard procedure HIGH is summarized below.

HIGH

Form:

   HIGH(array)

Rules:

1. The standard procedure HIGH returns the CARDINAL value that is the highest subscript value of the first dimension of an array.

2. Although most commonly used with open arrays, HIGH can be used with "regular" arrays as well. Thus given

```
VAR
     A : ARRAY [6..10],[19..20] OF INTEGER
```

HIGH(A) returns a value of 10 if A is visible and 4 if it is not.

8.5 Function Procedures

Example

A function procedure is one that RETURNs a result that replaces the expression invoking the procedure. Many of the standard procedures such as ABS, ORD and HIGH are function procedures. This section describes how to declare and use function procedures. Because VAR parameters return values to the calling procedure, a function procedure can always be replaced by an equivalent nonfunction procedure provided appropriate changes are made in the calling procedure.

The following is a function procedure called BIGGER that returns the larger of two INTEGER values.

```
PROCEDURE Bigger(   X : INTEGER;
                    Y : INTEGER) : INTEGER;

    BEGIN
        IF X > Y THEN
            RETURN X;
        ELSE
            RETURN Y;
            END;
    END Bigger;
```

This example illustrates the three important differences between function and nonfunction procedures.

1. The type of the function result is appended to the formal parameter list. For example, the value of the Bigger function is INTEGER. A function may return any type of result.

2. A RETURN statement specifies the result that replaces the calling expression and then terminates procedure execution.

3. A function procedure is invoked by the appearance of the procedure name and actual parameters (called the function designator) in an expression in the calling procedure. The function result is substituted for the function designator and execution continues with further evaluation of the expression. For example, given appropriate declarations, Bigger could be used in the following program body.

```
BEGIN
    WriteString('Enter the first integer:  ');
    ReadInt(A); WriteLn;
    WriteString('Enter the second integer: ');
    ReadInt(B); WriteLn;
    WriteString('The larger integer is: ');
    WriteInt(Bigger(A,B),8);
    WriteLn;
END BiggerTest;
```

A function procedure without formal parameters must still use parentheses to enclose its (empty) parameter list. For example, if Bigger obtained its values from global variables, its procedure header would be

```
    Bigger () : INTEGER;
```

The next box summarizes the forms and rules of a RETURN statement. Note that RETURN (with no argument) transfers control back to the calling procedure from a nonfunction procedure. This usage, as suggested in the style guidelines, is not recommended.

The RETURN Statement

Purpose: To exit from the enclosing procedure or module body, and in the case of a function procedure to return the function value.

Forms:

RETURN   (* used with nonfunction procedures *)

RETURN expression (* used with function procedures *)

Rules:

1. RETURN is a reserved word.

2. If no expression follows "RETURN", execution continues with the statement following the procedure call.

3. If the expression is present, the value of the expression replaces the function designator (function-invoking expression) in the calling statement.

4. "RETURN expression" is mandatory in function procedures.

5. For nonfunction procedures, the use of RETURN is optional since procedure execution terminates following execution of the last statement in the body of the procedure.

6. A procedure may contain more than one RETURN statement.

RETURN Style

1. Unless logic is convoluted and complex, use only one RETURN statement and make it the last statement in the procedure body. (The example Bigger deliberately violated this guideline for pedagogical reasons.)

2. Do not use a RETURN statement with nonfunction procedures; let the procedure exit from the "bottom" of the procedure body.

8.6   Recursive Procedures

A recursive procedure is one that "turns back on itself" to accomplish its objective. That is, it invokes itself. Two examples follow. The first is the well-known factorial function; the second is a recursive procedure for sorting an array of values.

The Factorial Function

For a positive integer n, factorial n is the product of the first n integers and is often written "n!". Factorial 0 is defined to be 1. In general, n! = n (n−1)! and 0! = 1. A recursive factorial function procedure follows.

```
PROCEDURE Factorial(    N : CARDINAL) : CARDINAL;

    VAR
        Fact : CARDINAL;

    BEGIN
        IF N = 0 THEN
            Fact := 1;
        ELSE
            Fact := N * Factorial(N-1);
            END;
        RETURN Fact;
    END Factorial;
```

Comments.   Suppose "Factorial(3)" appears in an expression. The Factorial function will be invoked four times with values of 3, 2, 1 and 0. The first three times it is invoked, the ELSE clause is executed; the fourth time, the THEN clause is executed. All four invocations occur before any RETURN statement is executed. Successive RETURNs cause values of 1, 1, 2 and 6 to be substituted for the function designator "Factorial (N−1)".

When a procedure invokes itself, all local variables and expressions are stacked on top of those from the previous invocation. As each RETURN is executed, the top set of variables and expressions is peeled off the stack and the return value substituted for the function designator before resuming execution of the calling procedure.

Any recursive algorithm can be replaced by a nonrecursive one. While clarity and simplicity of logic are important, there are sometimes significant differences in execution times and memory requirements between recursive and nonrecursive algorithms. Careful analysis may be required when confronted with a specific problem.

Quicksort: A Recursive Procedure

A frequently encountered problem is that of arranging the elements of an array into an ascending (or descending sequence). One of the best techniques is called the quicksort algorithm.

    .1 Select any element.
    .2 Rearrange the values so that:
        .1 All values less than the selected element
            are to the left of the selected value
        .2 All values greater or equal to the selected
            element are to its right
    .3 Sort the values to the left of the selected element
        using the same approach
    .4 Sort the values to the right of the selected element
        using the same approach.

Steps 3 and 4 amount to sorting two subarrays and this is where the recursion comes in. Note also that following the rearrangement step, the selected element is in its correct position. (If it is the k'th largest value, there will be (k-1) elements to its left and (n-k) elements to its right. The step requiring further explanation is the rearrangement of values in Step 2. It may be done in a number of ways. A relatively efficient method is the following. Suppose the selected value is the value of the first element. (There is no loss of generality in doing this.) The general strategy is to repeat the following three steps.

1. Beginning with the highest subscript and working backward, find the first element with a value less than the selected value. (In the procedure, this subscript is called Top.)

2. Beginning with the lowest subscript, find the first element having a value greater than or equal to the selected value. (In the procedure that follows, this subscript is called Bottom.)

3. Exchange the values at positions Bottom and Top.

These three steps are repeated until Bottom = Top. When this happens, the common value represents the position at which the selected value belongs. The Rearrange procedure follows. For reasons to be given subsequently, it does not contain a formal parameter for the array of values. The parameters denote the subscripts delimiting the subrange of elements to be rearranged; the correct position of the first element is returned in the VAR parameter called CorrectPos.

```
PROCEDURE Rearrange(     LowBound   : CARDINAL;
                         HighBound  : CARDINAL;
                    VAR CorrectPos : CARDINAL);

    VAR
        Top    : CARDINAL;
        Bottom : CARDINAL;
        Value  : REAL;

    BEGIN
        Value      := InputArray[LowBound];
        CorrectPos := LowBound;
        Bottom     := LowBound;
        Top        := HighBound;
        REPEAT
            WHILE (Top > Bottom) AND
                  (InputArray[Top] >= Value) DO
                Top := Top - 1;
                END;
            CorrectPos := Top;
            IF Top <> Bottom THEN
                InputArray[Bottom] := InputArray[Top];
                WHILE (Bottom < Top) AND
                      (InputArray[Bottom] <= Value) DO
                    Bottom := Bottom + 1;
                    END;
                CorrectPos := Bottom;
                IF Top <> Bottom THEN
                    InputArray[Top] := InputArray[Bottom];
                    END;
                END;
            UNTIL Top = Bottom;
        InputArray[CorrectPos] := Value;
    END Rearrange;
```

Shown next is a procedure called QuickSort. It uses an internal procedure Sort that performs the sort recursively. Sort contains the Rearrange procedure defined previously.

```
PROCEDURE QuickSort(VAR InputArray : ARRAY OF REAL);

    (* ********************************** *)
    PROCEDURE Sort(    LowBound  : CARDINAL;
                       HighBound : CARDINAL);

        VAR PartitionPoint : CARDINAL;

        (*  Rearrange goes here *)

        BEGIN
            IF LowBound < HighBound THEN
                Rearrange(LowBound,HighBound,PartitionPoint);
                Sort(LowBound,PartitionPoint - 1);
                Sort(PartitionPoint + 1,HighBound);
                END;
        END Sort;
    (* ********************************** *)

    BEGIN
        Sort(0,HIGH(InputArray));
    END QuickSort;
```

Comments.

1. Is Sort necessary? Couldn't QuickSort call itself? Yes, but this would require a great deal of array passing and two extra parameters. By taking the approach shown, calling QuickSort needs only one parameter and thus is more user friendly.

2. The formal parameter InputArray is global with respect to the Sort and Rearrange procedures. This is a situation in which the use of a global variable makes sense in order to reduce the overhead with the (possibly frequent) procedure invocations.

Two final comments about recursion. First, recursive algorithms often make the program logic more visible. Second, recursion is generally inefficient. Since a recursive algorithm can always be replaced by a nonrecursive one, thought should be given to which approach to use especially if the solution will involve many executions of the recursive procedure.

Recursion is not limited to single procedures. That is a group of procedures, say A, B and C may be mutually recursive. This would occur if A calls B which calls C which Calls A or if any other sequence of calls forms a loop. In order to avoid (theoretically) infinite recursion, some procedure must terminate the calling sequence at execution time.

8.7   Procedure Types and Variables

This section may be omitted on first reading.

A variable may have a procedure type and be assigned procedure identifiers. Consider the following declarations.

```
TYPE
    Example1Proc = PROCEDURE (REAL);
    Example2Proc = PROCEDURE (VAR CHAR, CARDINAL) : BOOLEAN;

VAR
    P1 : Example1Proc;
    P2 : Example2Proc;
```

As with any type, a procedure type defines a family of values. In the example

o Example1Proc represents all procedures having one formal REAL value parameter.

o Example2Proc includes all function procedures that have two formal parameters. The first of which is a VAR parameter of type CHAR; the second a CARDINAL value parameter; the function returns a BOOLEAN value.

Why have procedure types? Consider the following problem. A program is required which will tabulate (calculate and print) the values of <u>any</u> integer-valued function f(x) for x=0, 1, 2, ..., 20. Specifically let us use it to tabulate values of the following two functions.

Sum(n) = n (n+1)/2   and   SumSq(n) = n (n+1) (2n+1)/6

You may recognize these as being the sum and sum of squares of the first n natural numbers. These functions are defined by the following Modula-2 function procedures:

```
PROCEDURE Sum(    N : CARDINAL) : CARDINAL;
    BEGIN
        RETURN N * (N+1) DIV 2;
    END Sum;

PROCEDURE SumSquares(    N : CARDINAL) : CARDINAL;
    BEGIN
        RETURN N * (N+1) * (2*N + 1) DIV 6;
    END SumSquares;
```

Both of these function procedures have a single CARDINAL value parameter and return a CARDINAL result. The program to perform the two tabulations follows. The procedure "Tabulate" tabulates one function.

```
MODULE ProcVariables;

FROM InOut IMPORT WriteCard, WriteLn;

TYPE
    CardFunctionProc = PROCEDURE (CARDINAL) : CARDINAL;

PROCEDURE Tabulate(    F : CardFunctionProc);

    VAR
        N : CARDINAL;

    BEGIN
        FOR N := 0 TO 15 DO
            WriteCard(N, 10);
            WriteCard(F(N), 10);
            WriteLn;
            END;
    END Tabulate;

    (* procedures Sum, SumSquares go here *)

BEGIN
    Tabulate (Sum);
    Tabulate (SumSquares);
END ProcVariables.
```

Comments. The Tabulate Function is called twice using a different procedure identifier as an actual parameter. The "value" of the formal parameter F is replaced successively by Sum, SumSquares and SumCubes.

The rules of procedure types and variables which are given next, state that a procedure variable cannot be assigned the value of a standard procedure. This restriction is easily circumvented. For example ABS cannot be assigned to a procedure variable but MyABS below can.

```
PROCEDURE MyABS (X : INTEGER): CARDINAL;
    BEGIN
        RETURN ABS(X)
    END MyABS;
```

Procedure Types and Variables

Forms:

```
TYPE
     name = PROCEDURE (formal-type-list)

     name = PROCEDURE (formal-type-list) : type

     name = PROC
```

where the formal-type-list is a sequence of zero or more type identifiers optionally preceded by VAR and separated by commas.

Rules:

1. The first form is used for nonfunction procedures; the second for function procedures; the third for parameterless procedures.

2. PROC is a standard type and is equivalent to PROC=PROCEDURE.

3. A procedure variable may be assigned a compatible procedure identifier. Compatibility means the source identifier has the same order, type and mode (function or nonfunction) of formal parameters as the target procedure variable.

4. Standard procedures are not assignable to procedure variables.

5. Procedures that are assigned to procedure variables must be declared at the outermost level of a program.

6. Invoking a procedure variable invokes the procedure assigned to it.

An internal procedure or module should not assign any of its procedures to a global procedure variable. This would permit an attempt to execute a nonexistent procedure once the assigning procedure finished execution.

8.8 Procedures: A Summary

This section summarizes procedure invocations and declarations.

Procedure Invocation

Forms:

procedure-name

procedure-name (actual-parameter-list)

Algorithm:

1. Each parameter expression in the actual parameter list is evaluated.
2. Local variables in the called procedure are allocated memory and value parameters are assigned the values of their corresponding actual parameters.
3. The procedure body is executed.
4. Memory for local variables is released.
5. If the procedure is a function procedure, the value RETURNed replaces the function designator; If a nonfunction procedure, control returns to the statement following the invocation.

Rules:

1. The procedure-name is either the name of a declared procedure or a procedure variable (procedure variables are described in Section 8.7).

2. The parentheses can be present even if the parameter list is empty. The parentheses must be present in the case of a function designator with no parameters.

3. The actual parameters must agree in order and type with the corresponding formal parameters. Furthermore, if the formal parameter is a:

   a) Value parameter, then the actual parameter must be assignment compatible with the formal parameter.(Assignment compatibility is defined in Section 7.8.)

   b) VAR parameter, then the actual parameter must be a compatible variable. The formal parameter is an alias for the actual parameter.

   c) Procedure parameter, then the formal parameter is an alias for the actual parameter procedure.

Procedure Declarations. The following chart contains the form and rules of procedure declarations.

Procedure Declarations

Form:

```
PROCEDURE name formal-parameters;
    local declarations
    BEGIN
        statement sequence
    END name;
```

where

1. The formal-parameters are optional and have the following forms.

   ```
   (parameter-section; parameter-section;...)
   ```

   ```
   (parameter-section; parameter-section;...) : type
   ```

   and each parameter-section is either

   ```
   - a value parameter list, namely:
         identifier-list: formal-type
   - or a variable parameter list, namely:
         VAR identifier-list: formal-type
   ```

   and a formal-type is either a type identifier or an open array. An open array has the form

   ```
   ARRAY OF type-identifier
   ```

2. The local declarations may include declarations for constants, types, variables, procedures and modules (local modules are described in Chapter 10).

Vocabulary:

1. PROCEDURE, BEGIN and END are reserved words.

2. The construct "PROCEDURE name formal-parameters;" is called the procedure header.

3. If a procedure type specification is part of the formal parameters, the procedure is called a function procedure. If omitted it is a nonfunction or standard procedure.

Style Guidelines for Procedure Form

   Procedure Style

   1. Indent the procedure block.

   2. Use function procedures only when the purpose of the
      procedure is to return a single result.

   3. Use verb oriented names for nonfunction procedures and
      noun-oriented names for function procedures.

   4. Style guidelines for formal parameter lists are found in Section
      8.2.

8.9 Summary

1. Procedures are used to partition logic into functional units.   Each
   procedure should have an easily stated, well-defined purpose.

2. Communication among procedures and the mainline process is
   accomplished using either or both of shared (global) variables and
   parameters.

3. The formal parameters of a procedure are surrogates for values or
   variables. The binding of formal parameters is done at execution time.

4. A value formal parameter is a surrogate for a value. A copy of the
   value is assigned to the formal parameter when the procedure is
   invoked. Changes in the value are not returned to the calling procedure.

5. A VAR formal parameter is an alias for the corresponding variable in
   the actual parameter list.

6. A procedure may perform the role of a function. In this case the calling
   expression is replaced by the value RETURNed by the procedure.

7. Procedures may be recursive.

8.10   Exercises and Programming Problems

1. Exercise. For each block in the following program structure, state the variables that are local to the block, those that are global to it, and those that are inaccessible to the block.

```
MODULE BLOCK1;
VAR
    A, B : INTEGER;
PROCEDURE BLOCK2(    C : BOOLEAN);
  VAR
      D : CHAR;
  PROCEDURE BLOCK3(    E : REAL);
    VAR
        F : CHAR;
    BEGIN END;
  BEGIN END;
PROCEDURE BLOCK4;
  VAR
      G : REAL;
  BEGIN END;
BEGIN END BLOCK1.
```

2. Exercise. For each of the procedures in Exercise 1, state which procedures can be invoked. If a procedure cannot invoke another procedure, give the reason.

3. The greatest common divisor (GCD) of two numbers M and N can be calculated in the following way (Euclid's Algorithm). Divide the larger by the smaller. If the remainder is zero, the GCD is the smaller. If not, divide the smaller by the remainder. If zero, the remainder is the GCD. If not, continue dividing the remainder into the previous remainder until a remainder of zero is obtained. The GCD is the value of the last nonzero remainder. Write a program to find the GCD of any two INTEGER values. Test your program by reading a pair of data values. Stop when a pair of zeros is read.

4. Tabulate values of the function

$$z = \frac{x^2 - 2xy + 3y^2}{xy + 3x + 2y + 4}$$

using all pairs of x and y values in the ranges x=1,2,3,...,6; y=1,2,3,4,5. Use a pair of nested FOR-loops to generate the x and y values.

5. For security purposes it is occasionally necessary to "star out" dollar amounts. For example to replace "$19475.52" with "$*****.** ". Develop an algorithm and write a program to replace the digits in dollar amounts with a '*'. Test your program on the following passage. In a company of 75 employees, salaries of $20000 or more are not uncommon. The president makes over $45000.00 while the mail clerk has an hourly rate of $5.25.

6. Write a program that reads a sequence of words separated by blanks and determines how many of them are valid Modula-2 identifiers. Echo each word read and print a line of the form "There are X valid identifiers".

7. Suppose the value of the function Bigger(X,Y) is the larger of the two parameter values. Does the expression Bigger(X, Bigger (Y,Z)) involve recursion or not? Explain.

8. One method of generating INTEGER "random" numbers is as follows. Pick a large integer value, say 1792534165. Square it and extract the middle 5 digits (those in the thousands through the ten millions positions). Call this number N1. Square N1 and take the middle five digits calling the result N2. Continue the process of squaring and extracting. The sequence of numbers N1,N2,N3,... is often one that has no detectable or predictable pattern. Such a random sequence of numbers -- N1,N2, etc. -- can be converted to numbers that lie in the interval (I,J) by calculating I + N MOD (J-I+1) for each number in the sequence. Write a program to generate thirty random numbers in the range 7 through 15. On each line print the value of N1 and the derived number in the (7,15) range. Use a function for the step in the algorithm that squares and extracts the five-digit number.

9. The area of a regular polygon of N sides in which each side has a length "s" is equal to Ns^2 cot(180/N)/4. Write a function called PolygonArea having parameters N and s to calculate the area. Test PolygonArea by writing a mainline that uses the function to calculate the areas of regular polygons of perimeter 1 having 3, 4, 5, ..., 20 sides.

10. Write three functions called SinD, CosD and TanD to produce the sine, cosine and tangent values of an angle in degrees. Use the functions in a program that prints a table of the cosecant, secant and cotangents of angles of 10, 20, 30, ..., 80 degrees.

11. Write a function that will round off any REAL value greater than 0.1 correct to N decimal places. Assume N is positive. This can be done by adding $5*10^{-N}$ to the value; multiplying by 10^N using the function TRUNC; dividing by 10^N .. Test your function by rounding the value of 12.73469 correct to 1, 2, 3, and 4 decimal places.

12. Write a function called LogB having two parameters X and B. The value of the function is the logarithm of X using base B. Note that

$$\log_B X = \log_A X / \log_A B$$

Use LogB to print a table of the logs of the values one through ten using bases 2, 4, 6, 8, and 10. Make use of the MathLib0 ln function which calculates logarithms using base e.

13. Write a function called Kroniker that has two INTEGER parameters M and N. The value of Kroniker should be zero if M and N are unequal and one if M equals N. Make up your own program to test the function.

14. The value of the inverse sine of x radians (x must be between plus and minus pi/4) is given by the following expression.

$$\sin^{-1}x = x + \frac{1}{2 \cdot 3}x^3 + \frac{1 \cdot 3}{2 \cdot 4 \cdot 5}x^5 + \frac{1 \cdot 3 \cdot 5}{2 \cdot 4 \cdot 6 \cdot 7}x^7 + \ldots$$

Write a function that calculates the inverse sine of a value of 0.25. (What angle is such that its sine equals 0.25?) Obtain the result correct to three decimal places.

15. In the Julian calendar, the days of the year are numbered sequentially from 1 to 365 (in nonleap years). Develop a function having two parameters called Month and Day that returns the Julian day for any given month–day pair. Use the function in a program to print a Julian calendar having 12 columns, one for each month, and 31 rows. The entry in the Ith row and Jth column should be the Julian day for the Ith day in the Jth month.

16. (Recursion) The Fibonacci sequence of numbers is 0, 1, 1, 2, 3, 5, 8, ... where each number except the first two is the sum of its immediate two predecessors. Write a function with the header:

    PROCEDURE Fibonacci(N : INTEGER) : INTEGER;

    that produces the Nth number in the sequence. Use recursion to get the function value. Test your function by writing a program that uses Fibonacci to generate the first ten Fibonacci numbers.

17. (Recursion) The Kth triangular number has the value $1 + 2 + 3 + ... + K$. Its value is therefore K plus the (K-1)th triangular number. Write a function that calculates the Kth triangular number recursively. Test the program by printing the first twelve triangular numbers on four lines of three numbers each.

18. Suppose the equations of two straight lines are

    $$A_1x + B_1y = C_1$$
    $$A_2x + B_2y = C_2$$

    For any given values of A_1,B_1,C_1 and A_2,B_2,C_2 the lines may be parallel, coincident, perpendicular or oblique depending on the values of the A's, B's and C's. The mathematical relationships are as follows.

Orientation	Mathematical Relationship
parallel	$A_1*B_2 = B_1*A_2$
coincident	parallel and $A_1*C_2 = C_1*A_2$
perpendicular	$A_1*A_2 = -B_1*B_2$
oblique	not parallel and not perpendicular

    Write a program that reads an unspecified number of A,B,C triples. For each pair of triples read, use a procedure to print the two equations and one to print one of "Parallel", "Coincident", "Perpendicular" or "Oblique". Stop when an out-of-data condition is detected. Note that there will be an even number of input lines. Test the program on at least the following four pairs of lines.

2x + 3y = 4	2x - 3y = 4
8x + 12y = 16	6x + 4y = 12
5x + 13y = 0	4x - y = 8
13x + 5y = -65	64x - 16y = 1

    In the program, use a procedure to READ each pair of input lines describing the two lines; a procedure to check parallelism and one to process nonparallel lines.

19. What triples of integer values (x, y, z) have the property that $x^2+y^2=z^2$? A rigorous way of generating such values is to choose any pair of values m and n such that: m and n are relatively prime (one is not a multiple of the other); m is even and n is odd or m is odd and n is even. If m and n satisfy these conditions then set

$$x = 2mn, \quad y = m^2 - n^2, \text{ and } z = m^2 + n^2$$

For example, set m=2 and n=1. The values of x, y, and z are x=4, y=3 and z=5. Note that $3^2+4^2=5^2$. Write a program to generate all possible triples using values of m and n of five or less that satisfy the given conditions.

20. Suppose a brick is 8 inches long, 4 inches wide, 2 inches thick and weighs 1 kilogram. A number of bricks are piled one on top of the other so that each brick extends to the right of the one below it forming a staircaselike structure. If L denotes the length of the brick suppose the centers of the second, third, fourth, ... bricks are 1/2 L, 3/4 L, 7/8 L, ... inches to right of the center of the bottom brick. Write a program to determine the horizontal center of gravity of piles of one to ten bricks.

21. Charlie has just bought a new 10 ounce bottle of shampoo. Each time he shampoos, he uses 1/2 ounce of liquid. After removing the half-ounce, he replaces it with a half-ounce of water and then shakes the bottle. Thus the shampoo gets weaker and weaker after each use. He repeats this procedure until the shampoo is half the original concentration and then uses it at half-strength until it is gone. Determine how many shampoos Charlie gets. Print the concentration and volume remaining after each use.

22. Write a function called Determinant that calculates the value of the determinant of a two-by-two matrix. The function will have a single parameter, the name of the two-by-two matrix of REAL values.

23. Write a procedure that has two parameters -- K, an array of twenty INTEGER values, and Insert. Values in K and the value of Insert are passed to the procedure. The procedure should insert the value of Insert into the array K so that values in K are nondecreasing (increasing order of magnitude except for ties) and then return control to the calling block. Write a mainline that initializes an array of twenty INTEGER values called Data to zero and then reads one INTEGER value from each of twenty input lines. After each value is read, use the procedure to insert the value in the proper position in Data. After the twenty values have been read, print the values in Data and verify that they have been stored in order of increasing magnitude.

24. Write a procedure to assign an array of M*N REAL values stored in a vector to the first M rows and N columns of a matrix. Assume M and N are less than ten. The mainline should read values of M and N, then MN more values. The procedure should assign the first N values to row one of the parameter matrix, the next N values to row two, etc.. The procedure will have four variables in the parameter list: the values of M and N; the vector containing the MN values, and the matrix in which the values are to be stored.

25. Suppose a sentence on an input line has less than fifty characters and contains N words (where N is determined by the program). Write a program that reads the sentence and prints it N times such that on the first line the first word starts in print position 60, on the second line the second word starts in print position 60, etc.. For example, if the sentence is "Programming is easy", the following output would be produced. ▪

```
                              60
                               ↓
                              Programming is easy
              Programming is easy
          Programming is easy
```

26. A 5 by 5 matrix and its inverse are shown:

```
1 1 1 1 1          2 -1  0  0  0
1 2 2 2 2         -1  2 -1  0  0
1 2 3 3 3          0 -1  2 -1  0
1 2 3 4 4          0  0 -1  2 -1
1 2 3 4 5          0  0  0 -1  1
```

The pattern shown for the inverse may be extended to any N by N matrix having the form of the matrix on the left. Read a value for N (assume N is 8 or less); generate the matrix and its inverse and then multiply them to test the correctness of the pattern generation routines. (The product must have ones down the diagonal, and zeros elsewhere.) Use separate procedures called GenMatrix, GenInverse, PrintMatrix and Test in your program.

27. The Arithmetic Mean (ArithMean), Geometric Mean (GeoMean) and Harmonic Mean (HarmMean) of a set of N values X1, X2, X3, ..., Xn are defined as:

$$\text{ArithMean} = \frac{X1 + X2 + X3 + \ldots + Xn}{N}$$

$$\text{GeoMean} = \sqrt[N]{X1 \; X2 \; X3 \; \ldots \; Xn}$$

$$\text{HarmMean} = \frac{N}{\dfrac{1}{X1} + \dfrac{1}{X2} + \dfrac{1}{X3} + \ldots + \dfrac{1}{Xn}}$$

Write a program called Means in which ArithMean, GeoMean, and HarmMean are functions used to calculate the corresponding means of a set of N numbers. The functions should have two parameters -- the value of N and the array of values.

28. Solve Problem 27 but have the mainline pass a value to a Means function which is one of the values in the enumerated type (ArithMean, GeoMean, HarmMean). The Means function should contain three function blocks called ArithMean, GeoMean, and HarmMean. One of these is invoked to obtain the required value.

29. A programming project. In physics, five commonly used equations describe the relationships between distance (s), acceleration (a), final velocity (v), time (t) and initial velocity (u) of a moving body. Each of the five equations can be identified by the variable that does not appear in the equation. For this reason, they are sometimes known as the "SAVTU" equations. The equations are as follows.

```
"S" equation:    a = (v - u)/t
"A" equation:    v = t(u + v)/2
"V" equation:    s = ut + (at²)
"T" equation:    v² = u² + 2as
"U" equation:    s = vt - (at²)/2
```

Write a procedure called SAVTU that has the parameters Data and Codes defined by:

```
VAR
     Data : ARRAY [1..5] OF REAL;
     Code : ARRAY [1..5] OF INTEGER;
```

Let the values in Data be the values of distance, acceleration, final velocity, time and initial velocity. The values in Code indicate which values are known and which are to be calculated. If Code[I] is zero it means the value of Data[I] is to be calculated by the procedure and stored in Data[I]. If Codes[I] is 1, it means Data(I) can be used in the calculation of the unknown values. Note that in any call to the procedure, at least three values in Code must equal 1. Use any method you like in the procedure to calculate the unknown values. Test your procedure on at least the ten different ways that three values of the five can be specified as known. Include in your procedure a return code that indicates if fewer than three of the Code values are 1.

30. If several forces are acting on a body at rest, they can be replaced by a single equivalent force. Suppose each force is represented by a value (x,y) where the magnitude of the force is given by the distance between the origin and the point (x,y). The direction of the force is represented by the angle between the x-axis and the ray through the origin and the point (x,y). Assume the body upon which the forces are acting is at the origin. The resultant force is simply the sum of the force vectors. Write a program that reads a value of N and then N pairs of REAL numbers representing the magnitude and direction of the forces. Calculate the resultant force and print its magnitude and direction.

CHAPTER 9

CONCURRENT PROGRAMMING

Questions Answered In This Chapter

1. What is concurrent programming?

2. How do the coroutine facilities in Modula-2 permit simulation of true concurrent processes?

3. What are the two ways Modula-2 processes communicate?

This chapter may be omitted on first reading.

9.1 Concepts.

Many human activities involve performing more than one task at a given time. For example, when playing the piano, the left and right hands perform their tasks separately but concurrently. On a football team, running of a play may be viewed as the simultaneous execution of eleven concurrent processes (one per player). Similarly, the different components of a computer may perform input-output and mathematical calculations in parallel.

A programming language that provides concurrent programming facilities allows a programmer to specify that certain procedures should or may execute in parallel.

Is this an important capability? The answer is "that depends". It depends on whether your computer has more than one processor or CPU (central processing unit). Since most have only one CPU, true concurrency is not possible. What is possible however, is to write programs as if more than one processor were available. Modula-2 allows you to do this. In effect what happens is the single processor is shared sequentially among the "simultaneously" executing processes. This is called time multiplexing. It is also called pseudo-concurrency.

Why would you want to use (parallel) processes when programming? Consider the problem of programming the actions to describe the execution of a football play. It is far easier to write eleven different routines describing the behavior of each man in the play than to write one routine that describes what everybody is doing at a given time. That is, when the function of a program is more easily defined by describing the actions of independent (but perhaps coordinated) active entities, concurrent programming is a natural vehicle to use.

9.2 Coroutines and Processes

A coroutine is a procedure that executes independently of other coroutines and/or procedures in the program. Although viewed as executing in parallel, coroutines are in fact quasi-concurrent processes in that they share a single physical processor.

There are three significant ways in which a coroutine (also called a process in this chapter) differs from an "ordinary" procedure.

1. A process is defined via the NEWPROCESS procedure imported from the SYSTEM module.

2. Termination of a process terminates the program (hence most processes are defined as infinite loops).

3. Transfer of control from one process to another may be done explicitly using the TRANSFER procedure or implicitly via the SEND and WAIT procedures.

Other aspects and rules of concurrent processing in Modula-2 are illustrated and explained in the two examples that constitute the rest of this chapter.

Before providing the details, there are two concurrent programming facilities found in some languages that are not found in Modula-2. The first is the ability to dynamically create a new process at execution time. (Recall however that variables can be created at execution time using the NEW procedure). Second, Modula-2 has no provision for the use of semaphores. Semaphores are an alternative method of communication among processes. For the interested reader an excellent reference is the article "Concepts and Notations for Concurrent Programming" by G. Andrews and E. Schneider found in ACM Computing Surveys Vol.15, no.1, March '83, pp. 3-43.

9.3 Basic Operations: NEWPROCESS and TRANSFER

A Problem. During a 12-hour period, print the times at which the big hand and the little hand of a clock are essentially overlapped. We will do this by defining two processes -- BigHand and LittleHand that execute concurrently.

The solution illustrates the use of global variables to communicate between processes and the explicit transfer of control from one process to another via the TRANSFER procedure.

Analysis. The position of the hands will be calculated each minute. Observe the following. Since the 360 degrees of the clock face are traversed in 60 minutes by the big hand, the big hand moves 6 degrees each minute. On the other hand, the hour hand moves 30 degrees each hour or half a degree each minute.

The basic procedure to define the operation of the big hand is given next. All variables used are declared outside the procedure.

```
PROCEDURE BigHand; (* procedure for the MinuteProcess *)

    BEGIN
        LOOP (* forever *)
            Time         := Time + 1;
            BigPosition := BigPosition + BigChange;
            TRANSFER(MinuteProcess, HourProcess);
            IF BigPosition >= 360.0 THEN
                BigPosition := 0.0;
                END;
            END; (* LOOP *)
    END BigHand;
```

The procedure for the little hand is similar except the increment is 0.5. How will we determine if the two hands overlap? Because the big hand moves 6 degrees each minute, it must be within 3 degrees of the hour hand during the minute in which overlap occurs. Thus, if the difference in angular positions is less than 3 degrees we shall say the hands overlap.

The following program contains two procedures -- BigHand and LittleHand. They express the logic of the processes MinuteProcess and HourProcess respectively. Control is transferred back and forth between the two processes using the TRANSFER procedure imported from the SYSTEM module. The body of the program: creates the two processes using NEWPROCESS; initializes the global variables; and then transfers control to BigHand. The program terminates when the little hand has gone once around the clock.

```
MODULE ClockHands;

FROM SYSTEM IMPORT WORD,ADR,SIZE,ADDRESS,NEWPROCESS,TRANSFER;

FROM InOut IMPORT  Write,WriteString,WriteLn,WriteCard;

CONST
    BigChange    = 6.0;           (* minute hand increment *)
    LittleChange = 0.5;           (* hour hand increment *)
    CloseEnough  = 3.0;

VAR
    BigPosition   : REAL;
    LittlePosition : REAL;
```

```
    Time              : CARDINAL;  (* elapsed time in minutes *)

    Main              : ADDRESS;   (* the mainline process *)
    MinuteProcess     : ADDRESS;   (* the little hand process *)
    HourProcess       : ADDRESS;   (* the hour hand process *)
    MinuteWorkArea    : ARRAY[0..499] OF WORD; (* workareas *)
    HourWorkArea      : ARRAY[0..499] OF WORD;

PROCEDURE BigHand; (* procedure for the MinuteProcess *)

    BEGIN
        LOOP (* forever *)
            Time         := Time + 1;
            BigPosition := BigPosition + BigChange;
            TRANSFER(MinuteProcess, HourProcess);
            IF BigPosition >= 360.0 THEN
                BigPosition := 0.0;
                END;
            END; (* LOOP *)
    END BigHand;

PROCEDURE LittleHand; (* procedure for the HourProcess *)

    BEGIN
        LOOP
            LittlePosition := LittlePosition + LittleChange;
            IF ABS(BigPosition - LittlePosition)
               < CloseEnough THEN
                WriteString('The hands overlap at time ');
                WriteCard(Time DIV 60,3); Write(':');
                WriteCard(Time MOD 60,2); WriteLn;
                END;
            IF LittlePosition < 360.0 THEN
                TRANSFER(HourProcess,MinuteProcess);
            ELSE
                TRANSFER(HourProcess,Main); (* stop program *)
                END;
            END; (* LOOP *)
    END LittleHand;

BEGIN (* ClockHands *)
    NEWPROCESS(BigHand,ADR(MinuteWorkArea),
               SIZE(MinuteWorkArea),MinuteProcess);
    NEWPROCESS(LittleHand,ADR(HourWorkArea),
               SIZE(HourWorkArea), HourProcess);
    Time           := 0;
    LittlePosition := 0.0;
    BigPosition    := 0.0;
    TRANSFER(Main,MinuteProcess);
END ClockHands.
```

This is the output produced when the program is executed.

The hands overlap at time   1: 5

The hands overlap at time   2:11

The hands overlap at time   3:16

The hands overlap at time   4:22

The hands overlap. at time   5:27

The hands overlap at time   6:33

The hands overlap at time   7:38

The hands overlap at time   8:44

The hands overlap at time   9:49

The hands overlap at time   10:55

The hands overlap at time   12:00

Before looking at the detailed rules of usage for procedures, let us summarize the main points exemplified in the preceding program.

First, the body of the program module calls NEWPROCESS twice to create the processes used in the module. In fact, the program body is itself a process (referred to as "Main" in the example).

Second, each process has a name, a work area and an associated procedure. Consider for example the process MinuteProcess. The associated procedure is BigHand. It defines the local variables and logic to perform the minute hand function. The work area -- called MinuteWorkArea -- is needed to store the values of local variables and state of the procedure when control transfers out of the procedure. The size and memory address of the work area are specified in the call to NEWPROCESS.

Third, control is explicitly passed from one process to another using the TRANSFER procedure. A TRANSFER is absolute in the sense that no return is implied. Should control be TRANSFERed back however, execution resumes from the departure point.

Fourth, communication between MinuteProcess and HourProcess is achieved via global variables. Observe that this would allow the BigHand procedure to change the variable HourPosition and vice versa which is not desirable. A preferred method employs a "monitor" an example of which is found in the next section. Now for the details.

The Procedure NEWPROCESS

NEWPROCESS

Form:

```
NEWPROCESS (    p            : PROC;
                workaddress  : ADDRESS;
                worksize     : CARDINAL;
            VAR processname  : ADDRESS)
```

Rules:

1. The "p" is the procedure that contains the logic of the process. It must be declared at the outermost level of the module.

2. The "workaddress" specifies the address of the area of memory used to store the parameters, local objects and state of the procedure. A work area is normally created by declaring an array having WORD elements. (A WORD is a unit of memory capable of storing two characters. See Chapter 12 for a complete explanation). The address of the work area is usually obtained using the built-in function ADR. Both WORD and ADR are imported from the SYSTEM module.

3. The "worksize" is the size of the work area in bytes. (See Chapter 12 for a discussion of memory units). The worksize value is most easily provided by using the SIZE function imported from SYSTEM.

4. The "processname" is a variable of the type ADDRESS. The ADDRESS type is imported from SYSTEM. The process name is used in TRANSFER and other procedures that require processes as parameters. Each process name must be declared as a variable with the type ADDRESS at the outermost level of the module.

Size of the Work Area. How big should a process work area be? The question is difficult to answer. An approximate minimum is found by adding: the memory sizes of the procedure parameters, the memory requirements for the locally declared objects; and the work area sizes needed for any internally declared procedures. Memory sizes for different types of values and variables are discussed in Chapter 12. A crude approximation is to reserve four words (8 bytes) for each constant, simple variable, array element, field and pointer in the procedure. Precise information can only be obtained by examining a memory map of the compiled program. There is also a memory requirement that is

implementation dependent.   For instance in the Logitech implementation,
400 bytes of overhead must be provided.   Unless memory availability is a
problem, employ a significant safety factor in selecting a work area size.

The Procedure TRANSFER

TRANSFER

Form:

```
TRANSFER (VAR fromprocess : ADDRESS;
          VAR toprocess   : ADDRESS)
```

Rules:

1. The "fromprocess" is the process containing the TRANSFER
   statement.

2. Control is transferred from the fromprocess statement to the
   "toprocess".

3. The status of process that is exited is stored in the fromprocess
   variable.   Because this status update occurs after the toprocess
   is entered, the "fromprocess" and "toprocess" can be the same
   variable.   For example TRANSFER (x, x) is legal but not
   recommended.

Before leaving the clock hands example, it is always wise to ask the
question "Was this the best way to solve the problem?"   Although the
example illustrates the basics of process creation and use, all the logic
could more easily have been contained in a single nonprocess procedure
that used FOR loop to increment time.   Even better would be an algebraic
rather than iterative solution technique.   Specifically, the exact times at
which   overlap   occurs   can   be   found   by   solving   the   equation
$5(t-60n) = 0.5t$ for t for n=0, 1, 2, ..., 11.

9.4   Monitors and Process Synchronization

Monitors

Communication among processes can occur in three distinct ways -- via
global variables as was done in the first example; via signals as will be
illustrated in this section; and via semaphores as is done in some
programming languages (but not Modula-2).

The problem with shared variables is that should two processes be operating concurrently and should each be accessing and possibly changing a shared variable, the integrity of the variable's value could be lost. The solution to this problem is to create a separate module that: contains all variables needed for intraprocess communication; and contains procedures for performing all required operations on these shared variables.

Such a module is called a <u>monitor</u>. Because the monitor can only be executing one procedure at a given time, only one process can have access to the shared variables at any instant. Thus a monitor is a protection against simultaneous updating of shared variables.

As an example, suppose there is a "producer" who creates widgets and a "consumer" who consumes widgets. Each time the producer creates a widget it is placed in a storage area; the consumer consumes a widget by removing it from the storage area. Assume the rates of production and consumption are not constant so that the supply of widgets in the storage area goes up and down.

This producer-consumer activity occurs in many real-world and programming environments. In queuing situations production takes the form of arrivals to the queue; consumption relates to the servicing of queue elements. In a computing milieu, the producer is often the program which generates lines of output for the printer; the print lines are consumed by the printer; the communication between the processes is accomplished using a print buffer.

In order to model the producer and consumer as separate processes, the monitor must contain the shared variable (i.e. the storage or buffer) and the two procedures that access the buffer. They will be called Deposit and Fetch corresponding to the production and consumption activities.

For purposes of illustration, let us suppose the objects produced and consumed are integers. The essential features of the Producer and Consumer procedures are

```
PROCEDURE Producer;          PROCEDURE Consumer;
   BEGIN                        BEGIN
      LOOP                         LOOP
         ReadCard(X);                 Fetch(X);
         Deposit(X);                  WriteCard(X,10);
      END                          END
   END Producer;                END Consumer;
```

How does processing stop? We can easily add logic so that an input value of zero causes the Producer to exit from the procedure (and hence terminate execution).

More important questions are "What happens if the Consumer attempts to Fetch a value and the buffer is empty? Likewise, what happens if the Producer has a value but finds the buffer full?" These questions are answered in the next subsection.

Process Synchronization with SIGNALs.

Frequently a process requires that a certain condition or state exists in order for it to begin or continue execution. In Modula-2, the presence of a condition can be represented by variables of the type SIGNAL. Furthermore a signal can be sent using SEND to indicate that a particular condition has arisen. Likewise a process (by employing WAIT) can suspend execution until a condition arises in the form of a particular signal.

The use of signals to control the execution of processes is one means of process synchronization. When signals are used, at any instant, each process is in one of three states:

executing The processor is executing the statements in the associated procedure.

blocked Execution is suspended until a condition arises (a signal is given).

ready Not executing but ready to execute when the processor becomes available.

In Modula-2, the implementation-supplied Processes module contains the tools necessary for synchronizing process execution using signals. The Processes module is listed in Appendix C. In particular it contains:

o The type SIGNAL

o Procedures

Init	–	initializes a SIGNAL
WAIT	–	suspends execution until a signal is given
SEND	–	sends a signal
Awaited	–	indicates if any processes are waiting for a particular signal
StartProcess	–	defines and transfers control to a process

The form and rules for these procedures are given following the program that illustrates their use.

The ProduceConsume module that follows contains:

o IMPORT statements which import: the signal-processing routines from the Processes module; the shared variable, Deposit and Fetch from the monitor module; standard input-output procedures.

o Declarations for the signals Forever and Finished which are used to control process termination.

o The procedures Producer and Consumer.

o The body of the module which initializes the two process and then waits until the Finished signal is sent.

Further comments follow the program.

```
MODULE ProduceConsume;

(* This module tests the producer-consumer scenario *)

FROM Processes IMPORT SIGNAL, SEND, WAIT,
                      StartProcess, Init, Awaited;

FROM ProduceConsumeMonitor IMPORT Fetch, Deposit;

FROM InOut    IMPORT Write, Read, WriteString, WriteLn, EOL;

VAR
    Finished : SIGNAL; (* Sent when run is finished *)
    Forever  : SIGNAL; (* Takes a process out of action *)

PROCEDURE Producer;

    (* A continuous loop which obtains a character from the
       keyboard and deposits it in the buffer using the
       Monitor procedure called Deposit. Exits from
       the loop after a return character is entered
    *)

    VAR
        X : CHAR;

    BEGIN (* Producer *)
        REPEAT
            WriteString ('Enter a character or Return: ');
            Read(X); Write(X) ; WriteLn;
            Deposit (X);
            UNTIL X = EOL;
        WAIT (Forever)
    END Producer;

PROCEDURE Consumer;

    (* Continuously obtains the next element in the buffer
```

```
    using the procedure Fetch. Exits from the loop
    after retrieving an EOL character
*)

VAR
    X : CHAR;

BEGIN (* Consumer *)
    REPEAT
        Fetch (X);
        UNTIL X = EOL;
    SEND (Finished)
END Consumer;

BEGIN (* ProduceConsume *)
    Init (Finished);
    Init (Forever);
    StartProcess (Consumer, 500);
    StartProcess (Producer, 500);
    WAIT (Finished);
    WriteString('*** End of Producer-Consumer Run ***');
    WriteLn;
END ProduceConsume.
```

The first few lines of execution-time output are shown next.

```
Enter a character or Return to exit: 1
1 has been deposited
1 has been retrieved
Enter a character or Return to exit: 2
2 has been deposited
2 has been retrieved
etc.
```

An explanation of the mainline steps follows

1. Consider the program body. The Init statements "Init(Finished)" and "Init(Forever)" assign the value NIL to the signals Finished and Forever (A SIGNAL is actually a pointer value)

2. The statement StartProcess(Consumer, 500) does the following:

   o Creates a process descriptor record (Appendix C has details).

   o Executes NEWPROCESS (the "500" controls the size of the workarea -- see the StartProcess rules later in this section).

   When control returns from Consumer (recall the buffer is initially empty) the Producer process is defined and invoked.

3. The Producer and Consumer processes "do their thing" until an end-of-line character is entered at which time Procedure executes "WAIT(Forever)". This takes Producer out of the ready queue since nobody sends a Forever Signal. This is the recommended way of terminating a process without terminating the program. Recall that the first process to terminate stops all program execution.

4. The Consumer completes its work until it Fetches a value of zero at which time it sends the Finished signal.

5. Since the Main process is WAITing for a Finished signal, Consumer is suspended and execution continues with the program body's wrap-up message and subsequent termination.

The preceding discussion ignores the processing done by the monitor module called ProduceConsumeMonitor. This is the first example of a program which involves two user-written modules. The first is the program module ProducerConsumer which has just been discussed; the second is the ProduceConsumeMonitor module from which the procedures Deposit and Fetch are IMPORTed.

The Monitor Module. Concepts, varieties, details, and guidelines for use of modules are found in the next chapter. The following information is intended only to provide what you need to know to create a monitor module.

The ProduceConsumeMonitor is written and compiled completely independently of the program module. Such a separately compiled module has two components -- a DEFINITION module and an IMPLEMENTATION module. The definition module specifies what the module exports; the implementation module contains the logic to create the exported quantities.

Shown next is the definition module for ProduceConsumeMonitor.

DEFINITION MODULE ProduceConsumeMonitor;

(* Exports Deposit and Fetch procedures *)

PROCEDURE Fetch(VAR X : CHAR);   (* retrieves a character *)

PROCEDURE Deposit(X : CHAR);   (* deposits a character *)

END ProduceConsumeMonitor.

From this module, it is clear what the ProduceConsumeMonitor does -- it exports two objects called Fetch and Deposit. Furthermore we know Fetch is a procedure that has a single INTEGER VAR parameter. Similarly, deposit is a procedure with a one INTEGER value parameter. What is not known is how Fetch and Deposit perform their functions. That is precisely the purpose of the corresponding implementation module given next. Observe that it contains all the declarations necessary to support the Deposit and Fetch operations. It also contains a module body that performs initialization of the module's variables. The constant BufferSize denotes the size of the storage area. If the buffer has three widgets, it is full and Deposit is blocked from producing any more widgets. Likewise, Fetch is prohibited from retrieving a value if the buffer is empty.

```
IMPLEMENTATION MODULE ProduceConsumeMonitor[1];

(* Implements Deposits and Fetches to and from a character
   buffer. Deposits are accepted if the Buffer is not full;
   Fetch requests are serviced if the Buffer is not empty.
*)

FROM Processes IMPORT SIGNAL, SEND, WAIT, Init;

FROM InOut     IMPORT Write, WriteString, WriteLn;

CONST
    BufferSize = 3; (* the size of the shared storage *)

TYPE
    ElementType      = CHAR; (* the type of values deposited *)
                                and fetched *)
    BufferIndexRange = [0 .. BufferSize - 1];
    BufferArray      = ARRAY BufferIndexRange OF ElementType;

VAR
    BufferCount : [0 .. BufferSize];
    NotFull     : SIGNAL; (* sent when buffer less than full *)
    NotEmpty    : SIGNAL;  (* sent when buffer's at least one *)
    NextIn      : BufferIndexRange; (* Index for next deposit *)
    NextOut     : BufferIndexRange; (* Index for next fetch *)
    Buffer      : BufferArray;

PROCEDURE Deposit (X : CHAR);

    (* Puts value X in location NextIn in the buffer *)

    BEGIN (* Deposit *)
        IF BufferCount = BufferSize THEN   (* no room *)
            WAIT (NotFull);
            END;
        Buffer[NextIn] := X; (* store value in the buffer *)
        Write(X); WriteString(' has been deposited'); WriteLn;
        (* get ready for next deposit *)
        NextIn := (NextIn + 1) MOD BufferSize;
        SEND(NotEmpty);
    END Deposit;

PROCEDURE Fetch (VAR X : CHAR);
```

```
    (* Retrieves value X from NextOut in the buffer *)

BEGIN (* Fetch *)
    IF BufferCount = 0 THEN   (* buffer is empty *)
        WAIT (NotEmpty);
        END;
    X := Buffer[NextOut];           (* retrieve the value *)
    (* get ready for next Fetch *)
    NextOut := (NextOut + 1) MOD BufferSize;
    Write(X); WriteString(' has been retrieved'); WriteLn;
    SEND (NotFull); (* signal that deposits can be made *)
END Fetch;

BEGIN (* ProduceConsumeMonitor *)
    BufferCount := 0;     (* buffer is empty *)
    NextIn     := 0;      (* location of first deposit *)
    NextOut    := 0;      (* location of first withdrawal *)
    Init (NotFull);       (* initialize NotFull signal *)
    Init (NotEmpty);      (* initialize NotEmpty signal *)
END ProduceConsumeMonitor.
```

Comments.

1. Aside from Deposit and Fetch, which are exported, the objects declared within the implementation module are hidden from outside viewing. These include the buffer itself and the signals NotFull and NotEmpty.

2. The implementation module contains a module body that puts the buffer in an empty state and initializes the two signals using the Init procedure imported from the Processes model. This module body is executed prior to executing the first statement in the main program.

3. Fetch logic is straightforward. If the buffer is empty, Fetch suspends the Consumer process that called it until a NonEmpty signal is sent. When the buffer contains at least one value, the "oldest" (first-in-first-out) value is returned and the signal NotFull is sent.

4. The Deposit logic is equally simple. If the Buffer is full, the procedure (and hence the Producer process that called it) waits until a NotFull signal is received. At that time, it stores the value to be deposited and SENDs a NotEmpty signal.

5. One last point. Note the "[1]" following the module name in the module header. It is called a module priority. The default priority of a module is null. A nonnull priority means the module cannot be interrupted by any module with a lower priority. In this example, it means a call to Fetch cannot interrupt a Deposit and vice-versa. Because concurrency is only simulated by Modula-2, an interrupt of the monitor processing could not occur and hence the priority could be omitted. Priorities are significant when using the IOTRANSFER procedure. It is described in Chapter 12.

Consider again the output produced when the characters '1', '2', '3' etc. are entered when input is requested.

```
Enter a character or Return to exit: 1
1 has been deposited
1 has been retrieved
Enter a character or Return to exit: 2
2 has been deposited
2 has been retrieved
etc.
```

The sequence of steps that produces the first pair of outputs is: (refer also to the listing of the ProducerConsumer program module).

1. The body of the implementation module is executed.

2. The program body begins execution.

    .1 Finished is initialized
    .2 Forever is initialized
    .3 The Consumer process is created and the Consumer procedure
        begins executing; the main process (program body)
        is suspended but is in the ready state.

3. Fetch is called and, because the buffer is empty, executes WAIT(NotEmpty); the Consumer process is therefore suspended.

4. Because the main process is the only one ready, it resumes execution and starts the Producer process.

5. Producer procedure calls Deposit

    .1 Deposit prompts for and reads a value from the
        keyboard and stores it in Buffer [0].
    .2 NextIn is set to 1.
    .3 The signal NotEmpty is sent. Because a process
        is waiting for NotEmpty, Producer suspends execution
        but remains in the read state. Thus the main
        process and Deposit are in the ready queue.

6. Fetch resumes;

    .1 X is obtained from the buffer and "A is deposited"
        is printed.
    .2 NextOut is updated
    .3 The signal NotFull is sent but because no process is
        waiting for NotFull, execution continues with Fetch
        which returns control to the Consumer procedure.

7. Fetch, finding the buffer empty, executes WAIT(NotEmpty). At this point, both the main process and Producer are in the ready queue, with the main process first. Thus control transfers to the mainline.

8. The statement WAIT(Finished) is executed, suspending the main process. Control transfers to Producer since it is the first and only process in the ready queue.

From this point on, the Producer and Consumer processes WAIT and SEND signals which result in an alternating sequence of deposits and fetches. When the end-of-line character is entered, and the appropriate message printed, Fetch sends the Forever signal. This causes the main process to resume execution. It prints the wrap-up message before terminating.

Note that the buffer never has more than one element. Every deposit is followed by an immediate Fetch because Deposit always sends NotFull which activates the Consumer process. Because of the overhead involved in switching processes and the strong coupling of the processes, a preferred implementation of Deposit and Fetch uses the "sleeping barber" algorithm. The algorithm is described in Exercise 2 at the end of the chapter.

The rules and logic for the procedures in the Processes module follows. A listing of the statements in its IMPLEMENTATION module is found in Appendix C.

```
StartProcess (    pname    : PROC;
                  worksize : CARDINAL)
```

Rules:

1. The "pname" is the name of the procedure that specifies the process logic. It must be declared at the outermost level of the module.

2. The "worksize" is the size (in bytes) of the work area needed for the procedure parameters, locally declared objects and status information. See the description of NEWPROCESS for guidelines in determining workarea sizes.

3. StartProcess performs the following functions

   a) Creates a process descriptor record for storing status and queueing information.

   b) Executes the NEWPROCESS procedure.

   c) TRANSFERs control to the newly created process.

4. The process that executes the StartProcess changes its state from executing to "ready".

```
    Init   (VAR signal : SIGNAL)
```

Rules:

1. All variables of the type SIGNAL must be initialized using Init.

2. SIGNAL is declared as a pointer to a process descriptor record. Init sets the signal to NIL.

```
    Awaited  (    signal : SIGNAL) : BOOLEAN;
```

Rules:

1. Returns TRUE if any processes are waiting for the given signal; otherwise returns FALSE.

```
    WAIT  (VAR signal : SIGNAL)
```

Rules:

1. The "signal" represents a condition that must be true in order for the currently executing process to continue execution.

2. The calling process is placed at the end of the queue of those processes waiting for the named signal. It changes its state from executing to "blocked".

3. Control transfers to the process at the head of the "ready" queue.

4. If, following a WAIT, no process is "ready", (all processes are blocked), program execution terminates.

```
    SEND  (VAR signal : SIGNAL)
```

Rules:

1. Control transfers to the process at the head of the queue of processes waiting for the given signal. The calling process suspends execution and goes to the end of the "ready" queue.

2. If no process is waiting for the given signal, the calling process continues execution.

Processes Module Initialization

Like all modules, the body of Processes module is executed before the body of the program module begins execution. The Processes body creates a process descriptor record which has the effect of making a process out of the program body. For the interested reader, the statements executed are:

```
BEGIN
    ALLOCATE(CallingProcess,TSIZE(ProcessDescriptor));
    WITH CallingProcess^ DO
        NextSignal    := CallingProcess;
        ReadyState    := TRUE;
        WaitingQueue := NIL;
        END;
END Processes.
```

The Problem of Deadlock

Deadlock occurs if all processes are waiting for signals that can only be sent by blocked processes. A trivial case occurs when a process waits for a signal that is only sent by itself. A more interesting case is the "dining philosophers" problem which involves a numer of philosophers seated around a circular dining table. Only one fork is provided at each place. In order to eat, each person requires two forks. If each person is programmed as a separate process then deadlock occurs if each process contains "WAIT(leftfork); WAIT(rightfork)". A discussion of the solution is found in most books on concurrent programming.

9.5 Summary

1. Concurrent programming involves the concept of executing more than
one process (sequence of statements) simultaneously. It is becoming
more important for two reasons. First, some newer computers --
mainly experimental -- contain more than one processor thus
permitting true concurrency. Second, many programming problems,
particularly those involving real-time applications, are more easily
programmed using a collection of independent but coordinated
processes.

2. Modula-2 provides facilities for quasi-concurrent programming in the
form of coroutines. Coroutines -- called processes in this chapter --
are similar to regular procedures with two differences. First, a process
is created at execution time; it has a workspace for storing status
information and an associated procedure that defines its logic. Second,
when control TRANSFERs out of a process, there is no implicit return.

3. There are two ways Modula-2 processes communicate and synchronize
their actions. The lowest level involves global (shared) variables and
use of the TRANSFER function exported from the SYSTEM module. The
higher level employs the procedures in the Processes module. It
involves the use of the SIGNAL type to coordinate process actions
through the SEND and WAIT procedures.

4. Monitors. A monitor is a module that contains data structures shared
by concurrent processes. It also contains all the procedures for
processing the shared data. A module is given a higher priority than
the modules that use its services. Use of monitor modules prevents
simultaneous updating of shared variables.

5. Modules may be written and compiled separately and subsequently
linked together. A separately compiled module is made up of two
parts -- a DEFINITION module which describes the exported items, and
an IMPLEMENTATION module which contains the logic. Modules are
described in detail in Chapter 10.

9.6   Exercises and Programming Problems

> For the programming problems in this chapter, use processes to perform the actions specified.

1. Exercise. In each of the following scenarios, describe what elements of the system could be programmed as processes. Indicate how the processes should be synchronized.

   a) Airport activity. Planes are arriving and departing; baggage handling trucks, fuel trucks, and catering services are performing their tasks; the control tower is communicating and giving directions to aircraft.

   b) A job shop. A small manufacturing firm has a number of work centers (machines) through which various jobs flow. Different jobs require different sets of operations in different sequences.

   c) A computer operating system. A permanently resident program is required that among other functions must accept requests for computer resources under its control. These include access to devices such as the keyboard, screen, and disk files as well as requests for memory needed to execute application programs.

2. Exercise. The Producer-Consumer monitor employed a "flip-flop" algorithm in the Deposit and Fetch procedures. That is each deposit was followed by SEND (NotEmpty) and each fetch was followed by a SEND (NotFull). This resulted in an alternating sequence of Deposits and Fetches. A better algorithm is the "Sleeping Barber Algorithm" in which the buffer count is permitted to have an extended range of values. Specifically, if the count is −n, it means n consumers are waiting. If the count is greater than the buffer size, the value of (count−size) indicates how many production units are waiting. Finally, if the buffer count is between 0 and the buffer size, it simply denotes how many slots are full. Using this algorithm and Deposit and Fetch only SEND a signal if a request for the other service is waiting. Rewrite the ProduceConsume Monitor module to "wake up" more than one waiting process? Explain.

3. Here is a game you can try with a friend. Each player writes down three nonnegative integer numbers that add up to five. Examples are (0 0 5), (1 3 1) and (2 2 1). Compare your numbers with those of your opponent. The person who has the higher first number gets seven points (no points if a tie). The higher second number is worth five points and the higher third number is worth four points. Play ten times. The winner is the one with the highest total number of points. Write a program that generates all possible triples of numbers that can be used in the game. Use these to identify the rows and columns of a

matrix. In the (i,j)th element of the matrix, store the point value that would be obtained by someone who chose the triple associated with row i if his opponent chose the triple associated with column j. Print the values in the matrix with appropriate row and column headings. Use a separate process for each player.

4. At time zero, Fifi, the cat, is located at point (0,10) in the xy plane. Fido, the dog, is at the origin. Fifi runs parallel to the x-axis at a rate of 0.8 units per second. Fido runs at a rate of 1 unit per second with his head down in the direction of Fifi. At the end of each second he lifts his head up, sees where Fifi is, and runs in that direction during the next second. How long, to the nearest second, does it take Fido to catch Fifi? Print the positions of Fifi and Fido at 1-second intervals during the chase. Use separate processes for Fifi and Fido.

5. Suppose computers could only multiply and divide by 2. (In fact, this isn't far from the truth!) The product of any two numbers M and N can still be done using the "Russian" method of multiplication. It consists of successively dividing the smaller number by 2 (ignoring any remainder) and successively multiplying the larger value by 2. As this process is being carried out, add to a total only those multiples of the larger value for which the division of the smaller produced an odd quotient. For example, to multiply 37 by 65 the following results would be obtained.

```
37              65
18             130  (not added to total)
 9             260
 4             520  (not added to total)
 2            1040  (not added to total)
 1            2080
              ----
              2405  (the total)
```

If you don't believe it, what is 37 times 65? Write a Modula-2 program that reads a pair of values and calculates their product using the preceding technique. Use a separate process to perform the multiplication and division. Have them communicate using signals.

6. Four bees are located at the corners of a square having a side of one-half mile. Each bee flies toward the bee next to it in a clockwise direction for 5 seconds at a rate of 20 miles an hour. Each bee then changes its direction to reflect the new position of its target. How long does it take the bees to converge in the center of the square? Use four different processes -- one for each bee. If the bees changed their direction continuously, can you think of an easy way to answer the question without using the computer?

CHAPTER 10

PROGRAM AND LOCAL MODULES

Questions Answered In This Chapter

1. What are the four kinds of modules in Modula-2? What is the purpose of each?

2. How do local modules differ from procedures? When should you use a module? When should a procedure be used?

3. How do you create a module that can be used by several other modules?

4. What are the rules for importing and exporting objects from modules?

This chapter describes the role of modules in the Modula-2 language. It provides detailed rules for creating and using local, library and program modules.

10.1   Module Types

Outside the world of programming, the word "module" has connotations of independence, containment and cohesiveness. These notions are also present in modules belonging to the Modula-2 programming language.

Thus far, we have only defined and used one type of module -- the program module. There are in reality four types of modules:

program modules
> a separately compiled sequence of statements that can be executed.

local modules
> declared within other modules and/or procedures; allows explicit control of access to objects both within and outside its boundaries.

definition modules
> describe the objects exported from a module that makes services (procedures, constants, types, variables) and software tools available to other modules.

implementation modules
> always paired with a corresponding definition module. Contains the logic to support the exports defined by its definition module.

As well as these four, some implementations of Modula-2 have callable or subprogram modules. These are not a standard feature of Modula-2.

   Library Modules. All implementations of the Modula-2 language provide a library of precompiled definition and implementation modules for performing input-output tasks, mathematical routines and interfacing with memory resources. Library modules are described in Chapter 11.

10.2   Program Modules

Form. Each stand-alone computer program written in the Modula-2 programming language has one and only one program module. It has the following form:

```
MODULE name priority;
imports;
    block
name.
```

where:

o "MODULE" is a reserved word.

o The "name" is the name of the program module.

o The "priority" is optional. It is significant for modules performing concurrent operations and when controlling external devices that "interrupt" the execution of a program. (Concurrency is described in Chapter 9. Device interrupt processing is described in Chapter 12.) If present, the priority must be a CARDINAL constant enclosed in brackets. "[2]" is an example of a module priority.

o A "block" consists of declarations and a module body that terminates with "END".

o A program module ends with the module name and a period.

   A program module is one type of compilation unit. The other two compilation units are definition modules and implementation modules.

Imports. Every meaningful program module contains at least one IMPORT statement. Why? Recall that all input-output facilities are provided through imported procedures. Therefore, a program module cannot communicate with the outside world unless input-output procedures are imported from other modules.

Exports. A program module cannot export identifiers. Only local modules and definition modules can export objects.

Declarations. A program module normally contains declarations for constants, types, variables, procedures and modules used in the performance of its task. A program module cannot export any of its objects.

Body. The body of a program module contains the executable statements that accomplish its task. When a program module is executed, control transfers from the operating system to the program module. This causes the memory needed for locally declared objects to be allocated, and local modules to be initialized (see the next section) prior to executing the program module body.

10.3   Local Modules

An Example

A local module is a module declared within another module or procedure. The following program module prints ten random numbers between 0 and 1. It is complete except for the the local module containing the RandomNum procedure referred to in the program body.

```
MODULE RandomProgram;

(* This program demonstrates the use of a local module which
   exports a function  for producing random numbers between
   0 and 1
*)

FROM InOut      IMPORT WriteCard, WriteString, WriteLn;

FROM RealInOut IMPORT WriteReal;

VAR
    i : CARDINAL;

(* the local module Random is inserted here *)

BEGIN (* RandomProgram body *)
    FOR i := 1 TO 10 DO
        WriteReal(RandomNum(),8);
        WriteLn;
        END;
END RandomProgram.
```

How are the random numbers to be calculated? There are many ways of generating a sequence of such values. One of these is the following. Each value is calculated from the previous value using the formula

```
next = (current + increment) MOD modulus
```

where "increment" and "modulus" are constants. With appropriate choices of the increment, modulus and initial value, a sequence of integers in the range 0 .. (modulus-1) is produced that exhibit properties of true random sequences. For example, if the modulus is 9; the increment is 14 and the first value is 1 then the next values are 6, 2 and 7.

Should a programmer have to be concerned about the parameters of a random number generator? No. This is one important reason for using a module to provide a random value. That is, unnecessary details can be hidden from the calling procedure.

Shown next is a module called Random that EXPORTs the function procedure RandomNum. It is inserted in the program module following the other declarations. The output statements are present purely for expository purposes and can be deleted.

```
MODULE Random;

(* A local module which exports the function Random *)

IMPORT WriteCard, WriteString, WriteLn;

EXPORT RandomNum;

CONST
    Modulus    = 7415;   (* upper bound of the raw values *)
    Increment  = 25543;  (* added to previous raw value *)

VAR
    RawValue : [0 .. Modulus-1];

PROCEDURE RandomNum() : REAL;

    (* Returns a real value in the range 0 to 1  *)

    BEGIN (* RandomNum body *)
        RawValue := (RawValue + Increment) MOD Modulus;
        WriteString('The next raw value is ');
        WriteCard(RawValue,7); WriteLn;
        (* return a converted value to REAL 0-1 *)
        RETURN FLOAT(RawValue) / FLOAT(Modulus);
    END RandomNum;

BEGIN (* Random initialization *)
    RawValue := 6789;  (* 1st raw value in the sequence *)
END Random;
```

Comments.

1. Observe the IMPORT statement. IMPORTed objects must always be obtained from the immediately surrounding environment. In this example, the enclosing "procedure" is the program module Random. This requirement is the reason WriteCard and WriteString are IMPORTed at the outer (program) level even though they are not used in the program body. For example, it would be illegal to include the following statement in the local module.

   FROM InOut IMPORT WriteCard, WriteString;

   Full rules of the IMPORT statement are found later in this chapter.

2. The statement "EXPORT RandomNum" indicates that the purpose of the local module is to export an object called RandomNum. The EXPORT statement (there can only be one in a module) lists the objects which can be referenced outside the module. EXPORT must follow any IMPORT statements. Recall that a program module cannot EXPORT anything.

3. The declarations of the local module contains no surprises. They include constants, a variable and the exported procedure.

4. The body of the local module contains the assignment statement "Raw Value := 6789". It is clear that this defines the first raw value in the range 0 to 7415. The question is "When is the local module body executed?" The answer is "when the immediately enclosing procedure or module is activated". The Random module is enclosed by the program module. Hence the body of Random is executed automatically when the program itself is loaded into memory. This is consistent with the idea that declarations are processed prior to executing a body.

Local Modules Versus Procedures

This section summarizes the key differences between procedures and local modules.

Purpose. The purpose of a local module is entirely different from that of a procedure. A procedure is written to perform some well-defined task. The purpose of a module is to define rather than do; to specify rather than perform; to declare rather than execute. A local module provides information for the compiler whereas a procedure is an execution-time phenomenon. The body of a local module simply performs initialization actions that set values for variables rather than mainstream operations.

The Random module's primary purpose was to define the procedure RandomNum. By enclosing its specifications within a module, details of how random numbers are generated are hidden from the user. All the user needs to know is that by importing the procedure called RandomNum a means is available for obtaining random numbers, in the range 0 to 1.

Aside from purpose, there are five key differences between procedures and local modules, described next.

First, is the form. The PROCEDURE header and MODULE header are different. Both contain declarations and a body. Procedures may not contain IMPORT and EXPORT statements.

Second, and most critical, is the visibility of identifiers. A procedure may use any identifier in any procedure that encloses it. All such identifiers are global with respect to the procedure. On the other hand, a module may only access external objects that are imported. From the outside-looking-in perspective; only objects exported from a module are visible. This is the primary difference between procedures and modules. With procedures, visibility of objects is implicit; with modules, visibility in both directions is explicitly stated.

Third, communication between a procedure and its surrounding environment is accomplished via a parameter list. In a module, communication is via IMPORTed and EXPORTed objects. An important ramification is that procedures can be written without knowing the names of the corresponding identifiers that will be used in the surrounding environment. On the other hand, when a module is used, you must know both the exact names of all imported objects and also where they will be coming from. This has a very important consequence which is explained below.

Fourth, the rules of existence of procedures and modules are different. All objects in a procedure are re-created each time the procedure is called. Furthermore, when a procedure terminates, all its values are lost. A module, however, remains in existence and hence is able to retain its values as long as its enclosing module or procedure is active.

Fifth, the body of a procedure is executed when the procedure is called. A module's body is executed when the enclosing module or procedure is activated.

Local Module Imports and Exports

Imports to a program module from a library module such as InOut were described in the previous section. Library module imports and exports are described in the next section. In this section we limit the discussion to local module imports and local module exports. We shall use the terms "enclosing module", "local module" and "library module". The "enclosing module" is normally the program module but it could be enclosed by another procedure or module. Likewise the local module could enclose other modules but the rules are transitive. A "library module" is any separately compiled module other than the one containing the local module of interest. Because a local module can only pass and receive objects from its immediately enclosing environment, the rules are relatively simple.

Local Module Import Rules. The rules that follow refer to a "qualified identifier". An example is "InOut.WriteString". That is a qualified identifier is formed by prefixing the identifier with a module name and a period. Qualified identifiers are only used when referencing objects IMPORTed without "FROM". Further comments follow the rules.

1. A local module can import any object declared by or imported to its enclosing module.

2. A local module cannot import the identifier of the enclosing module in an attempt to import all available objects. The only module identifiers that can be imported are those of library modules. Hence "FROM" is (optionally) used only when referring to a library module.

3. References to imported objects declared in an enclosing module are never qualified. Therefore a local module's declared objects must be different from its imported identifiers.

These rules are illustrated with reference to the following program fragment:

```
MODULE A;
IMPORT InOut;
FROM RealInOut IMPORT ReadReal;
VAR
    X : REAL;

    (* *************** *)
    MODULE B;
    IMPORT X, InOut;
    VAR
        Read : CHAR;
    (* rest of B *)
    END B;
    (* *************** *)

(* rest of A *)
END A.
```

Comments.

1. Rule 1 says that Module B can import InOut, ReadReal or X but it cannot import WriteReal for example because WriteReal is not known in the enclosing module A.

2. Rule 2 says B cannot import "A" but can import "InOut". A second IMPORT statement using FROM could be used in B to selectively unqualify specific objects in InOut.

3. Rule 3 says references to X cannot be qualified as in "A.X". Hence B cannot declare X. B however can and does declare "Read" as a CHAR

variable. B can therefore reference InOut.Read and Read without ambiguity.

4. Note that A does not have an EXPORT statement. EXPORT is an outward directed operation. All objects declared in or imported by an enclosing module are candidates for import by a local module.

Local Module Export Rules.

1. Objects exported from a local module are automatically available in the enclosing module.

2. Since only one EXPORT statement is permitted in a module, all exports are either QUALIFIED or not qualified.

3. Qualified exports from a local module mean that the enclosing module:

   a) must prefix the exported object with the local module name

   b) may declare an object with the same name

4. Unqualified exports from a local module mean that the enclosing module cannot declare a object having the exported name.

5. The identifiers in an export list cannot be qualified.

   The following program fragments illustrate these rules.

```
MODULE NoQualA;                  MODULE QualA;
EXPORT X;                        EXPORT QUALIFIED X, QualB;
    (* ************** *)         VAR X : CHAR;
    MODULE NoQualB;                  (* ************** *)
    EXPORT X;                        MODULE QualB;
    VAR X : CHAR;                    EXPORT QUALIFIED X;
    (* rest of B *)                  VAR X : CHAR;
    END NoQualB;                     (* rest of QualB *)
    (* ************** *)             END QualB;
  (* rest of NoQualA *)              (* ************** *)
  END QualA;                       (* rest of QualA *)
                                   END QualA;
```

Comments.

1. The local modules on the left do not qualify exports -- those on the right do.

2. Consider the "NoQual" example.

   a) Because NoQualB exports X unqualified, reference to this object in NoQualA can be "X" or "B.X". "A.X" is illegal.

   b) NoQualA cannot declare a meaning for X.

c) NoQualA exports X without qualification. Hence outside NoQualA, B's X is still referenced as "X". If the export statement in NoQualA had been "EXPORT QUALIFIED X", then outside NoQualA, B's X would be referenced as A.X.

3. Consider the Qual example.

a) Because B's export of X is QUALIFIED, QualA must reference the object as "QualB.X" and not "X".

b) QualA declares a meaning for X. Within A therefore, A's X and B's X are referenced as X and QualB.X respectively.

c) QualA exports QUALIFIED its 'X' and the module QualB. Thus outside of QualA the 'X's are referenced as QualA.X and QualA.QualB.X

d) Because the export list must not have qualified identifiers, "QualB.X" cannot be used instead of "QualB" in the EXPORT statement. That is, an enclosing module cannot export a subset of a local module's identifiers unless they have unique names -- a practice we highly recommend.

4. If the name of a local module appears in an enclosing module's export list, all objects exported by the local module are exported by the enclosing module. Therefore, because the local module NoQualA only exports one item the export statement in NoQualA could be replaced by the following equivalent statement.

```
EXPORT NoQualB;   (* goes in NoQualA *)
```

Local Module Initialization.

A module body is executed when its enclosing module or procedure is activated. In the case of local (perhaps nested to several levels) the initialization occurs in order of physical appearance of the <u>bodies</u> in the program. Because a module's declarations precede its body, this has the effect of initializing the modules from the innermost outwards. Put another way, a local module is initialized before its enclosing module. An implication or this ordering is that there is little purpose in importing a variable to a local module unless the purpose of the local module is to initialize the variable. Otherwise it cannot be used.

10.4   Separately Compiled Modules

This section describes how to create modules that can be compiled independently of, but still accessed by, a program module and/or other modules. Why would you want to do this? There are two main reasons. First, you can build a library of commonly required services (procedures and data structures) that can be imported as needed by other modules. Hence separately compiled, nonprogram modules are called <u>library</u>

modules. These service modules can be updated and maintained independently of the modules that use them. Second, computing overhead is reduced because the service or utility modules are stored in compiled form and only need to be linked to the modules that use them. The alternative would be to imbed the service module as a local module in every program requiring its facilities. This would not only increase compile times, but also tempt people to tamper with the source code leading to perhaps many versions of the same logic. It would also make it difficult to protect proprietary or confidential software.

The relationship between service/utility modules and application modules that employ their services is shown in Figure 10.1.

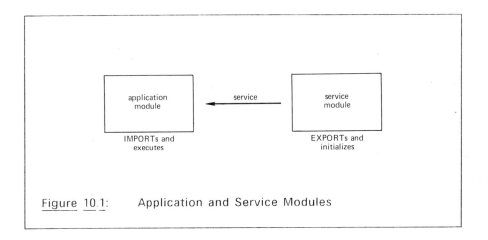

Figure 10.1:   Application and Service Modules

Every implementation of the Modula-2 language comes with a library of modules. These provide input-output services, resource services such as memory allocation and special purpose services such as string handling, graphics and type transformations. Additional information about these modules is found in Chapter 11.

The purpose here is to explain how the module library can be extended by modules of your choosing. Separately compiled modules have one of three principal purposes.

1. Data conversion. The service module exports procedures for transforming data from one representation to another. Examples are: a module that transforms real or integer data into dollars-and-cents formats; or one that reads a character string and returns a year, month and day.

2. Data hiding. The procedures in the module require access to a body of data that is either proprietary or of no interest to the user. An example is a module that exports a procedure to validate passwords.

The list of valid passwords can be hidden from the user in the service module because the user doesn't see the source form of the password module. The user, however, can import a procedure that will check a password to see if it is valid.

3. High level data types and operations. The service module contains a definition of a nonstandard data type. It exports both the type and all procedures used for processing the type. An example is a module that defines a type called "queue". it exports "queue" and the procedures "Join", "Leave", and "Count" for manipulating the queue. The user need not be concerned with how queues are actually represented in terms of numbers and data structures in order to make effective use of them. An example is given later in this chapter in which "car" is defined as a type.

10.5   DEFINITION and IMPLEMENTATION Modules

A separately compiled module has two cooperating parts -- a definition module and an implementation module. The two parts are compiled separately but the definition module must be compiled first. The definition module essentially lists the constants, types and variables, which are exported along with the headers of exported procedures. The implementation module contains the details of the exported procedures.

Definition modules, implementation modules and program modules are the three types of compilation units in Modula-2.

An Example

To illustrate the mechanics of creating a service module, we will transform the local module Random described in the previous section into a pair of DEFINITION and IMPLEMENTATION modules. Many important ideas are illustrated by this example.

For ease of reference the module Random as used previously is shown next.

```
MODULE Random;

(* A local module which exports the function Random *)

IMPORT WriteCard, WriteString, WriteLn;

EXPORT RandomNum;

CONST
    Modulus     = 7415;    (* upper bound of the raw values *)
    Increment   = 25543;   (* added to previous raw value *)

VAR
    RawValue : [0 .. Modulus-1];
```

```
PROCEDURE RandomNum( ) : REAL;

    (* Returns a real value in the range 0 to 1  *)

    BEGIN (* RandomNum body *)
        RawValue := (RawValue + Increment) MOD Modulus;
        WriteString('The next raw value is ');
        WriteCard(RawValue,7); WriteLn;
        (* return a converted value to REAL 0-1 *)
        RETURN FLOAT(RawValue) / FLOAT(Modulus);
    END RandomNum;

BEGIN (* Random initialization *)
    RawValue := 6789;   (* 1st raw value in the sequence *)
END Random;
```

The Definition Module. When transformed to a separately compiled module, the DEFINITION module is:

```
DEFINITION MODULE Random;

(* This module exports the real-valued function - RandomNum *)

PROCEDURE RandomNum( ) : REAL;

END Random.
```

Comments.

1. The reserved word "DEFINITION" precedes the word MODULE and the module name.

2. The declarations of the constants, variables, and types in the DEFINITION module have the same form and rules as those in any other module. In the case of exported procedures only the procedure header is given in the definition module; the procedure body is found in the corresponding implementation module.

3. A definition module contains no module body nor may it contain local module declarations. Every compilation unit ends with a period.

4. The example definition module contains precisely enough information to explain what it does -- it exports a single object called RandomNum. RandomNum is a procedure with no parameters which returns a REAL value.

Shown below is the corresponding IMPLEMENTATION module.

```
IMPLEMENTATION MODULE Random;

(* This implementation module implements the random number
   procedure RandomNum() which produces a pseudo-random number
   in the range 0 .. 1.
*)

CONST
    Modulus    = 7415;    (* the upper bound of the raw values *)
    Increment  = 25543;   (* added to the previous raw value   *)

VAR
    RawValue : [0 .. Modulus-1];

PROCEDURE RandomNum() : REAL;

    BEGIN (* RandomNum body *)
        RawValue := (RawValue + Increment) MOD Modulus;
        (* convert to REAL 0 to 1 *)
        RETURN FLOAT(RawValue) / FLOAT(Modulus);
    END RandomNum;

BEGIN (* Random initialization *)
    RawValue := 6789;  (* the first raw value in the sequence *)
END Random.
```

It is similar to the local module Random. However, there are four small
but important differences.

1. The word "IMPLEMENTATION" precedes the word MODULE in the
   header.

2. The IMPORT statement begins with FROM InOut. This not only
   specifies the source of the imported objects but also "unqualifies" the
   imported identifiers. An unqualified identifier can be used without
   reference to the module from which it was obtained. Complete details
   are found in the rules of the IMPORT statement given later in the
   chapter.

3. The implementation module contains no EXPORT statement. This is the
   purpose of the corresponding DEFINITION module.

4. The compilation unit terminates with a period. A local module is
   followed by a semicolon to separate it from the next program
   component.

Qualified Identifiers

To complete the picture, the following is a program module that imports RandomNum. The random numbers generated are identical to those produced when Random took the form of a local module. The new feature illustrated is the IMPORT statement which does not include the word FROM. It demonstrates the use of qualified identifiers. These are explained in the comments following the end of the program.

```
MODULE RandomProgram2;

(* This program imports the procedure RandomNum from the
   separately compiled module Random. It also illustrates
   the use of qualified identifiers
*)

IMPORT Random, RealInOut, InOut;

VAR
    i : CARDINAL;

BEGIN
    FOR i := 1 TO 10 DO
        RealInOut.WriteReal(Random.RandomNum(),8);
        InOut.WriteLn;
        END;
END RandomProgram2.
```

Comments.

1. The IMPORT statement is:

```
    IMPORT Random, InOut, RealInOut
```

It does not indicate what objects are imported from the three modules. Importing an entire module has two consequences. First all objects in the imported module are assumed to be imported. Second, because the imported module's objects are not explicitly named, references to them must be qualified (prefixed by the name of the exporting module). This is necessary so that the compiler knows where their meanings can be found.

2. In the example, three qualified identifiers are found. They are Random.RandomNum, RealInOut.WriteReal and InOut.WriteLn. A qualified identifier has the form

```
    modulename . objectname
```

Qualified identifiers must be used whenever an IMPORT statement simply contains a module name. Put another way, FROM has the effect of unqualifying identifier references. That is an import statement of the form.

FROM modulename   IMPORT   identifierlist

means the identifiers can be used without qualification. Recall that objects declared in a DEFINITION module are automatically qualified exports. That is, the exported identifiers must be qualified outside the module unless unqualified by "FROM". The rule that all objects exported from a definition module must be qualified at export time is necessary to resolve two otherwise potentially ambiguous situations.

o An importing module may have declared an object with the same name as an object that it imports. The qualification is necessary to distinguish the locally declared object from the imported object.

o Two different modules may export identifiers with the same name. Qualification resolves the ambiguity.

The Rationale For Separate Compilation

The somewhat lengthy explanation associated with the preceding example may provoke the questions such as "Why go to all the trouble of separating the definition and implementation parts?" "Why not just compile the local module and store it in a library?" There are four good reasons:

1. The purpose of a module is separated from how that purpose is achieved.

2. The implementation part can be changed without changing the definition part. This means improvements in efficiency or method can be made that are transparent to the user because the implementation part is private. Definition modules on the other hand are public.

3. When designing a large software system, the function of the system can be decomposed into a hierarchy of subfunctions. By specifying these subfunctions in the form of definition modules, members of the programming team have a well-defined set of functional interfaces.

4. Modula-2 contains facilities that automatically match the "version numbers" of a definition module and any module that imports its services. This has the effect of preventing a change in a definition module from unknowingly affecting any of its clients. Version checking is described later in this chapter.

The only time EXPORT may be used without QUALIFIED is in a local module. In this case, the local module is completely contained within its environment, and hence it is the programmer's responsibility to ensure identifiers are unique.

Library and Program Module Imports

This subsection summarizes the form and rules of imports to program, DEFINITION and IMPLEMENTATION modules.

Forms:

    IMPORT modulelist

    FROM modulename IMPORT identifierlist

Purpose: To make constants, types, variables, procedures and modules declared in other modules available to the importing module.

Rules:

1. A module may have more than one IMPORT statement.

2. All IMPORT statements must precede the EXPORT statement.

3. Implied imports

   a) Importing an array type automatically imports its index type(s).

   b) Importing a RECORD type automatically imports all its field names.

   c) Importing an enumerated type automatically imports the constants of the type.

   d) Importing a pointer type automatically imports the identifiers associated with the referenced object.

4. Modula-2's standard identifiers are automatically imported into every module.

5. Qualified import. The form is:

    FROM modulename IMPORT identifierlist

   a) The identifiers in the identifier list must be different from each other and from other identifiers declared within or imported to the module.

   b) The identifiers in the list cannot be qualified.

6. Unqualified import. The form is

    IMPORT modulelist

   a) All identifiers exported from the named definition modules are available to the IMPORTing module.

b) Reference to the imported objects must be qualified by prefixing the name of the object with the definition module name and a period.

7. Objects exported from a definition module are automatically imported into its corresponding implementation module.

8. Objects imported by a definition module are not automatically visible in the implementation module.

The following pair of statements shows how to selectively unqualify imported objects.

```
IMPORT InOut;
FROM InOut IMPORT WriteLn;
```

The effect is that InOut objects other than WriteLn must be qualified. For example, WriteString must be referenced as InOut.WriteString.

Order of Module Initialization

Case 1: When large numbers of modules specify imports, the order of module initialization is chosen so that (subject to Case 2) imported modules are initialized prior to importing modules. A second rule is that a module is only initialized once, even if several modules import objects from the same module.

Case 2 – Mutually importing modules. It is possible though not common, that a pair of modules each import one or more objects from the other. In this case, the order of module initialization is unspecified.

The program module is always inititalized last. Initialization of the program module is in effect execution of the program.

10.6   Opaque Types.

An opaque type is a type exported by a definition module, the internal representation of which is unknown without examining the corresponding implementation module.   Along with the type, the definition module exports all procedures used to manipulate objects of that type.   Opaque types are one of the most powerful features of the Modula–2 language because they allow you to define and perform operations on nonstandard types that are meaningful in the context of the problem to be solved.

An Example. Let us define the type "car." Suppose that three operations are possible with a car. purchase, drive and sell. Further let us suppose: that the purchase information includes its size; that driving requires specifying the miles driven and that selling a car requires knowing how many months a car has been owned. Beginning with these assumptions, let us define a definition module that exports the enumerated CarSizeType and the opaque type CarType and the procedures Purchase, Drive and Sell. The definition module follows:

```
DEFINITION MODULE CarModule;

(* This module illustrates the use of an abstract data
   type called CarType
*)

TYPE
    (* CarType is not defined here, it is an opaque type *)
    CarType;

    (* CarSizeType is an enumerated type *)
    CarSizeType = (Compact, MidSize, FullSize);

PROCEDURE Purchase(VAR Car      : CarType;
                       CarSize : CarSizeType;
                       Price   : CARDINAL);

PROCEDURE Drive(    Car   : CarType;
                    Miles : CARDINAL);

PROCEDURE Value(    Car : CarType;
                    Age : CARDINAL) : CARDINAL;

END CarModule.
```

The CarModule definition module clearly shows what can be done with a car but gives no clue how CarType is implemented.

Before looking at the implementation module, let us assume that a car loses 5 percent of its value as soon as it is purchased; that its value decreases by 1 percent of the purchase price each month; and that the value decreases by an additional 10 percent if the mileage is over 1000 miles per month at the time the car is sold.

The CarModule implementation module is given next. Note that a car's information is actually stored in a RECORD structure but this fact is transparent to a user.

```
IMPLEMENTATION MODULE CarModule;

(* Implements the abstract data type "CarType" *)

FROM Storage IMPORT ALLOCATE;  (* required for NEW *)

TYPE
    CarType = POINTER TO CarRec;

    CarRec  = RECORD
        CarSize  : CarSizeType; (* Compact, mid or full *)
        CarPrice : CARDINAL;    (* in dollars *)
        CarMiles : CARDINAL;    (* cumulative miles driven *)
        END;
```

```
PROCEDURE Purchase(VAR Car   : CarType;
                       Size  : CarSizeType;
                       Price : CARDINAL);

    BEGIN
        NEW (Car);  (* create a car rec *)
        WITH Car^ DO
            CarPrice := Price;
            CarSize  := Size;
            CarMiles := 0;
            END;
    END Purchase;

PROCEDURE Drive(   Car   : CarType;
                   Miles : CARDINAL );

    BEGIN
        Car^.CarMiles := Car^.CarMiles + Miles
    END Drive;

PROCEDURE Value(   Car : CarType;
                   Age : CARDINAL) : CARDINAL;

    VAR
        Salvage : REAL;  (* the price when sold *)

    BEGIN
        WITH Car^ DO
            (* initial depreciation *)
            Salvage := 0.9 * FLOAT(CarPrice);
            (* age effect *)
            Salvage := Salvage - 0.05 * FLOAT(CarPrice)
                                      * FLOAT(Age);
            IF CarMiles > 1000 * Age THEN
                (* include mileage effect *)
                Salvage := Salvage - 0.1 * FLOAT(CarPrice);
                END;
            END; (* WITH *)
        IF Salvage < 0.0 THEN
            Salvage := 0.0;
            END;
        RETURN TRUNC(Salvage);
    END Value;

BEGIN
    (* no module initialization is required *)
END CarModule.
```

Comments.

1. The implementation module provides the missing details concerning the type CarType. It shows that CarType is in fact a pointer to a record describing attributes of a car.

2. Note that an implementation module implicitly imports all objects exported from its corresponding definition module.

A program module that purchases a car, drives it for a while and then sells it is given next.

```
MODULE CarUse;

(* This module illustrates the use of an abstract data type
   called CarType
*)

FROM CarModule IMPORT CarType, CarSizeType, Purchase, Drive,
                      Value;

FROM InOut      IMPORT Read, Write, WriteString, ReadCard,
                      WriteCard, WriteLn;

VAR
    Price        : CARDINAL;     (* purchase price *)
    CarSizeCode  : CHAR;         (* 'C', 'M', or 'F'
                                    to denote car size *)
    CarSize      : CarSizeType;  (* denotes compact,
                                    mid or fullsize *)
    Miles        : CARDINAL;     (* miles driven in one trip *)
    Age          : CARDINAL;     (* age of car in months *)
    MyCar        : CarType;      (* a car *)

BEGIN
    (* 1 - Get price and size *)
    WriteString('Enter purchase price of the car: ');
    ReadCard(Price); WriteLn;

    WriteString('Enter car size code ("C", "M" or "F"):');
    Read(CarSizeCode); Write(CarSizeCode); WriteLn;

    CASE CAP(CarSizeCode) OF
        'C' : CarSize := Compact;
      | 'M' : CarSize := MidSize;
      | 'F' : CarSize := FullSize;
        END;
    Purchase(MyCar, CarSize, Price);
```

```
    (* 2 - Drive the car *)
    LOOP
        WriteString('Enter miles driven (0 to exit): ');
        ReadCard(Miles); WriteLn;
        IF Miles = 0 THEN
            EXIT;
            END;
        Drive(MyCar,Miles);
        END;

    (* 3 - Sell the car *)
    WriteString('How many months have you owned the car? ');
    ReadCard(Age); WriteLn;
    WriteString('The car can be sold for $');
    WriteCard(Value(MyCar,Age), 7); WriteLn;
END CarUse.
```

Comments.

1. The module imports all five identifiers exported from the CarModule. Had the IMPORT statement been "IMPORT CarModule", qualified identifiers would have to be used.

2. The CASE construct is necessary to convert the input to the appropriate CarSizeType constant. Recall that enumerated constants cannot be read directly although you can write a pair of procedures to perform input-output for any enumerated type.

3. Observe that the three exported procedures Purchase, Drive and Value give no clue as to how CarType is implemented. This is why such types are called opaque types.

Opaque Types - A Summary

The following points summarize the rules and details about opaque types.

1. An opaque type is a type that is exported from a definition module but is defined in the implementation module.

2. In the definition module, the type declaration takes the form

        TYPE   typename;

3. The only operations that can be performed on values of an opaque type are those defined by the procedures exported with the type. Most implementations also permit assignment and comparison (for equality) of variables of the same opaque type.

4. The actual implementation of the type must usually be a POINTER.

5. An <u>abstract</u> <u>type</u> is an opaque type together with the procedures for processing the values of the type.

10.7   Module Rules: A Summary

DEFINITION Modules:

1. The form is

```
DEFINITION MODULE name;
IMPORT statements; (* optional *)
declarations
END name.
```

IMPLEMENTATION Modules

1. The form is:

```
IMPLEMENTATION name priority;
IMPORT statements; (* optional *)
    block
name.
```

The priority is optional. If present, it must be a CARDINAL constant enclosed in brackets.

2. An IMPLEMENTATION module must have a DEFINITION module with the same name.

3. An IMPLEMENTATION module is not required if a DEFINITION module only exports fully declared types.

4. Objects exported from a definition module are automatically imported into the corresponding implementation module.

Local Modules

1. The form is

```
MODULE name priority;
EXPORT statement;  (* optional *)
IMPORT statements; (* optional *)
    block
name;
```

2. A local module may only import from and export to its immediately enclosing procedure or module.

Program Modules

1. There may be only one program module.

2. A program module is indistinguishable from a local module except that:

   a) A program module may not contain an EXPORT statement.

   b) A program module ends with a period instead of a semicolon.

10.8   Version Checking

The Problem. Suppose the author of a service module that you have been using in an application program removes or changes one of the exported objects. If you were not informed of the change and if there was no automatic checking, unexpected results could occur the next time you recompiled and attempted to execute your application program. Fortunately, Modula-2 has automatic "version checking" to insure this problem will not arise. The method involves the use of module keys.

Module Keys

When a DEFINITION module is compiled, it produces a symbol file that contains information about the exported objects. The symbol file also contains a value called the module key which changes each time the definition module is compiled. Depending on the implementation, the module key may be a sequential number, a random number or a number based on date and time.

When an implementation or program module is compiled, it produces a code file containing the machine language representation of the declarations and statements in the module. The code file also contains the names and keys of all modules that it imports. Thus every code file in the system is tied to the specific symbol files that it imports. This binding occurs at compile time.

In order to execute a program, the code files must be linked together to form a load file. The load file is then executed. For each module that is linked, the module keys in the corresponding symbol and code files must match or a "version mismatch" occurs. This guarantees that the constituent components of the load file are using the same definitions.

Order of Compiling

No problems arise by adhering to the following rules.

1. Initial order of compilation

   a) DEFINITION module

   b) IMPLEMENTATION module

c) client (application) modules

2. Recompiling

a) If a definition module is recompiled, the implementation and <u>all</u> of its client modules must be recompiled.

b) If an implementation module is recompiled, the program must be relinked but application modules need not be recompiled.

c) If an application module is recompiled, only a relink is required.

A Warning. Module imports often form chains. For example 'A' imports 'B' which imports 'C' etc., forms a chain of imports. Thus a hierarchy of imports exists in a module library. Changing a definition module at any level in the hierarchy requires recompilation of all modules below it in the hierarchy.

10.9   Exercises and Programming Problems

1. The game of ten-pin bowling is divided into ten "frames". In each frame, the player has at most two chances to knock down all ten pins. The score in any frame is determined as follows.

Name	# of balls thrown	Pins knocked down	Score
strike	1	10	10 + pins knocked down on next 2 throws
spare	2	10	10 + pins knocked down on next throw
open frame	2	<10	# of pins knocked down

Should a bowler get a spare or strike in the tenth frame he throws one or two additional balls respectively in order to obtain his score for the tenth frame. The largest number of balls a player can throw in one game is therefore 9*2+3=21.

Write a program that reads the number of pins knocked down on each throw and prints the frame-by-frame score. Use at least one nontrivial procedure in the program. Test your program on the following three cases

```
 8  1  7  3  9  1  9  0  9  1 10 10  7  1  7  3  9  1  9
 9  1  9  0  8  2  8  2  7  2 10  6  0 10  9  0  9  0
10 10  7  2  9  1 10 10 10  7  0  8  2 10 10  4
```

2. Write a local module called Merge to "merge" two arrays of names. Each name is stored in a record containing a name field and an age field. (The array elements are records.) The number of records used in each array should be imported. If the names of the two arrays are "S1" and "S2" and if they have M and N records, respectively, the logic should create a third array of M+N records made up of the union of the values in S1 and S2. The values in the merged array should also be in alphabetical order. For example, if the records in the first array contain Ann, Charlie, Ted and Zeke, and if those in the second contain Dave, Pat and Tom, then the merged records will contain Ann, Charlie, Dave, Pat, Ted, Tom and Zeke. The merging process can be done efficiently by processing elements in S1 and S2 in order and selecting the lower value of the two being considered as the next value to be put in the merged set. In the mainline, assume M and N are less than ten.

3. Use the procedure written to solve Problem 2 to merge K sets of values. Assume K is 5 or less. This can be done by having the mainline: read the value of K; read the data for the first pair of arrays; merge them using the procedure; read the next array of values; merge it with the previous result; read the next array; etc. The input data should each contain the number of records in the array followed by the values. (The first input value contains the number of sets.)

4. One method of storing a list of words in alphabetical sequence consists of prefixing each word with a number indicating how many characters from the previous word are used at the beginning of the current word. For example, to store the words APPLE, APPLICANT, APPLICATION, APPRAISE, BOX, BOXER, the following string would be used.

    0APPLE4ICANT7TION3RAISE0BOX3ER$

Assume that a dollar sign follows the last character of the last word. Problem: Create an appropriate string to store the following words: atom, atomic, backtracking, body, boundary condition, box model, call, catchall, character, circular definition. Write a program that prompts for a word or phrase as input and prints a line of the following form:

    _____ is (not) in the list

Assume that case is not significant. That is "Cat" and "cat" are the same. The program should terminate when a null (empty) string is entered. Test your program on at least the following words: boundary, boxmodel, a, characters, boxing, atom, catch.

5. Write a procedure called FlipSet that, given two sets A and B produces a set with the common members removed. Use the procedure to solve the following problem.

    Suppose a set of doors numbered 1 to 25 is initially closed. Twenty-five people successively pass down the line of doors and reverse the status (open or closed) of one or more doors according to the following rules. The first person reverses every door; the second person then flips the status of the even-numbered doors; the third person flips every third door, and so on. (The 25th person will simply change the status of the 25th door.) What doors are open after the 25th pass? What is the general rule that determines the status of any given door after N passes?

6. The game of Keno is a popular gambling game in many places. A player pays $1.20 for each game and then chooses eight numbers in the range 1 .. 80. The house randomly picks twenty numbers in the same range. If the player matches five numbers, he wins $10; if he matches six, he wins $100; seven is worth $2200 and matching all eight wins $25000. Write a program to play ten games of Keno. The first ten lines of input data contain the players guesses. Use either of the random number generator described in the problems of the text to generate the house numbers. Assume the player starts with $25. Print a report showing the cumulative position of the player after each game.

7. Acme parking lots charges $0.50 per hour for a parking space. Suppose a line of data is recorded for each car using the lot. It contains: the license number (an INTEGER), the arrival time (a pair of INTEGERs denoting hours and minutes), and a departure time in hours and minutes. Assume that hours range from 0 to 24 and that no one leaves after midnight. (The departure time is always greater than the arrival time).

a) Develop an algorithm and write a program to read each line of data (stop when a license number of zero is found); compute the charges for each car and print a report in the following form:

```
            ACME PARKING LOT
    LICENSE #      TIME IN       TIME OUT      CHARGE

      XXXXX        XX  XX        XX  XX        X.XX
      XXXXX        XX  XX        XX  XX        X.XX
        .
        .
      XXXXX        XX  XX        XX  XX        X.XX

    TOTAL NUMBER OF CARS = X
    TOTAL CHARGES          = $ XXX.XX
```

Test your program using the following lines of data.

```
    3527    8    0    11    0
    1469    10   15   14    45
    2750    0    27   20    27
    1986    17   53   18    45
    7787    15   15   15    59
       0
```

b) Assume the parking charge should be rounded to the nearest five cents. Modify and run the program. c) Assume the charge is "$0.50 per hour or any fraction thereof". Modify and run the program. d) Use a set to keep track of the number of cars in the lot at any given time. Print a report showing the cars in the lot at the end of each hour. Assuming the parking lot has twenty-five spaces, calculate the percent utilization of the lot for the periods midnight to 8 a.m., 8 a.m. to 6 p.m. and 6 p.m. to midnight.

8. A real estate firm wants to be able to match clients searching for homes with appropriate houses for sale. To do this, two files have been prepared -- a client file, and a house file. Information in these files consist of the following record types.

```
ClientRec = RECORD
      RefNum     : INTEGER;
      Bedrooms   : [1..6];
      PriceCode  : [1..10];
      Wooded     : [-1..+1]; (*see note below*)
      Pool       : [-1..+1];
      School     : [-1..+1];
      END;
```

Note: A preference code of -1 means the feature is not wanted; zero means the client is indifferent and +1 means the client must have it.

The House file has records of the following type

```
HouseRec = RECORD
      RefNum     : INTEGER;
      Bedrooms   : [1..6];
      PriceCode  : [1..10];
      Wooded     : BOOLEAN;
      Pool       : BOOLEAN;
      Schools    : BOOLEAN;
      END;
```

For example if Schools is TRUE it means there are schools nearby.

The problem. Create a client file and a house file containing a mixture of client preferences and house characteristics. Then, for each client list the houses that are suitable, meaning that the house must have at least the number of bedrooms needed, a price code no greater than that specified by the client, all of the features required by the client and none of the features not wanted by the client.

9. A consumer has $15,000 and is debating whether to buy a small foreign car or a large domestic car. The relevant data is as follows.

	Small	Large
purchase price	$10,000	$15,000
miles/gallon	35	22
annual maint. cost	400	350
depreciation/year	15%	10%

Assume that the car will be driven 12,000 miles per year; the cost of gas is currently $2.00/gal and will increase 10 percent per year; the difference in purchase prices ($5,000) could be invested at 8 percent per year, and the depreciation applies to the value of the car at the start of each year. Write a program thath determines the net position of the consumer at the end of each of the next five years.

10. Suppose, while practicing your basketball shooting you perform the following drill. Starting 1 foot away from the basket you take a shot. If you make the shot, you step back 1 foot and shoot again. As long as you keep making the shot you move back one more foot for the next shot. As soon as you miss, you return to the 1-foot mark and start again. Suppose the probability of making a shot from N feet away is $(1 - 0.01N)$. Use simulation to answer the following questions.

a) During 100 shots, how many are taken from 1 foot, 2 feet, 3 feet, ...?

b) What is the average number of shots that must be taken before being successful at a distance of 15 feet. (Run the simulation ten times, stopping each time the first successful shot from 15 feet occurs. Average the ten counts.)

c) Given that a shot has just been successful from 5 feet away, what is the probability of making an 8-foot shot without any intervening misses.

d) Answer questions (a), (b), (c) above using the rule that when a miss occurs, you move 1 foot closer rather than return to the start. Assume that if you miss at 1 foot, you stay there until a shot is made.

11. A friend has watched you play the game described in Problem 10 and offers you the following bet. After each of your shots, he will take one shot from the foul line which is 12 feet from the basket. If he misses before you do, he will pay you $5. If you miss any shot up to and including a shot from the foul line, you pay him $10. Suppose the probability of his making a foul line shot is 0.9. Should you take the bet? Does it make any difference if he has to shoot first? How would you determine a fair payoff for the game?

CHAPTER 11

INPUT-OUTPUT SERVICES

Questions Answered In This Chapter

1. What is the Modula-2 approach to input-output?

2. What are the standard input-output service modules?

3. How is a file-to-file transfer performed?

4. How are direct access file operations done?

Chapter 3 provided descriptions of the Read procedures used to obtain single values of the basic types. It also explained how to use the OpenInput and OpenOutput to change the standard input and standard output device assignments.

This chapter describes how to perform general input- output operations such as reading records from a file of records stored on an external device such as a floppy disk drive.

11.1   Modula-2's Approach to Input-Output

The Modula-2 language unlike almost all other programming languages contains no imbedded facilities for performing input-output operations. That is there are no statements or standard procedures for reading and writing data. Instead, all input-output facilities must be imported from one or more modules. These service modules are members of a library of modules supplied with every implementation of the language. You can add to this library using the methods described in the previous chapter.

Why does Modula-2 take this approach? Like almost every decision made by the designer of a language, there are both advantages and disadvantages. The disadvantages include:

o All input-output procedures (e.g., Read), types (e.g. "File"), variables (e.g. "termCH"), and constants (e.g. EOL) must be imported into every module needing them.

o The syntax of input-output operations is restricted to what can be accomplished using the syntax of procedure calls. For example, a procedure cannot have a variable number of parameters.

o Although the language's designer has recommended that certain
   "standard" input-output procedures be supplied with every installation,
   implementors and users of the language have freedom to create
   procedures and tools that seem most appropriate to them.
   Consequently, there is a low probability that programs are portable
   from one implementation to another.

Advantages of the service module approach to input-output include the
following:

o The language is smaller and simpler. This permits a smaller compiler.

o The code generated by the compiler is often more compact than would
   be the case if input-output was part of the language.

o There is no restriction on the kinds of devices with which a Modula-2
   program can communicate. Support is open ended.

o Because modules can form a hierarchy, higher and higher levels of
   abstraction can be built. This permits not only extremely high level
   procedure calls of the type "UpdateMasterFile" but allows programmers
   to enter the hierarchy at a level that is most appropriate for the task at
   hand.

11.2   Input-Output Service Modules

The implementors of Modula-2 have agreed to some extent to offer the
same set of input-output utilities with the software they distribute.
Nonetheless, there are differences -- some significant -- in the various
implementations. Because the authors used the Logitech implementation
to develop and test the examples found in this book, we will briefly
outline the contents and functions of the main input-output facilities
found in that implementation. More complete information can be found
in Appendix C and you should use the reference documentation supplied
with your compiler as the final authority. The main modules are
described in the following subsections.

InOut

The InOut module is found in all implementations. Its facilities perform
general input-output tasks using the standard input and standard output
devices. The objects exported by InOut are:

```
EOL,            - end of line constant
Done,           - return status
in,             - standard input file
out,            - standard output file
termCH,         - termination character

CloseInput,     - close input file
CloseOutput,    - close output file
```

```
OpenInput,       - open input file
OpenOutput,      - open output file
Read,            - read a character
ReadCard,        - read a cardinal
ReadInt,         - read an integer
ReadString,      - read a string
ReadWrd,         - read a word
Write,           - write a character
WriteCard,       - write a cardinal
WriteHex,        - write a value out in hexadecimal
WriteInt,        - write an integer
WriteLn,         - write an end of line character
WriteOct,        - write a value out in octal
WriteString,     - write a string
WriteWrd;        - write a word value
```

The parameters required by each procedure are found in Appendix C.

RealInOut

The RealInOut module is supplied with most implementations. Its procedures perform input-output of REAL values. The exported objects are:

```
Done,            - status
ReadReal,        - read in real value
WriteReal,       - write real in 'e' notation
WriteRealOct;    - write real value out in octal
```

Further details are found in Appendix C.

FileSystem

All implementations have a module called "FileSystem" or "Files" or "FileStuff" or something similar. It contains the tools for creating, reading from, writing to and deleting named collections of data stored on external devices. The two remaining sections of this chapter illustrate sequential and direct access file processing.

The objects exported by the Logitech FileSystem module are:

```
Command,          - commands passed to DiskFiles
DirectoryProc,    - proc type - entire file operations
File,             - file control block for DiskFiles
FileProc,         - proc type - internal file operations
Flag,             - status for file operations
FlagSet,          - status flag set
MediumType,       - medium name (A, B...
Response,         - result of a file operation
Again,            - return char to buffer for retry
Close,            - close a file
Create,           - create temporary file
CreateMedium,     - install medium in file system
Delete,           - delete a file
Doio,             - do various i/o operations on file
FileNameChar,     - check char legality in MSDOS
GetPos,           - get current byte position in file
Length,           - length of file in bytes
Lookup,           - look for a file
ReadByte,         - read one byte from file
ReadChar,         - read one character from file
ReadNBytes,       - read number of bytes from file
ReadWord,         - reads word at current position
RemoveMedium,     - remove medium from file system
Rename,           - rename a file
Reset,            - open and position to start of file
SetModify,        - set for read/write w/o position chg
SetOpen,          - open file without position change
SetPos,           - set current position in file
SetRead,          - set for read w/o position change
SetWrite,         - set for write w/o position change
WriteByte,        - write one byte to file
WriteChar,        - write one character to file
WriteNBytes,      - write number of bytes to file
WriteWord;        - write one word to file
```

One of the most important objects in the preceding list is the File type. The type "File" is an opaque type meaning that its definition is hidden in the implementation module. An examination of that module reveals that a variable of the type File is a record containing information about the file. In particular, the type is declared as follows:

```
TYPE
    File = RECORD
              bufferadr   : BuffAdd;
              buffersize  : CARDINAL;
              validlength : CARDINAL;
              byteindex   : CARDINAL;
              statusflags : FlagSet;
              eof         : BOOLEAN;
              result      : Response;
              lastdata    : CARDINAL;
              medium      : MediumType;
              internal    : CARDINAL;
              internal    : MediumHint;
              CASE commandcode : Command OF
                    lookup :
                          new      : BOOLEAN;
                  | setpos, getpos, length :
                          highpos : CARDINAL;
                          lowpos  : CARDINAL;
              END;
          END;
```

The fields in a file record generally contain either attribute descriptions or
status information. For example the "bufferadr" field points to the area of
memory containing the data being sent or received. The "eof" field on
the other hand indicates if the last record in the file has been read.

Other Input-Output Modules

Some of the other modules commonly found are as follows:

Terminal: performs input-output specifically for terminals

Display: low-level routines used by terminal to write to a screen device

Keyboard: low-level routines used by terminal to obtain input from a
keyboard

RS232: one or more modules that send and receive data over a
communication line using the RS232 protocol.

A complete list of modules and their contents is found in the
documentation describing your implementation.

11.3 Sequential File Input-Output

The purpose of this section is to illustrate how the input-output modules are used to perform a simple file-to-file transfer. The problem is simply to print the contents of a file containing textual (ASCII) information. The name of the input file is to be obtained from the keyboard. For those with knowledge of the MS-DOS operating system, our objective is to execute the DOS command "COPY c:filename.ext PRN:".

Analysis. The main algorithm is straightforward.

```
.1  Get the name of the file to be printed
.2  If it can be opened then
        .1 Open the output (printer) file
        .2 Repeat
                .1 Read a character
                .2 Write the character
            Until the end of the input file
.3 Close the input and output files
```

The tools needed to do the job require imports from the modules FileNames, Terminal and FileSystem. Specifically,

```
FROM FileNames IMPORT ReadFileName, FNParts, FNPartSet;
```

where:

1. ReadFileName is a procedure that returns the name of a file as a character string.

2. FNParts is an enumerated type having values that correspond to the components of a file identifier. In the MS-DOS operating system the four positive components are a disk drive, a search path, a file name and a file extension.

3. FNPartSet is a type defined as SET OF FNParts. A variable of this type can be used to determine which components of a file id were entered.

The single import from Terminal is given by:

```
FROM Terminal IMPORT Read
```

The Read procedure reads a single character from the standard input device (the keyboard). It is required in order to read the character (usually EOL) that terminated the end of the filename input.

The imports from FileSystem are specified by

```
FROM FileSystem IMPORT File, ReadChar, WriteChar, Lookup,
                       Close, Response;
```

where:

1. ReadChar and WriteChar are procedures to read and write one character from a variable of the type File.

2. Lookup is a powerful procedure to determine if a file exists and if not to create or erase it. More about Lookup later.

3. Close makes a file unavailable for further processing.

4. Response is an enumerated type containing the constants "done" and "notdone" among others. By examining a variable of the type Response after an attempted input-output operation, you can determine if the operation was successfully performed.

The following is a complete (except for the SetUpFiles procedure) program for solving the problem. Further comments follow the listing.

```
MODULE Print;

FROM FileSystem IMPORT Lookup, Close, ReadChar,
                       WriteChar, File, Response;

FROM FileNames  IMPORT ReadFileName, FNParts, FNPartSet;

FROM InOut      IMPORT Write, WriteString, WriteLn;

FROM Terminal   IMPORT Read;

VAR
    InputChar       : CHAR;
    InputFile       : File;
    InputFileId     : ARRAY[0..14] OF CHAR;
    InputFileIdParts : FNPartSet;
    OutputFile      : File;

    (* SetUpFiles procedure goes here *)

BEGIN
    IF SetUpFiles() THEN
        LOOP
            ReadChar(InputFile,InputChar);
            IF InputFile.res <> done THEN
                EXIT;
                END;
            WriteChar(OutputFile,InputChar);
            END;
            Close(InputFile);
            Close(OutputFile);
        END;
END Print.
```

Comments.

1. In the VAR declarations, two files are declared called InputFile and OutputFile. The variable InputFileId will contain the character string identifying the input file. The InputFileIdParts is required by the ReadFileNames procedure but is not otherwise used in the program.

2. The body of the program uses the procedure SetUpFiles (given next) to see if the appropriate files have been found and opened and if so executes the read-write loop.

3. After an attempt is made to read the next character in the file, the field "res" in the InputFile record is examined to see it if has a value of "done". When the end of file has been reached, the res variable -- which has the type Response -- will have a value of "notdone". Thus the loop can be EXITed.

Now for the SetUpFiles procedure. It has three main steps. First, it solicits the name of the input file using the ReadFileName procedure. Second it attempts to open the input file. Third it attempts to open the printer file. The procedure returns a value of TRUE if all steps are completed satisfactorily. Additonal comments follow the listing.

```
PROCEDURE SetUpFiles() : BOOLEAN;

    VAR
        ReturnCode : BOOLEAN;

    BEGIN
        LOOP
            ReturnCode := FALSE;
            WriteString("Enter source file identifier: ");
            ReadFileName(InputFileId,"",InputFileIdParts);
            Read(InputChar);
            WriteLn;
            Lookup(InputFile,InputFileId,FALSE);
            IF InputFile.res = notdone THEN
                WriteString("Source file does not exist");
                WriteLn;
                EXIT;
                END;
            Lookup(OutputFile,"PRN",FALSE);
            IF OutputFile.res <> done THEN
                WriteString("Unable to open printer");
                WriteLn;
                EXIT;
                END;
            ReturnCode := TRUE;
            EXIT;
            END;
        RETURN ReturnCode;
    END SetUpFiles;
```

Comments.

1. In the ReadFileName invocation, the second parameter is null. If desired, it can contain a default file extension, which would be used if and is not entered via the keyboard.

2. In the Logitech implementation, Lookup is the procedure used to open a file. In other implementations it may have a different name and/or number of parameters. When attempting to open the input file, the statement is:

   ```
   Lookup (InputFile, InputFileId, FALSE);
   ```

   The first parameter is the record containing information about the file. Fields including "res" are assigned values as a result of executing Lookup. The second field is a string that contains the identification of the file to be searched for as in "C:EXAMPLE1.LST". The third parameter is BOOLEAN and indicates what to do if the file is not found. "TRUE" causes the file to be created and "res" set to "done"; "FALSE" means assign "notdone" to the res field. Thus the FALSE in the preceding example means do not create the file if it cannot be found.

3. The opening of the printer file is accomplished with the following statement.

   ```
   Lookup (OutputFile, "PRN", TRUE);
   ```

   The "PRN" specifies the printer. In the case of the printer, the third parameter (TRUE) is irrelevant since one cannot create a printer at execution time. The variable OutputFile.Res is compared to "done" and appropriate action taken. This avoids having the program abort when conditions are not as expected.

11.4   Direct–Access Input–Output

Concepts. A direct access file is one in which the collection of data in the file is usually partitioned into chunks having distinct keys. Given the value of a key, the desired chunk of data -- usually a record -- can be retrieved or written by computing a record address from the key. The length of the data (the number of bytes in the chunk) is either fixed or recorded as part of the data itself. Thus, in a direct access file, instead of searching through the file for the record of interest, one can go directly to the data.

Two schemes used to assign records to storage locations are indexing and hashing. For example, the index in a book tells you where to find material about a given topic. A hashing scheme performs a mathematical transformation of a key to obtain the address of the data.

Before presenting an example to illustrate direct access processing in Modula-2, the general approach will be described.

Low-level Direct Access Procedures

The characters in a file can be viewed as a one long sequence of characters numbered consecutively starting from zero. For example, a file of thirty-six characters containing the letters of the alphabet followed by the ten digits has characters in positions 0 through 35. Suppose now we partition these thirty-six characters into four records of nine characters each as follows:

ABCDEFGHI JKLMNOPQR STUVWXYZO 123456789

record 1   record 2   record 3   record 4

To obtain the data in record i, we need to know the starting position of record i and the number of characters to read. Observe that the record size is 9. If we number the positions starting from zero, record i starts at position (i-1)*9. This starting position for a record is called its record offset. Listed next are the steps needed to read or write a record. The parentheses contain the names of the FileSystem procedures that perform the operations.

.1 Open the file (Lookup)
.2 Prepare the file for reading or writing (SetRead or SetWrite)
.3 Calculate the offset and length (problem dependent)
.4 Move to the correct position (SetPos)
.5 Read or write N characters (ReadNBytes or WriteNBytes)

When the data is transferred from the device to memory, it is assigned to a buffer (an area of memory) specified in the ReadNBytes procedure. Similarly, prior to performing a write operation, the characters must be stored in a buffer such as a record variable.

The following problem illustrates these principles.

Problem Description and Analysis

We will create and store five records of financial information. The record key will be the record number. Thus, we will perform operations of the type "read record 3", "write record 4", etc. The record fields include the key, a name, an amount, and a date. The declaration follows:

```
TYPE
    SampleRecord = RECORD
        Key    : INTEGER;
        Name   : ARRAY [0..11] OF CHAR;
        Amount : CARDINAL;
        Date   : CARDINAL;
        END;
```

The mainline processing is described by the following algorithm.

```
.1  Open a file for storing the records
.2  For i = 1 to 5
        .1  Get data for record i
        .2  Write record i
.3  Display all records
.4  Update the file
        .1  Loop forever
                .1  Get a record number
                .2  If a valid record number then
                        .1 Get new data for the record
                        .2  Write it on the file
                        .3  Display all records
                    Otherwise
                        .1  Exit
```

The program will be developed in bits and pieces. A listing of the complete program is found in Appendix D.

The program that is used could be significantly simplified if we were to assume all file operations were carried out successfully. This is a very dangerous assumption! Consequently, this example checks all file operations and exits gracefully if any fail. The approach taken is to have each procedure return a TRUE or FALSE result to indicate if it was successful in performing its task. For example, "DisplayRecord(i)" returns TRUE if it was successful in displaying the contents of record i.

Procedures Used In The Solution

We now have the tools needed to solve the problem. The imports needed are found in the following five statements.

```
FROM FileSystem IMPORT Lookup, Close, ReadChar, ReadNBytes,
                       WriteNBytes, SetRead, SetWrite,
                       SetModify, SetOpen, Reset, SetPos,
                       GetPos, Length,
                       WriteChar, File, Response;

FROM FileNames  IMPORT ReadFileName, FNParts, FNPartSet;

FROM InOut      IMPORT Write, WriteString, WriteLn,
                       WriteInt, ReadInt, WriteCard, ReadCard,
                       ReadString;

FROM Terminal   IMPORT Read;

FROM SYSTEM     IMPORT WORD, TSIZE, ADR, ADDRESS, SIZE;
```

Global Variables. Along with the type SampleRecord described previously, we will use the following global variables.

```
VAR
    Buffer          : SampleRecord; (* input-output area *)
    DirectFile      : File;         (* the data file     *)
    RecSize         : CARDINAL;     (* length of a rec   *)
    RecNumber       : CARDINAL;     (* reference number  *)
    RecPtr          : ADDRESS;      (* location of a rec *)
    RecCount        : CARDINAL;     (* records/file      *)
```

The program uses eight nonimported procedures. In the following list, indentation indicates the procedure called by a given procedure. The underlined identifiers are library procedures; boldface identifiers are written for this problem.

SetUpFile– prompts for a file name and creates an empty file

    ReadFileName– gets name of file from keyboard

    LookUp– creates the file

CreateFile– prompts for and writes five data records

    InputFields– prompts for name, amount and data

    WriteRecord– writes a record on the file
        SetWrite– puts the file in write mode
        CalcPos– determines the record offset
        SetPos– positions file at offset
        WriteNBytes– writes the record

Reset– repositions the file at the beginning

DisplayAllRecords– displays the contents of all records in the file
    DisplayRec– displays the date in one record

        ReadRecord– retrieves one record from the file
            SetRead– readys the file for reading
            CalcPos– determines the record offset.
            SetPos– positions the file at the offset
            ReadNBytes– performs the read

InputFields– prompts for name amount and date

WriteRecord– writes updated record (see above)

DisplayAllRecords– displays file contents (see above)

We now examine the mainline and the procedures one-by-one.
Comments precede each listing.

Mainline. The most important point to note is that the procedures
SetUpFile, CreateFile, DisplayRecs and WriteRecord are function
procedures that return a value of TRUE or FALSE. If any task fails, it
returns a value of FALSE which causes the program to terminate.

```
BEGIN
     LOOP
         IF NOT SetUpFile(DirectFile) THEN EXIT END;

         WriteString("Five records will be created");
         WriteLn;
         RecCount := 5;
         IF NOT CreateFile(DirectFile,RecCount) THEN EXIT END;
         Reset(DirectFile);
         IF DirectFile.res <> done THEN EXIT END;
         IF NOT DisplayAllRecords() THEN EXIT END;

         WriteString('Enter record number to update: ');
         ReadCard(RecNumber);
         WriteLn;
         InputFields(RecNumber,RecSize,RecPtr);
         IF NOT WriteRecord(DirectFile,RecNumber,
                            RecSize,RecPtr) THEN
             EXIT;
             END;
         IF NOT DisplayAllRecords() THEN EXIT END;
         EXIT; (* LOOP *)
         END;
END DirectIO.
```

SetUpFile. After getting a file name using ReadFileName, the SetUpFile procedure creates an empty file using the Lookup procedure. If the file exists, SetUpFile returns a value of false.

```
PROCEDURE SetUpFile(VAR DataFile : File) : BOOLEAN;

    VAR
        ReturnCode  : BOOLEAN;
        InputChar   : CHAR;
        FileId      : ARRAY[0..14] OF CHAR;
        FileIdParts : FNPartSet;

    BEGIN
        LOOP
            ReturnCode := FALSE;
            WriteString("Enter file identifier: ");
            ReadFileName(FileId,"",FileIdParts);
            Read(InputChar);  (* logitech peculiarity *)
            WriteLn;
            Lookup(DataFile,FileId,FALSE);
            IF DataFile.res = done THEN
                WriteString("Target file already exists");
                WriteLn;
                Close(DataFile);
                EXIT;
                END;
            Lookup(DataFile,FileId,TRUE);
            IF DataFile.res = notdone THEN
                WriteString("Target file cannot be opened");
                WriteLn;
                EXIT;
                END;
            ReturnCode := TRUE;
            EXIT;
            END;
        RETURN ReturnCode;
    END SetUpFile;
```

CreateFile. The CreateFile procedure reads the data for five records and writes them as records 1 through 5 in the file.

```
PROCEDURE CreateFile(VAR DataFile    : File;
                         NumOfRecords : CARDINAL) : BOOLEAN;

    VAR
        LocalIndex    : CARDINAL;
        NBytes        : CARDINAL;
        RecordNumber  : CARDINAL;
        RecordSize    : CARDINAL;
        RecordAdr     : ADDRESS;
        ReturnCode    : BOOLEAN;

    BEGIN
        ReturnCode := FALSE;
        LOOP
            FOR LocalIndex := 1 TO NumOfRecords DO
                InputFields(LocalIndex,RecordSize,RecordAdr);
                IF NOT WriteRecord(
                        DataFile,LocalIndex,RecordSize,RecordAdr)
                    THEN EXIT;
                    END;
                END;
            ReturnCode := TRUE;
            EXIT;
            END;
        RETURN ReturnCode;
    END CreateFile;
```

DisplayRecs and DisplayRec. These procedures are very straightforward.

```
PROCEDURE DisplayAllRecords () : BOOLEAN;

    VAR
        ReturnCode : BOOLEAN;
        LocalIndex : CARDINAL;

    BEGIN
        ReturnCode := TRUE;
        FOR LocalIndex := 1 TO RecCount DO
            IF NOT DisplayRecord(LocalIndex) THEN
                ReturnCode := FALSE;
                END;
            END;
        RETURN ReturnCode;
    END DisplayAllRecords;
```

```
PROCEDURE DisplayRecord(     RecordNumber : CARDINAL) : BOOLEAN;

    VAR
        ReturnCode : BOOLEAN;

    BEGIN
        ReturnCode := FALSE;
        IF ReadRecord(DirectFile,RecordNumber,SIZE(Buffer),
                ADR(Buffer)) THEN
            WITH Buffer DO
                WriteInt(Key,8);
                Write(" ");
                WriteString(Name);
                WriteCard(Amount,8);
                WriteCard(Date,8);
                END;
            WriteLn;
            ReturnCode := TRUE;
            END;
        RETURN ReturnCode;
    END DisplayRecord;
```

InputFields. The InputFields procedure does not use any file-oriented procedures. It simply solicits the three fields of information and stores them in the record variable called Buffer.

```
PROCEDURE InputFields(     RecordNumber : CARDINAL;
                       VAR RecordSize   : CARDINAL;
                       VAR RecordPtr    : ADDRESS);
                                          .

    BEGIN
        WriteString("Name(CHAR) Amount(CARD) Date(CARD): ");
        WITH Buffer DO
            Key := RecordNumber;
            RecordNumber := Key;
            ReadString(Name);
            Write(" ");
            ReadCard(Amount);
            Write(" ");
            ReadCard(Date);
            END;
        WriteLn;
        RecordPtr  := ADR(Buffer);
        RecordSize := SIZE(Buffer);
    END InputFields;
```

WriteRecord. In the WriteRecord procedure, the first statement (SetWrite(DataFile)) puts the file in write mode. CalcPos is passed the record number and returns with <u>two</u> offsets High and Low. In this example, High will always be zero. Its meaning follows the description of CalcPos. SetPos positions the file to write at the offset position and then WriteNBytes transfers the data in the buffer to the file.

```
PROCEDURE WriteRecord(VAR DataFile      : File;
                          RecordNumber   : CARDINAL;
                          RecordSize     : CARDINAL;
                          BufferAddress : ADDRESS) : BOOLEAN;

    VAR
        High       : CARDINAL;
        Low        : CARDINAL;
        NBytes     : CARDINAL;
        ReturnCode : BOOLEAN;

    BEGIN
        ReturnCode := FALSE;
        LOOP
            SetWrite(DataFile);
            IF DataFile.res <> done THEN EXIT END;
            CalcPos(RecordNumber,RecordSize,High,Low);
            SetPos(DataFile,High,Low);
            IF DataFile.res <> done THEN EXIT END;
            WriteNBytes(DataFile,BufferAddress,
                        RecordSize,NBytes);
            IF DataFile.res <> done THEN EXIT END;
            ReturnCode := TRUE;
            EXIT;
            END;
        RETURN ReturnCode;
    END WriteRecord;
```

ReadRecord. The ReadRecord procedure is identical to WriteRecord except that SetRead is used instead of SetWrite and ReadNBytes replaces WriteNBytes. Here it is.

```
PROCEDURE ReadRecord(VAR DataFile      : File;
                         RecordNumber  : CARDINAL;
                         RecordSize    : CARDINAL;
                         BufferAddress : ADDRESS) : BOOLEAN;

    VAR
        High        : CARDINAL;
        Low         : CARDINAL;
        NBytes      : CARDINAL;
        ReturnCode  : BOOLEAN;

    BEGIN
        ReturnCode := FALSE;
        LOOP
            SetRead(DataFile);
            IF DataFile.res <> done THEN EXIT END;
            CalcPos(RecordNumber,RecordSize,High,Low);
            SetPos(DataFile,High,Low);
            IF DataFile.res <> done THEN EXIT END;
            ReadNBytes(DataFile,BufferAddress,
                        RecordSize,NBytes);
            IF DataFile.res <> done THEN EXIT END;
            ReturnCode := TRUE;
            EXIT;
            END;
        RETURN ReturnCode;
    END ReadRecord;
```

CalcPos. The CalcPos procedure is passed a record number and record size. It returns two offsets -- High and Low. Why two? Recall that the largest whole number is MaxCard which is 65535 (64k) on most microcomputers. The question then is how to handle files that have more than 64k of data. The answer is to use two offsets. The High offset denotes which 64k chunk; the Low value designates the position within that chunk.

In the CalcPos procedure the following statements calculate the High and Low offsets.

```
RecPerChunk := MaxCard DIV RecordSize;
High := RecordNumber DIV RecPerChunk;
Low  := ((RecordNumber -1) MOD RecPerChunk) * RecordSize;
```

Suppose for example a file has 100 records of 1k each. In our program, the first record is number 1. From the maximum number of bytes allowed in a chunk (64k), it is obvious that there can be 64 records per chunk if each is 1k. Consider record number 70. The High offset is 70/64 or 1 meaning that the record is found in the second 64k chunk. Low is 5k meaning the seventieth record begins at the 5kth character in the chunk. The CalcPos procedure given does not permit records to span 64k boundaries. It will start the record in the next 64k chunk.

```
PROCEDURE CalcPos(     RecordNumber : CARDINAL;
                       RecordSize   : CARDINAL;
                   VAR High         : CARDINAL;
                   VAR Low          : CARDINAL);

    CONST
        MaxCard = 65535;

    VAR
        RecPerChunk : CARDINAL;

    BEGIN
        RecPerChunk := MaxCard DIV RecordSize;
        High := RecordNumber DIV RecPerChunk;
        Low  := ((RecordNumber MOD RecPerChunk) - 1)
                  * RecordSize;
    END CalcPos;
```

This somewhat rather lengthy discussion of the example provides an insight into how to define and process direct- access files. It is intended to serve as a template for other direct- access applications. A listing of the complete program is found in Appendix D.

Comments.

1. The tools for direct access processing are found in the FileSystem module.

2. In order to retrieve or write records, you must know the starting position (offset) and length of the data to be processed.

3. You should check the "res" field in the file record after every invocation of a FileSystem procedure.

4. By having higher-level procedures such as ReadRecord and WriteRecord return a Boolean value, error checking is simplified and program structure is streamlined.

11.5   Summary

1. All input-output facilities in Modula-2 are found in library modules. There are both advantages and disadvantages to this approach.

2. The tools for processing external files of data are often found in a module called FileSystem. It contains a type called "File" which is implemented as a record structure containing various attribute and status fields.

3. Sequential input-output requires use of the Lookup procedure to open or create files. Subsequent reading and writing is done one character or byte at a time.

4. Direct access processing has additional overhead. You must be at the correct position in the file before reading or writing data.

A Warning. Although the data in a direct access file are viewed as a contiguous sequence of characters, in actual fact, there may gaps or holes in the data stored in the file. These are created by the implementation in order to start fields on full-word boundaries (even-numbered addresses), to avoid spanning a 64k memory address; or other implementation-dependent reasons. You should carefully read the relevant implementation documentation and thoroughly test direct access routines.

11.6   Exercises and Programming Problems

1. An input file contains several lines of text. Assume that a word begins with the first character after a blank and terminates with the first blank character thereafter. Write a program that reads the input file and reformats it so that no word starts to print after position 30 in an output line. Replace instances of multiple blanks in the input with a single blank in the output.

2. Write a program that reads a set of twenty INTEGER values; sorts them into increasing order of magnitude; and writes them in four groups of five values each on a file. Repeat this process for a second set of values and write the output on a different file. Using these two sets of values as input, perform a merge of the two files of values to produce one string of forty nondecreasing values. Write the merged values on a third file in records of four values per record. Print the values in the original sets and in the merged set.

3. Prepare a file of twenty-five records each of which has the following information. Assume the marks are integer values.

Positions	Item
1-5	student number
6	year of studies (1,2,3 or 4)
7-9	mark in course 1
10-12	mark in course 2
13-15	mark in course 3
16-18	mark in course 4
19-21	mark in course 5

a) Arrange the lines in order of increasing student number and write them on a file -- one record per student. Call this the student master file. b) Read the student master file and: (i) print the student number, marks, and average of each student. (ii) While reading the data from the file, accumulate statistics required to print the following report. Print the report at the end of the run. One page should be printed for each year. Assume a pass requires a 60 percent average.

Pass/Fail Report

	Year of Studies				Overall
	1	2	3	4	
Number of students	XX	XX	XX	XX	XX
Percent who passed	XX.X	XX.X	XX.X	XX.X	XX.X
Percent who failed	XX.X	XX.X	XX.X	XX.X	XX.X
Average mark	XX.X	XX.X	XX.X	XX.X	XX.X

4. Prepare several input lines of each of the following types. Each record is either an "add" or "delete" transaction that refers to the student master file created in Problem 3. Add records have the same data as the student records described in Problem 3 but in addition, have a "1" in position 25. Delete records have a student number in positions 1-5 and a "0" in position 25. Arrange the add/delete records in order of increasing student number. The inputs to the program are the student master file and the set of add/delete records. The output is a new student master file (written on a file that is different from the old student master file). The new master file should reflect the changes specified by the add/delete records. The program should detect and print error messages for the following conditions: an attempt to delete a student record that is not on the old student master file; an attempt to add a student who is already on the old student master file; an add or delete record that is out of sequence -- the student number on the add/delete card is less than the student number on the previous add/delete card. Once the new student master file has been written, reset the file and print the same two reports described in Problem 3.

5. Assume that each of twelve students takes two courses -- Math and English. Prepare a file of twelve records containing the following data.

Positions   Data

1-2   student number (range 01-99)
3-24   student name
25-26   math mark
27-28   English mark

Write a program that reads the twelve records and records the information on a file so that the information about the student having a student number of K is found in the Kth record of the file. On a second file write a single record containing the twelve valid student numbers in order of increasing magnitude. Display the contents of each record for future reference.

6. Using the data files created in Problem 5, print a report that, for each student, displays the student number, name, math mark, English mark, and average. Rewrite each student's record to include his or her average in the information kept in the file.

7. Given a file that contains 100,000 integers in the range 1 to 1 million, find an integer that is not in the file. Develop two algorithms. First assume you have lots of main memory. Second, assume you have very little memory but lots of file space. Test your algorithms using a small number of values.

8. Anagrams. Given a dictionary of words and a reference word, find all words in the dictionary that are formed by permuting the letters of the reference word. For example, given "stop" you would find "pots", "spot" and "tops".

9. Moving Billboard. An input file contains several messages -- one message per line. After each message is read display it on the screen as though it appeared on a moving billboard. That is it starts at the right edge of the screen and moves across the screen from right to left. Use a constant ScreenWidth in your program to define the width of the display window.

10. Create two files each of which contains twenty records of one INTEGER value each. The values in each file should be in order of nondecreasing magnitudes. Using these files as input, use sets to determine how many values are present in both sets and how many unique values there are in total. Use an algorithm such that each record needs to be read only once.

11. The input file contains a number of lines describing the
characteristics of individuals as follows.

Positions	Data
1-3	ID #
4-12	name
13-14	age
15	sex ('M' or 'F')
16	hair color (1=brunette, 2=blonde, 3=redhead, 4=bald)
17	eye color (1=brown, 2=blue, 3=hazel)
18-19	height
20	blank
21-23	weight

Prepare an input file containing several records. Read the data into an
array of records and print a report with appropriate headings showing
the data in the file.

Answer the following questions using set operations. Hint: For each
question, build one or more sets of ID#s and perform the set
operations with these. When the resultant set has been found, its
members can be used to search for the names in the array of data.

a) Who are the males?

b) What brown-eyed individuals are females?

c) Which people under 50 have either red hair and hazel eyes or blonde
hair and blue eyes?

d) For the first male, print the names of females who are within five
years of his age, are not taller than he is, and do not have red hair.

12. Suppose each student's answers to a true-false test of ten questions
have been recorded on the input file, one line per student. On each
line, positions one to six contain the student's ID number; positions
seven to ten are blank and positions eleven through twenty contain
"T's" and "F's" indicating the student's answers. Assume twelve
students took the test. Preceding the first student record is a line
containing the correct answers. This answer line has an ID number of
zeros and the correct answers in columns eleven through twenty. Write
a program that: a) Lists each student's answers and calculates the
percentage of right answers. b) Calculates the average mark on the
test. c) Prints the percentage of right answers for each question. d)
Determines how many students answered both of questions 3 and 7
correctly, and e) Determines those questions for which the students in
the bottom half of the class did as well as students in the top half of
the class. The problem should be solved making the assumption that
each student answered all questions. However, suppose now that a

blank in an answer column means that the student did not answer the question. Explain why this makes the programming problem more difficult. Can you solve the problem with this new assumption?

CHAPTER 12

LOW-LEVEL FACILITIES

Questions Answered In This Chapter

1. What low-level facilities exist in Modula-2?

2. How can you determine the size, location and contents of a variable?

3. How do you assign otherwise incompatible values to each other?

4. What facilities are available for managing the internal memory of a computer?

5. What means are available for low-level device control?

6. How can you interface with the operating system?

By definition, "low-level" means machine dependent. Hence the material in this chapter is primarily of interest to programmers who must interface directly with the hardware on which a Modula-2 program is run. The designer and implementors of Modula-2 have given a programmer access to and control over the fundamental resources of memory and devices. By providing low-level tools, Modula-2 becomes not only a high level language but also offers the facilities necessary for writing systems software such as operating systems.

Because Modula-2 runs on a variety of computer systems, the information in this chapter describes the general low-level facilities specified by the language's designer. We do not for instance, explain how to write a device driver for the Microsoft Mouse running on an IBM XT under MS-DOS (if that makes sense to you!). Specific implementations may provide more extensive capabilities. Most of the low-level facilities are found in a module called SYSTEM. Because the procedures and constants it contains are essentially "hard-wired" to the computer, they should be viewed more as an extension of the compiler than a library module.

The assumption is made that the reader of this chapter has a basic understanding of memory concepts and device management.

12.1   The Internal Representation of Data

This section describes how to determine three salient aspects of a
variable: its address, its size (in memory units) and the bit pattern
representing its value.

Memory Concepts

The internal memory of a computer is a contiguous sequence of bits.
Each bit has one of two values -- a one or a zero. A sequence of eight
consecutive bits is called a byte. On most microcomputers, two
consecutive bytes constitute a word of memory. The bytes in memory
are numbered consecutively starting from zero. The number is called the
address of the byte. The address of a word is the address of its leftmost
byte.

Most microcomputers partition the internal memory into 64K chunks.
(A "K" of memory is 2^{10} or 1024 bytes). Thus the addresses in 64K are 0
through 65535.

Attributes of Variables

For each variable declared in a program, the compiler reserves an area of
memory of the appropriate size to store its value. The address of the
variable can be determined by the ADR function; the size by the SIZE
procedure and contents by displaying the hexadecimal representation of
the value. Details follow.

ADR(variable). The ADR function returns the memory address of a
variable as an ADDRESS value. ADR must be IMPORTed from SYSTEM.

SIZE(variable). This standard function returns the size of a variable or
type in bytes or words depending on the implementation. Consider the
following declarations. The comments show the number of bytes used to
store the variable on a typical microcomputer.

```
VAR
     c  : CARDINAL;        (* 2 bytes *)
     i  : INTEGER;         (* 2 bytes *)
     r  : REAL;            (* 8 bytes *)
     ch : CHAR;            (* either 1 or 2 bytes *)
     b  : BOOLEAN;         (* either 1 or 2 bytes *)
```

Thus the SIZE function returns the following values:

```
SIZE (c)   = 2    because    SIZE (CARDINAL)   = 2
SIZE (i)   = 2    because    SIZE (INTEGER)    = 2
SIZE (r)   = 8    because    SIZE (REAL)       = 8
SIZE (ch)  = 1    because    SIZE (CHAR)       = 1
SIZE (b)   = 1    because    SIZE (BOOLEAN)    = 1
```

Some implementations provide a TSIZE function which can be imported from the SYSTEM library module. Unlike SIZE, the TSIZE parameters are restricted to types. In the case of CHAR and BOOLEAN values, the value may be allocated a full word of memory even though the value is stored in the left byte of the word. The contents of the right byte are unspecified. Check your implementation documentation.

Consider now the following data structures:

```
TYPE
      IntegerArray = ARRAY [0..5] OF INTEGER;
      String       = ARRAY [0..5] OF INTEGER;
      DataRec      = RECORD
          Fld1 : CARDINAL;
          CASE tagfield : BOOLEAN OF
                TRUE  : truefield  : CARDINAL
              | FALSE : falsefield : ARRAY [0..99] OF REAL;
            END;
          END;
VAR
      integers : IntegerArray;
      chstr    : String;
      rec      : DataRec;
      bset     : BITSET;
```

Array Sizes. The memory requirement for an array of N elements is in general N times the size of one element. In most implementations, each value in a CHAR or BOOLEAN array is stored in 1 byte even if a single value occupies two bytes. With respect to the example declarations therefore:

```
SIZE (integers) = 12  because  SIZE (IntegerArray)  = 12
SIZE (chstr)    =  6  because  SIZE (String)        =  6
```

Record Sizes. The memory requirements for a simple (nonvariant) record is the sum of the memory sizes of each field in the record. For a variant record as in the preceding example, there are two forms of the SIZE procedure call as shown below.

SIZE (DataRec, TRUE) = 6   because when the tagfield is TRUE the record has three fields of two bytes each

SIZE (DataRec, FALSE) = 804   because when the tagfield is FALSE, the variant part is an array of 800 bytes

SIZE (DataRec) = 804   because if no tagfield is specified, the maximum record size is returned.

If a record contains nested variants, SIZE may have additional parameters that specify subvariant tagfield values. For example an expression of the following form is possible.

```
SIZE (rectype, tag, subtag, subsubtag,...)
```

Set Sizes. The standard type BITSET occupies one word of memory. Thus SIZE(bset) is 2. This is the reason that many implementations limit the number of elements in the base type to 16. By doing so, it allows all sets to be processed using the BITSET processing routines.

12.2   The Type WORD

The WORD type is one of the most useful tools available to a low-level programmer. The SYSTEM module exports the type called WORD, which occupies one word of memory. A formal parameter of the type WORD is compatible with actual parameters occupying one word of memory. These typically include CARDINAL, INTEGER, BITSET and of course WORD. However, WORD can be used as a parameter in procedures which must operate on values of any type when a formal parameter is an open array of WORD components. This allows a formal parameter to be compatible with any actual argument including data structures.

Aside from use in formal parameter lists, WORD variables may only appear in assignment operations. That is, WORD variables are assignment incompatible with all non-WORD types. However, by using the type transfer functions described in the next section, this restriction is not severe.

Some Modula-2 implementations also include a type called BYTE. It is similar in many ways to WORD but works with 8 bits of memory.

We turn now to methods of overcoming the restriction that the left and right sides of an assignment statement must be assignment compatible.

12.3   Bit Pattern Assignments

In addition to the assignment statement and the read procedures, Modula-2 provides another method of assigning a particular bit pattern to a variable. It is accomplished using a type name as a procedure name and is called a type transfer function.

Type Transfer Functions

A type transfer function is one which returns the bit pattern of the function argument without modification. The result however has the type associated with the function name. Any of the standard types including CARDINAL, INTEGER, REAL, CHAR, BOOLEAN, BITSET and WORD can be used as a type transfer function. In each case the type is used as a function procedure having one argument. The argument value represents the bit pattern of interest. One example will be given.

A CARDINAL value and an INTEGER value each occupy two bytes. The pattern 1111 1111 1111 1100 represents an INTEGER value of -3 and a CARDINAL value of 65533. To assign the bit pattern of -3 to a CARDINAL variable C say the statement   C := -3   cannot be used because of incompatible types. When the target type (CARDINAL) is used as a type transfer procedure, the assignment can be performed. The following statement is valid.

```
C := CARDINAL(-3)
```

Every type can be used as a type transfer function provided the actual argument has the same size as the target type. That is an expression of the form:

```
type(argument)
```

is valid provided SIZE(type) = SIZE(argument). Thus CARDINAL(3.0) is invalid because SIZE(CARDINAL) is 2 and SIZE(3.0) is 8.

When a type transfer function is used, no change is made in the bit pattern of the actual parameter.

12.4   Displaying the Contents of Memory

The pattern of bits for any range of memory addresses can be displayed using a series of hexadecimal characters. Each hexadecimal character represents a 4-bit pattern as follows:

Hex	Pattern	Hex	Pattern
0	0000	8	1000
1	0001	9	1001
2	0010	A	1010
3	0011	B	1011
4	0100	C	1100
5	0101	D	1101
6	0110	E	1110
7	0111	F	1111

WriteHex(c,n). The procedure WriteHex displays four hexadecimal characters representing the bit pattern of the CARDINAL value c. The four hexadecimal characters are right justified in the "n" characters sent to the output device. WriteHex is exported from InOut.

Assume C is a CARDINAL variable with a value of 672. The statement "WriteHex(C,5)" results in the characters " 02A0" being displayed since the CARDINAL representation of the decimal value 672 is the bit pattern "0000001010100000" which when taken in groups of four bits is represented by the hexadecimal value "02A0".

InOut also contains the procedure **WriteOct** which displays six octal (base eight) characters. If needed, check with your implementation documentation.

The following procedure displays the bit pattern of any variable. It makes use of the HIGH procedure and an open array of word to accommodate the unknown actual parameter.

```
PROCEDURE ShowVariable(   X : ARRAY OF WORD);

    VAR
        i : CARDINAL; (* Array index *)

    BEGIN
        FOR i := 0 TO HIGH(X) DO
            WriteHex(CARDINAL(X[i]),6);
            END;
    END ShowVariable;
```

The use of CARDINAL as a type transfer function is required because WriteHex requires a CARDINAL parameter.

On most mini and micro computers, the order of the two bytes in a word of data are reversed. For example, the value 672 having a hexadecimal representation of 02A0 is actually stored as A002.

12.5   Memory Management

This section describes

o How to assign specific bit patterns to variables using hexadecimal constants.

o How to assign variables and/or values to specific memory locations.

Bit Pattern Definition

An integer (CARDINAL or INTEGER) constant can be defined using hexadecimal digits. In the examples below the final "H" specifies that the value is hexadecimal.

0H   —   the bit pattern   0000

1234H   —   the bit pattern 0001 0010 0011 0100

0BEACH —   the pattern 0000 1011 1110 1010 1100 The leading "0" is required in order to prevent the value from being interpreted as the identifier "BEACH".

Octal constants (base 8) can be defined by appending "B" to the octal digits. For example 123B represents the decimal value 1*64 + 2*8 + 3 or 83.

Character constants can be directly specified in terms of their ORD values by postfixing a "C" to the octal representation of the ORD value. For example, the letter "A" has an ORD value of 65 (base 10). Therefore, the expression "81C" can be used to define the literal "A" because 81 base 8 is 65 in the decimal number system.

Address Specificiation

Address specification details are implementation dependent. For an example, we shall use the Logitech implementation.

The address of a variable can be specified by enclosing the segment and offset within square brackets and putting it after the identifier in the declaration as illustrated in the following examples:

```
VAR
    X [OH:1008H]         : CARDINAL;
    Z [OH:100AH]         : ARRAY [0..99] OF CHAR;
    MonoCrt [0B000H:OH]  : ARRAY [0..80],[0..25],[0..1] OF CHAR;
    Color [0B000H:8000H] : ARRAY [0..16384] OF CHAR;
```

Notes:

1. The address is formed by a pair of hexadecimal constants separated by a colon. The first constant specifies the segment (64K chunk) and the second, the offset within the segment.

2. The address of the CARDINAL variable X and the CHAR array Z are 1008H and 100AH respectively.

3. The third example defines a map of the IBM-PC monochrome screen. The screen always displays the data stored in memory beginning at location 0B0000H. It consists of an 80 columns by two5 rows array of 2-character elements. The first character is called the status byte and control highlighting, blinking, etc. The second character of each pair is the bit pattern representing the character displayed on the screen. With reference to the MonoCrt variable for instance, an 'X' will be displayed in the bottom left-hand corner of the screen by executing the assignment "MonoCrt[0,25,1] := 'X'".

4. The Color variable can be used to reference the portion of memory used for the screen map of the standard IBM-PC color card. This memory map starts at 0B8000H. Note the way the segment is specified in the address constant as 0B000H, and not 0BH as you might assume. Use of this memory is described in Appendix E.

Direct address control is important when input-output is memory mapped, meaning that specific memory locations are reserved for communicating with particular devices.

The Type ADDRESS

The SYSTEM module exports the type ADDRESS which has the following definition.

```
TYPE
    ADDRESS = POINTER TO WORD
```

ADDRESS variables can be used in arithmetic expressions in order to calculate new addresses of interest. The contents of a word having a given ADDRESS are referenced by appending the pointer symbol "^" to the address value. For example, the procedure below displays the hexadecimal representation of N words of memory starting at address MemLocation.

```
PROCEDURE DumpMemory(    MemLocation : ADDRESS;
                         N           : CARDINAL);
    BEGIN
        WHILE N > 0 DO
            WriteHex(CARDINAL(MemLocation^),6);
            MemLocation := MemLocation + 2;
            N := N-2;
            END;
    END DumpMemory;
```

The foregoing assumes that ADDRESS has been imported and that a word is two bytes. The logic can easily be enhanced to display a fixed number of patterns per line, a line header showing the range of addresses and other formatting niceties.

12.6   Device Control With IOTRANSFER.

Concepts

Input-output devices attached to a computer system have the ability to perform their operations in parallel with those of the central processing unit. There are three steps in the sequence.

1. The main process initiates the device process which enables a specific type of interrupt and returns control to the main process.

2. When the interrupt occurs, control transfers to the device process.

3. The device process services the interrupt and then returns control to the main process.

Chapter 9 contains a description of processes in Modula-2. It is assumed the reader is familiar with this material. The new idea in this section is that completion of the main process causes an <u>unscheduled</u> transfer from the device process to another process.

In Modula-2, the procedure used to process an interrupt is called IOTRANSFER. It is exported by the SYSTEM module.

The example program that follows illustrates the use of IOTRANSFER. The program has a mainline process that prints a "*" after each 40000 iterations of a FOR loop. The "device" procedure interrupts the main process and prints "36" after every 36 "type 8" interrupts. A type 8 interrupt is a timeout signal which on the authors' machine is automatically generated seventeen times a second. Thus the output from the program is an continuous and uneven pattern of "*"s and "36"s. Further comments follow the program.

```
MODULE Timer;

(* This program demonstrates the use of IOTRANSFER *)

FROM InOut  IMPORT WriteString, WriteCard, WriteLn;

FROM SYSTEM IMPORT IOTRANSFER, WORD, ADDRESS, ADR,
                   NEWPROCESS, TRANSFER;

VAR
    StarCount   : CARDINAL; (* number of "*"s printed *)
    Index       : CARDINAL; (* FOR loop index *)
    Main        : ADDRESS;
    DeviceProc  : ADDRESS;  (* processes timer interrupts *)
    MainArea    : ARRAY [0..959] OF CHAR;  (* process workarea *)
    DevArea     : ARRAY [0..959] OF CHAR;  (* process workarea *)

PROCEDURE Device();

    VAR
        InterruptCount : CARDINAL;

    BEGIN
        InterruptCount := 0;
        LOOP
            IOTRANSFER(DeviceProc, Main, 8); (* '8' is clock *)
            InterruptCount := InterruptCount + 1;
            IF InterruptCount MOD 36 = 0 THEN
                WriteString(" 36");
                END;
            END;
        END Device;

(* continued on next page *)
```

```
BEGIN (* Main Process *)
    NEWPROCESS(Device, ADR(DevArea), 960, DeviceProc);
    TRANSFER(Main, DeviceProc);   (* to the device processor *)
    StarCount := 0;
    LOOP
        FOR Index := 0 TO 40000 DO (* nothing *)
            END;
        WriteString("  *");
        StarCount := StarCount + 1;
        IF StarCount MOD 8 = 0 THEN
            WriteLn;
            END; (* IF *)
        IF StarCount = 50 THEN
            EXIT;
            END;
        END;
END Timer.
```

Comments.

1. The main process creates the Device process and immediately transfers control to it.

2. The Device process contains an infinite loop. In each iteration, the statement below is the first one executed.

    IOTRANSFER (DeviceProc, Main, 8)

This statement does three things.

a) The DeviceProc process is suspended

b) Control is transfered to the Main process until a type 8 interrupt occurs

c) When a type 8 interrupt happens, Main is suspended and control returns to DeviceProc

In this example, "36" is printed after every 36 type 8 interrupts.

3. The irregular pattern of *'s and 36's results from the fact that the time between type 8 interrupts is not an exact divisor of the time taken to complete one iteration of the Main loop.

Priorities and LISTEN

Some interrupts have a higher priority than others in order to prevent loss of data. The built-in priority depends on the CPU being used. In order to prevent a low priority interrupt from interrupting a higher priority process, Modula-2 allows a priority specification to be appended to the module header. Consider the headers below.

MODULE A [3] ;   MODULE B [7] ;

Processes defined in Module B have a higher priority than those in module A and therefore, B-processes cannot be interrupted by A-processes. This rule can be overridden by using the LISTEN procedure exported by SYSTEM.

LISTEN temporarily lowers the priority of the enclosing module so that any pending interrupts of a lower priority may be serviced.

Module priorities can only be used with program and implementation modules. If no priority is specified in an implementation module, its exported procedures take on the priority of the importing module.

The form and rules of IOTRANSFER are summarized next.

IOTRANSFER

Form:

```
IOTRANSFER (VAR currentproc : ADDRESS;
            VAR deviceproc  : ADDRESS;
                interrupt   : CARDINAL)
```

Rules:

1. The process containing the IOTRANSFER (i.e., currentproc) is suspended and control transfers to the "deviceproc"

2. Execution of "currentproc" continues until an interrupt of the type "interrupt" occurs.

3. If the deviceproc has a priority equal to or greater than the currentproc process, "currentproc" is suspended and execution of "deviceproc" resumes (in order to process the interrupt).

4. The "interrupt" values are usually described in the implementation documentation or in the description of your operating system.

12.7   Operating System Interface

Concepts

Most modern programming languages provide a means of executing an operating system command from within a program. This operating system interface is <u>very</u> implementation dependent. If present, the modules providing operating system services contain procedures which duplicate one or more of the operating system's commands. Shown below is a procedure which employs the Logitech DOSCALL procedure to return the date. DOSCALL is exported by the Logitech SYSTEM module.

```
PROCEDURE GetDate(VAR Year      : CARDINAL;
                  VAR Month     : CARDINAL;
                  VAR Day       : CARDINAL);
VAR
    MonthDay : CARDINAL;
BEGIN
    DOSCALL(2AH,Year,MonthDay);
    Month := MonthDay DIV 256;
    Day   := MonthDay MOD 256;
END GetDate;
```

The first parameter is the hexadecimal constant "2A" which specifies that the date is the DOS function to be executed. The constants to use for different operating system functions are listed in the implementation documentation. Shown below is a procedure to return the current time.

```
PROCEDURE GetTime(VAR Hour      : CARDINAL;
                  VAR Minute    : CARDINAL;
                  VAR Second    : CARDINAL;
                  VAR MilliSec  : CARDINAL);
VAR
    HourMinute   : CARDINAL;
    SecMilliSec  : CARDINAL;
BEGIN
    DOSCALL(2CH,HourMinute,SecMilliSec);
    Hour     := HourMinute DIV 256;
    Minute   := HourMinute MOD 256;
    Second   := SecMilliSec DIV 256;
    MilliSec := SecMilliSec MOD 256;
END GetTime;
```

12.8   Assembler Language Interface

Implementations for which the compiler produces native code (e.g. Logitech) may include facilities for linking code files produced by another language compiler with code files produced by the Modula-2 compiler. A discussion of this topic is outside the scope of this book. The reader requiring knowledge of this topic is directed to the documentation describing his or her implementation.

12.9   Summary

1. Modula-2 contains facilities for low-level control of a computer's resources.

2. Low-level memory management tools found in the SYSTEM module include:

   o The type WORD, a generic type occupying a single word of memory. An open array of WORD is compatible with any actual parameter.

   o The address and size of entities can be determined using the function procedures ADR, and SIZE.

   o A type can be used as a function procedure that returns a value of the given type. The bit pattern of the actual argument is unmodified.

   o Contents of memory locations can be displayed using the WriteHex procedure which displays the hexadecimal digits of a single CARDINAL value.

   o Objects can be assigned to specific memory locations by appending the address as a hexadecimal constant to the identifier in the declaration.

   o Integer constants can be specified in terms of their hexadecimal or octal equivalents. A CHAR constant can be specified using its octal ORD value.

3. Interrupts can be enabled and serviced using the IOTRANSFER procedure. LISTEN procedure allows lower priority interrupts to be "heard".

4. Most implementations include one or more procedures for executing operating system commands from within a Modula-2 program.

12.10   Exercises and Programming Problems

1. Write a program that prompts for a starting memory address and a number indicating how many bytes of memory are to be displayed. The program should display a formatted report of the contents of memory in groups of four bytes, five groups per line. The report should display the date, time, page numbers, column and row headings. On the right of each line print the ASCII characters (in groups of four) represented by the hexadecimal patterns.

Appendix A

CHARACTERS, OPERATORS AND IDENTIFIERS

A.1   Introduction

This appendix contains general reference information about the character sets, punctuation usage, reserved words, and standard identifiers for Modula-2.

A.2   Character Sets

The characters used to construct identifiers in Modula-2 programs consist of the letters and digits. Upper and lower case letters are not equivalent.

The characters have an ordering called the collating sequence. The most popular collating sequence on micros and minis is the ASCII orderings which are defined below.

Ordinal, hexadecimal and octal values of the ASCII character set are:

ORD	HEX	OCT	CHAR	ORD	HEX	OCT	CHAR	ORD	HEX	OCT	CHAR
0	0	0	null	86	56	126	V	172	AC	254	
1	1	1	soh	87	57	127	W	173	AD	255	
2	2	2	stx	88	58	130	X	174	AE	256	
3	3	3	etx	89	59	131	Y	175	AF	257	
4	4	4	eot	90	5A	132	Z	176	B0	260	
5	5	5	enq	91	5B	133	[	177	B1	261	
6	6	6	ack	92	5C	134	\	178	B2	262	
7	7	7	bel	93	5D	135	]	179	B3	263	
8	8	10	bs	94	5E	136	^	180	B4	264	
9	9	11	ht	95	5F	137	_	181	B5	265	
10	A	12	lf	96	60	140	`	182	B6	266	
11	B	13	vt	97	61	141	a	183	B7	267	
12	C	14	ff	98	62	142	b	184	B8	270	
13	D	15	cr	99	63	143	c	185	B9	271	
14	E	16	so	100	64	144	d	186	BA	272	
15	F	17	si	101	65	145	e	187	BB	273	

ORD	HEX	OCT	CHAR	ORD	HEX	OCT	CHAR	ORD	HEX	OCT	CHAR
16	10	20	dle	102	66	146	f	188	BC	274	
17	11	21	dc1	103	67	147	g	189	BD	275	
18	12	22	dc2	104	68	150	h	190	BE	276	
19	13	23	dc3	105	69	151	i	191	BF	277	
20	14	24	dc4	106	6A	152	j	192	C0	300	
21	15	25	nak	107	6B	153	k	193	C1	301	
22	16	26	syn	108	6C	154	l	194	C2	302	
23	17	27	etb	109	6D	155	m	195	C3	303	
24	18	30	can	100	6E	156	n	196	C4	304	
25	19	31	em	111	6F	157	o	197	C5	305	
26	1A	32	sub	112	70	160	p	198	C6	306	
27	1B	33	esc	113	71	161	q	199	C7	307	
28	1C	34	fs	114	72	162	r	200	C8	310	
29	1D	35	gs	115	73	163	s	201	C9	311	
30	1E	36	rs	116	74	164	t	202	CA	312	
31	1F	37	us	117	75	165	u	203	CB	313	
32	20	40	blank	118	76	166	v	204	CC	314	
33	21	41	!	119	77	167	w	205	CD	315	
34	22	42	"	120	78	170	x	206	CE	316	
35	23	43	#	121	79	171	y	207	CF	317	
36	24	44	$	122	7A	172	z	208	D0	320	
37	25	45	%	123	7B	173	{	209	D1	321	
38	26	46	&	124	7C	174	|	210	D2	322	
39	27	47	'	125	7D	175	}	211	D3	323	
40	28	50	(	126	7E	176		212	D4	324	
41	29	51	)	127	7F	177	del	213	D5	325	
42	2A	52	*	128	80	200		214	D6	326	
43	2B	53	+	129	81	201		215	D7	327	
44	2C	54	,	130	82	202		216	D8	330	
45	2D	55	-	131	83	203		217	D9	331	
46	2E	56	.	132	84	204		218	DA	332	
47	2F	57	/	133	85	205		219	DB	333	
48	30	60	0	134	86	206		220	DC	334	
49	31	61	1	135	87	207		221	DD	335	
50	32	62	2	136	88	210		222	DE	336	
51	33	63	3	137	89	211		223	DF	337	
52	34	64	4	138	8A	212		224	E0	340	
53	35	65	5	139	8B	213		225	E1	341	
54	36	66	6	140	8C	214		226	E2	342	
55	37	67	7	141	8D	215		227	E3	343	
56	38	70	8	142	8E	216		228	E4	344	
57	39	71	9	143	8F	217		229	E5	345	
58	3A	72	:	144	90	220		230	E6	346	
59	3B	73	;	145	91	221		231	E7	347	
60	3C	74	<	146	92	222		232	E8	350	
61	3D	75	=	147	93	223		233	E9	351	
62	3E	76	>	148	94	224		234	EA	352	
63	3F	77	?	149	95	225		235	EB	353	

ORD	HEX	OCT	CHAR	ORD	HEX	OCT	CHAR	ORD	HEX	OCT	CHAR
64	40	100	@	150	96	226		236	EC	354	
65	41	101	A	151	97	227		237	ED	355	
66	42	102	B	152	98	230		238	EE	356	
67	43	103	C	153	99	231		239	EF	357	
68	44	104	D	154	9A	232		240	F0	360	
69	45	105	E	155	9B	233		241	F8	361	
70	46	106	F	156	9C	234		242	F2	362	
71	47	107	G	157	9D	235		243	F3	363	
72	48	110	H	158	9E	236		244	F4	364	
73	49	111	I	159	9F	237		245	F5	365	
74	4A	112	J	160	A0	240		246	F6	366	
75	4B	113	K	161	A1	241		247	F7	367	
76	4C	114	L	162	A2	242		248	F8	370	
77	4D	115	M	163	A3	243		249	F9	371	
78	4E	116	N	164	A4	244		250	FA	372	
79	4F	117	O	165	A5	245		251	FB	373	
80	50	120	P	166	A6	246		252	FC	374	
81	51	121	Q	167	A7	247		253	FD	375	
82	52	122	R	168	A8	250		254	FE	376	
83	53	123	S	169	A9	251		255	FF	377	
84	54	124	T	170	AA	252					
85	55	125	U	171	AB	253					

A.3   Special Punctuation Usage

There are a number of special meanings in Modula-2 given to single punctuation characters or groups of characters. They are either operators or delimiters.

+   - plus sign   - addition and set union

-      - dash or minus sign   - subtraction and set difference

*   - asterisk   - multiplication and set difference

/   - forward slash   - division and symmetric set difference

:=   - colon and equal sign   - used on assignment statements and FOR statements

&   - ampersand   - logical AND

=   - equals sign   - EQUAL

<>   - left and right arrows - NOT EQUAL

- number or hash sign   - same as <>

<	- left arrow	- LESS THAN
>	- right arrow	- GREATER THAN
<=	- left arrow and equal	- LESS THAN OR EQUAL
>=	- right arrow and equal	- GREATER THAN OR EQUAL
()	- left and right parens	- used for enclosing arguments to procedures and for enclosing enumerations
[]	- left and right square brackets	- used for enclosing array indexes and for enclosing subranges
{}	- left and right braces (curly brackets)	- used for enclosing sets
(* *)	- parens with asterisks	- used for enclosing comments
^	- carat	- used in pointer-based referencing
,	- comma	- used to separate lists of similar items
.	- period	- used on last END statement for module and with REAL constants
;	- semicolon	- indicates end of statement grouping and separates parameters in PROCEDURE statements
:	- colon	- used in VAR, CASE, and PROCEDURE statements
|	- vertical or OR bar	- used in CASE statements
..	- double periods	- used in subrange specifications
'	- single quote	- used to enclose strings
"	- double quotes	- used to enclose strings

A.4   Reserved Words

The reserved words in Modula-2 are:

AND	ELSIF	LOOP	REPEAT
ARRAY	END	MOD	RETURN
BEGIN	EXIT	MODULE	SET
BY	EXPORT	NOT	THEN
CASE	FOR	OF	TO
CONST	FROM	OR	TYPE
DEFINITION	IF	POINTER	UNTIL
DIV	IMPLEMENTATION	PROCEDURE	VAR
DO	IMPORT	QUALIFIED	WHILE
ELSE	IN	RECORD	WITH

A.5   Standard Identifiers and Procedures

The standard identifiers and procedures are:

ABS(x)   procedure to return absolute value of real or integer

BITSET   type - SET OF [0..15]

BOOLEAN   type - (TRUE,FALSE)

CAP(char)   procedure to force lowercase characters to to uppercase

CARDINAL   type - [0..65535]

CHAR   type - ordinal values [0..255]

CHR(card)   procedure to form a character from an ordinal value

DEC(var)   procedure to decrement an integer, cardinal, subrange character, and enumeration variable by 1

DEC(var,exp)   procedure to decrement an integer, cardinal, subrange character, and enumeration variable by an integer or cardinal expression

EXCL(set,exp)   procedure to perform set exclusion of single element

FALSE	boolean value
FLOAT(card)	procedure to form a real from a cardinal
HALT	procedure to terminate all processing
HIGH(array)	procedure to return high index in array
INC(var)	procedure to increment an integer, cardinal, subrange character, and enumeration variable by 1
INC(var,exp)	procedure to increment an integer, cardinal, subrange character, and enumeration variable by an integer or cardinal expression
INCL(set,exp)	procedure to perform set inclusion of a single element
INTEGER	type - [-32768..32767]
LONGINT	type - set of integers between MIN(LONGINT) and MAX(LONGINT)
LONGREAL	type - finite set of real numbers
MAX(type)	procedure returning maximum value of type
MIN(type)	procedure returning minimum value of type
NIL	special value for pointing to nothing
ODD(exp)	procedure to determine if integer or card value is mod(2)
ORD(exp)	procedure to determine ordinal number of a value in any enumeration type, cardinal integer, or character
PROC	type

REAL   type - implementation dependent for number of
                     digits, size of exponent, and how performed -
                     Logitech supports the IEEE Double Precision
                     Floating Point Standard which gives 15- to 16-
                     digit accuracy and exponents from -308 to 308

SIZE(var)   number of storage units occupied by variable

SIZE(type)   number of storage units occupied by a
                     variable of this type

TRUE   boolean value

TRUNC(real)   procedure to return integral part of real number

VAL(type,card)   procedure to determine the value with a specific
                     ordinal value in a specific enumeration type

Appendix B

MODULA-2 SYNTAX DIAGRAMS

B.1 Introduction

This appendix contains the syntax diagrams for the Modula-2 language as defined by N. Wirth in <u>Programming</u> in <u>Modula-2</u> (3rd edition, Springer-Verlag, New York, 1985). They are used with permission. The order of the diagrams is that of the Extended Backus Naur Form that Wirth uses to describe the language. Information on how to read these diagrams is found in Section 2.3.

B.2 Syntax Diagrams

ident

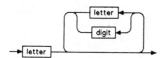

real

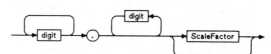

number

ScaleFactor

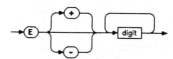

integer

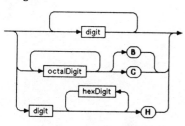

hexDigit

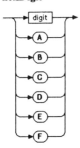

digit

qualident

octalDigit

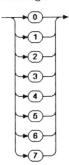

relation

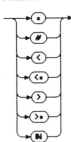

AddOperator

MulOperator

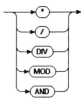

string

ConstExpression

TypeDeclaration

enumeration

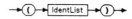

type

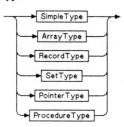

SimpleType

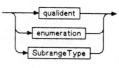

IdentList

SubrangeType

ArrayType

RecordType

FieldListSequence

FieldList

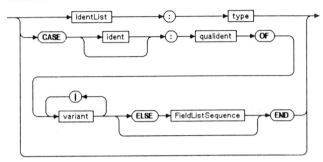

variant

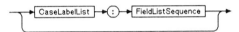

CaseLabelList

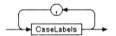

CaseLabels

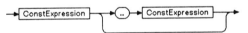

SetType

PointerType

→(POINTER)→(TO)→ type →

ProcedureType

→(PROCEDURE)→ FormalTypeList →

FormalTypeList

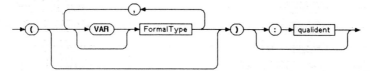

VariableDeclaration

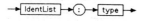

designator

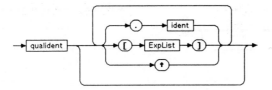

ExpList

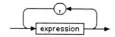

expression

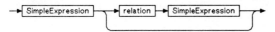

SimpleExpression

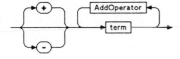

term

factor

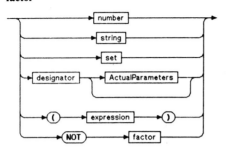

statement

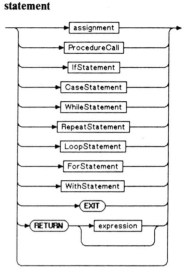

set

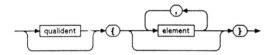

element

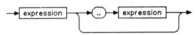

ActualParameters

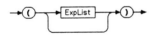

assignment

ProcedureCall

StatementSequence

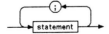

IfStatement

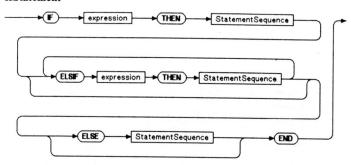

CaseStatement

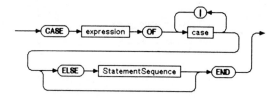

case

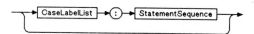

WhileStatement

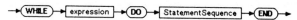

RepeatStatement

ForStatement

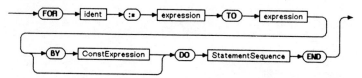

LoopStatement

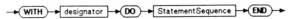

WithStatement

ProcedureDeclaration

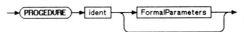

ProcedureHeading

block

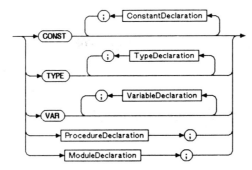

declaration

FormalParameters

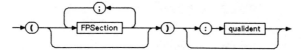

FPSection

FormalType

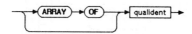

priority

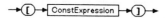

ModuleDeclaration

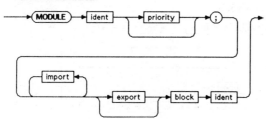

export

import

DefinitionModule

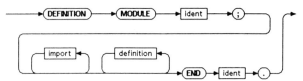

definition

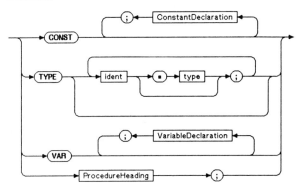

ProgramModule

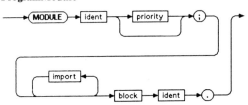

CompilationUnit

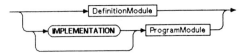

Appendix C

STANDARD LIBRARY MODULES

C.1 Introduction

This appendix contains detailed definitions for the library modules commonly found in Modula-2 implementations. Those listed are found in the Logitech Version 2.0 implementation may differ slightly from other implementations. In addition to the exploded definitions, a list of other modules often supplied by vendors is provided. The lists are intended to be used as a quick reference when programming and not as a replacement for vendor-supplied documentation.

The exported identifiers and procedure names are those found in the actual libraries. The procedure parameter names have been altered to be self-explanatory. For each definition, a brief commentary is given that describes the exported items. This documented format will not compile.

The following libraries are found in many implementations.

FileSystem	- random and sequential input and output support
InOut	- generalized input and output
MathLib0	- mathematical routines
Processes	- concurrent (coroutine) support (the implementation module for Processes is included in Appendix D, Section 5)
RealInOut	- input and output for real numbers
Storage	- memory management
SYSTEM	- low-level and system interface
Terminal	- input and output specifically for terminals

The following libraries from Logitech are itemized:

ASCII	- constants for nonprinting ASCII characters
Break	- handles the Ctrl-Break interrupt
CardinalIO	- input/output of cardinals in decimal and hex
Clock	- access the system date and time
Conversions	- convert from integer and cardinal to string
Devices	- logic for device and interrupt handling
Directories	- additional directory operations
DiskDirectory	- interface to directory functions of MS-DOS
DiskFiles	- interface to disk subfunctions of MS-DOS
Display	- low-level console output
FileMessage	- write file status/response to terminal
FileNames	- read a file specification from terminal
Keyboard	- default driver for terminal input

NumberConversion – conversion between numbers and strings
Options   – read a file specification with options
ProgMessage   – write program status message to the terminal
Program   – subprogram loading and execution
RealConversions   – conversion module for floating point numbers
RS232Code   – high-speed i/o via serial port
RS232INT   – iotransfer style i/o via serial port
RS232Polling   – polled i/o via serial port
Strings   – variable-length character strings handler
System   – additional system-dependent facilities
Termbase   – terminal i/o with redirection hooks

C.2   FileSystem

Command,   – commands passed to DiskFiles
DirectoryProc,   – proc type – entire file operations
File,   – file control block for DiskFiles
FileProc,   – proc type – internal file operations
Flag,   – status for file operations
FlagSet,   – status flag set
MediumType,   – medium name (A, B...
Response,   – result of a file operation

Again,   – return char to buffer for retry
Close,   – close a file
Create,   – create temporary file
CreateMedium,   – install medium in file system
Delete,   – delete a file
Doio,   – do various i/o operations on file
FileNameChar,   – check char legality in MSDOS
GetPos,   – get current byte position in file
Length,   – length of file in bytes
Lookup,   – look for a file
ReadByte,   – read one byte from file
ReadChar,   – read one character from file
ReadNBytes,   – read number of bytes from file
ReadWord,   – reads word at current position
RemoveMedium,   – remove medium from file system
Rename,   – rename a file
Reset,   – open and position to start of file
SetModify,   – set for read/write w/o position chg
SetOpen,   – open file without position change
SetPos,   – set current position in file
SetRead,   – set for read w/o position change
SetWrite,   – set for write w/o position change
WriteByte,   – write one byte to file
WriteChar,   – write one character to file
WriteNBytes,   – write number of bytes to file
WriteWord;   – write one word to file

TYPE

```
Buffadd    = POINTER TO ARRAY [0..0FFFEH] OF CHAR;

Command    = (create, close, lookup, rename, delete,
              setread, setwrite, setmodify, setopen,
              doio, setpos, getpos, length);

DirectoryProc = PROCEDURE (VAR File, ARRAY OF CHAR);

File       = RECORD
    bufferadr    : BuffAdd;
    buffersize   : CARDINAL;
    validlength  : CARDINAL;
    byteindex    : CARDINAL;
    statusflags  : FlagSet;
    eof          : BOOLEAN;
    result       : Response;
    lastdata     : CARDINAL;
    medium       : MediumType;
    internal     : CARDINAL;
    internal     : MediumHint;
    CASE commandcode : Command OF
          lookup :
                new     : BOOLEAN;
        | setpos, getpos, length :
                highpos : CARDINAL;
                lowpos  : CARDINAL;
        END;
    END;

FileProc   = PROCEDURE (VAR File);

Flag       = (er, ef,rd, wr, ag, txt);

FlagSet    = SET OF Flag;

MediumHint = CARDINAL;

MediumType = ARRAY [0..2] OF CHAR;

Response   = (done, notdone, notsupported, callerror,
              unknownmedium, unknownfile, paramerror,
              toomanyfiles, eom, userdeverror);

PROCEDURE Again        (VAR fileblock  : File);

PROCEDURE Close        (VAR fileblock  : File);

PROCEDURE Create       (VAR fileblock  : File;
                            mediumname : ARRAY OF CHAR);

PROCEDURE CreateMedium (    medium     : MediumType;
                            internalprc: FileProc;
```

```
                             wholeproc   : DirectoryProc;
                         VAR status      : BOOLEAN);

PROCEDURE Delete         (    fileid     : ARRAY OF CHAR;
                         VAR fileblock   : File);

PROCEDURE Doio           (VAR fileblock  : File);

PROCEDURE FileNameChar   (    chartocheck: CHAR)      : CHAR;

PROCEDURE GetPos         (VAR fileblock  : File;
                         VAR highpart    : CARDINAL;
                         VAR lowpart     : CARDINAL);

PROCEDURE Length         (VAR fileblock  : File;
                         VAR highpart    : CARDINAL;
                         VAR lowpart     : CARDINAL);

PROCEDURE Lookup         (VAR fileblock  : File;
                             fileid      : ARRAY OF CHAR;
                             newfilecmd  : BOOLEAN);

PROCEDURE ReadByte       (VAR fileblock  : File;
                         VAR target      : CHAR);

PROCEDURE ReadChar       (VAR fileblock  : File;
                         VAR target      : CHAR);

PROCEDURE ReadNBytes     (VAR fileblock  : File;
                             bufferadr   : ADDRESS;
                             sizetoread  : CARDINAL;
                         VAR sizeread    : CARDINAL);

PROCEDURE ReadWord       (VAR fileblock  : File;
                         VAR target      : WORD);

PROCEDURE RemoveMedium   (    medium     : MediumType;
                         VAR status      : BOOLEAN);

PROCEDURE Rename         (VAR fileblock  : File;
                             newfileid   : ARRAY OF CHAR);

PROCEDURE Reset          (VAR fileblock  : File);

PROCEDURE SetModify      (VAR fileblock  : File);

PROCEDURE SetOpen        (VAR fileblock  : File);

PROCEDURE SetPos         (VAR fileblock  : File;
                             highpart    : CARDINAL;
                             lowpart     : CARDINAL);
```

```
PROCEDURE SetRead       (VAR fileblock  : File);

PROCEDURE SetWrite      (VAR fileblock  : File);

PROCEDURE WriteByte     (VAR fileblock  : File;
                             source      : CHAR);

PROCEDURE WriteChar     (VAR fileblock  : File;
                             source      : CHAR);

PROCEDURE WriteNBytes   (VAR fileblock  : File;
                             bufferadr   : ADDRESS;
                             sizetowrite: CARDINAL;
                         VAR sizewritten: CARDINAL);

PROCEDURE WriteWord     (VAR fileblock  : File;
                             source      : WORD);
```

C.3   InOut

```
    EOL,            - end of line constant
    Done,           - return status
    in,             - standard input file
    out,            - standard output file
    termCH,         - termination character

    CloseInput,     - close input file
    CloseOutput,    - close output file
    OpenInput,      - open input file
    OpenOutput,     - open output file
    Read,           - read a character
    ReadCard,       - read a cardinal
    ReadInt,        - read an integer
    ReadString,     - read a string
    ReadWrd,        - read a word
    Write,          - write a character
    WriteCard,      - write a cardinal
    WriteHex,       - write a value out in hexadecimal
    WriteInt,       - write an integer
    WriteLn,        - write an end of line character
    WriteOct,       - write a value out in octal
    WriteString,    - write a string
    WriteWrd;       - write a word value

CONST
    EOL = 36C;

VAR
    Done    : BOOLEAN;
    in      : File;
    out     : File;
```

```
        termCH : CHAR;

PROCEDURE CloseInput    ();

PROCEDURE CloseOutput   ();

PROCEDURE OpenInput     (      defaultfid : ARRAY OF CHAR);

PROCEDURE OpenOutput    (      defaultfid : ARRAY OF CHAR);

PROCEDURE Read          (VAR target      : CHAR);

PROCEDURE ReadCard      (VAR target      : CARDINAL);

PROCEDURE ReadInt       (VAR target      : INTEGER);

PROCEDURE ReadString    (VAR target      : ARRAY OF CHAR);

PROCEDURE ReadWrd       (VAR target      : WORD);

PROCEDURE Write         (    source      : CHAR);

PROCEDURE WriteCard     (    source      : CARDINAL;
                             width       : CARDINAL);

PROCEDURE WriteHex      (    source      : CARDINAL;
                             width       : CARDINAL);

PROCEDURE WriteInt      (    source      : INTEGER);
                             width       : CARDINAL);

PROCEDURE WriteLn       ();

PROCEDURE WriteOct      (    source      : CARDINAL;
                             width       : CARDINAL);

PROCEDURE WriteString   (    source      : ARRAY OF CHAR);

PROCEDURE WriteWrd      (    source      : WORD);
```

C.4   MathLib0

```
arctan,      - arctangent
cos,         - cosine
entier,      - largest integer number less or equal x
exp,         - e to the x power
ln,          - natural log of a real
real,        - real representation of an integer
sin,         - sine
sqrt;        - square root
```

```
PROCEDURE arctan        (     source    : REAL)     : REAL;

PROCEDURE cos           (     source    : REAL)     : REAL;

PROCEDURE entier        (     source    : REAL)     : INTEGER;

PROCEDURE exp           (     source    : REAL)     : REAL;

PROCEDURE ln            (     source    : REAL)     : REAL;

PROCEDURE real          (     source    : INTEGER)  : REAL;

PROCEDURE sin           (     source    : REAL)     : REAL;

PROCEDURE sqrt          (     source    : REAL)     : REAL;
```

C.5   Processes

```
    SIGNAL,         - datatype for semaphore
    Awaited,        - test for someone waiting
    Init,           - initialize a semaphore
    SEND,           - send a semaphore
    StartProcess,   - start a process
    WAIT;           - wait for semaphore

TYPE
    SIGNAL;

PROCEDURE Awaited       (     signal    : SIGNAL)   : BOOLEAN;

PROCEDURE Init          (VAR signal     : SIGNAL);

PROCEDURE SEND          (VAR signal     : SIGNAL);

PROCEDURE StartProcess  (     procedure : PROC;
                              worksize  : CARDINAL);

PROCEDURE WAIT          (VAR signal     : SIGNAL);
```

C.6   RealInOut

```
    Done,           - status
    ReadReal,       - read in real value
    WriteReal,      - write real in 'e' notation
    WriteRealOct;   - write real value out in octal

TYPE
    Done = BOOLEAN;

PROCEDURE ReadReal      (VAR target     : REAL);
```

```
PROCEDURE WriteReal    (    source     : REAL;
                            width      : CARDINAL);

PROCEDURE WriteRealOct (    source     : REAL);
```

C.7   Storage

```
    ALLOCATE,      - allocate memory from system
    Available,     - test for enough memory
    DEALLOCATE,    - return memory to system
    InstallHeap,   - used internally by loader
    RemoveHeap;    - used internally by loader

PROCEDURE ALLOCATE     (VAR dataarea   : ADDRESS;
                            datasize   : CARDINAL);

PROCEDURE Available    (    size       : CARDINAL) : BOOLEAN;

PROCEDURE DEALLOCATE   (VAR dataarea   : ADDRESS;
                            datasize   : CARDINAL);

PROCEDURE InstallHeap  ();

PROCEDURE RemoveHeap   ();
```

C.8   SYSTEM

```
    AX,BX,CX,DX,   - constants referring to registers
    SI,DI,ES,DS,
    CS,SS,BP,SP,
    RTSVECTOR,     - runtime interrupt vector

    ADDRESS,       - datatype for memory addresses
    BYTE,          - datatype for 8 bit storage
    PROCESS,       - control block for processes
    WORD,          - datatype for word size storage

    ADR,           - obtain address of variable
    CODE,          - insert object code in-line
    CPMCALL,       - call an CPM-86 function
    DISABLE,       - disable interrupts
    DOSCALL,       - call an MS-DOS function
    ENABLE,        - enable interrupts
    GETREG,        - obtain value from register
    INBYTE,        - input an 8 bit value from a port
    INWORD,        - input a word value from a port
    IOTRANSFER,    - transfer on i/o interrupt
    LISTEN,        - lower priority temporarily
    NEWPROCESS,    - create a new process
```

```
        OUTBYTE,          - output an 8 bit value on a port
        OUTWORD,          - output a word value on a port
        SETREG,           - set a value into a register
        SIZE,             - obtain size of a variable
        SWI               - cause a software interrupt
        TRANSFER,         - transfer control to process
        TSIZE;            - obtain size of type

CONST
    AX = 0;   DX = 2;   ES =  8;   SS = 10;
    BX = 3;   SI = 6;   DS = 11;   BP =  5;
    CX = 1;   DI = 7;   CS =  9;   SP =  4;

    RTSVECTOR = 228;

TYPE
    ADDRESS;
    BYTE;
    PROCESS;
    WORD;

PROCEDURE ADR           (      variable   : any      ) : CARDINAL;

PROCEDURE CODE          (      byte1...   : BYTE);

PROCEDURE CPMCALL       (      function   : CARDINAL;
                               parm1...   : CARDINAL);


PROCEDURE DISABLE       ();

PROCEDURE DOSCALL       (      function   : CARDINAL;
                               parm1...   : CARDINAL);

PROCEDURE ENABLE        ();

PROCEDURE GETREG        (      register   : CARDINAL;
                        VAR targetword : BYTE or WORD);

PROCEDURE INBYTE        (      portnumber : CARDINAL;
                        VAR targetword : BYTE or WORD);

PROCEDURE INWORD        (      portnumber : CARDINAL;
                        VAR targetword : WORD);

PROCEDURE IOTRANSFER    (VAR current    : PROCESS;
                         VAR next       : PROCESS;
                             interrupt  : CARDINAL);

PROCEDURE LISTEN        ();

PROCEDURE NEWPROCESS    (      procedure  : PROC;
```

```
                                   dataarea    : ADDRESS;
                                   datasize    : CARDINAL;
                          VAR newprocess : PROCESS);

PROCEDURE OUTBYTE        (      portnumber : CARDINAL;
                                sourceword : BYTE or WORD);

PROCEDURE OUTWORD        (      portnumber : CARDINAL;
                                sourceword : WORD);

PROCEDURE SETREG         (      register   : CARDINAL;
                                sourceword : BYTE or WORD);

PROCEDURE SIZE           (      variable   : any      ) : CARDINAL;

PROCEDURE SWI            (      interrupt  : CARDINAL);

PROCEDURE TRANSFER       (VAR current      : PROCESS;
                          VAR next         : PROCESS);

PROCEDURE TSIZE          (      type, tag1.: any      ) : CARDINAL;
```

C.9   Terminal

```
    KeyPressed,    - test for a pressed key
    Read,          - read a character
    ReadAgain,     - put character back in buffer
    ReadString,    - read a complete string
    Write,         - display a character
    WriteLn,       - write end of line to terminal
    WriteString;   - display string

PROCEDURE KeyPressed    ()                              : BOOLEAN;

PROCEDURE Read          (VAR character   : CHAR);

PROCEDURE ReadAgain     ();

PROCEDURE ReadString    (VAR characters : ARRAY OF CHAR);

PROCEDURE Write         (      character  : CHAR);

PROCEDURE WriteLn       ();

PROCEDURE WriteString   (      characters : ARRAY OF CHAR);
```

Appendix D

OTHER USEFUL MODULES

D.1 Introduction

The following sections contain programs developed by the authors that not only demonstrate the recommended style and structure of good Modula-2 programs but also may serve as the starting point of your own module libraries. These examples of Modula-2 programming show how to combine the various concepts discussed throughout the text and also how to use the style guidelines to create code that is clear, concise, and easy to maintain.

Information on how to obtain a diskette containing the source code is found in the Preface.

The examples included are:

CaseFix: – Case Sensitivity. There are two source listings provided. The first is the program module for processing a Modula-2 source file and fixing all case sensitivity problems. The second file is the data file containing the CaseFix dictionary which provides the correct typing for reserved words etc. The data file presented is one that the authors use regularly when banging in the first draft of a program and includes common library names, variable names, etc. in addition to the normal Modula-2 identifiers. The CaseFix uses the generic ListHandler to build and maintain its lists, and also shows how hashing can be used to distribute an alphabetic stream of words into a dynamic structure to minimize search time.

EasyIO: – Easy Input and Output. This subsection lists the definition and implementation modules for an example of making IO easier in Modula-2. These routines package up the most common sequences of terminal input and output into one procedure call. An example program called Easy is listed that shows how EasyIO can be used.

ListHandler, TreeHandler: – Dynamic Structures. The definition and implementation modules for generic linked list and binary tree handling are found in this subsection. In addition to showing how dynamic structures are used, these modules illustrate the construction of library modules, data independent structures, pointer handling, and how one module (TreeHandler) can be built up using another library (ListHandler). A small utility routine called ListHelp is shown that illustrates how a simple tool can be built and included as a library and accessed time and time again. It provides the logic to dump link list elements in hexadecimal format. A short program called TreeTest, presented as the last program in this subsection, shows how easy it is to use a library like TreeHandler to build a binary tree.

Processes: – Coroutines. This module is essentially the Processes module described by N. Wirth and implemented in the Logitech version. There is one difference. The code has been rewritten in the authors' style in an attempt to make the code clear and self-documenting.

DirectIO: – Direct-access Input and Output. The DirectIO module illustrates how to use the Logitech implementation to achieve direct-access file support. The various Modula-2 implementations differ in how this is done, but they do use the same basic ideas. There are a number of procedures in DirectIO that are specific to the example record structure. The majority of routines are example independent and would serve as the basis for a direct access utility library.

D.2   Case Sensitivity – CaseFix

CaseFix Module

MODULE CaseFix;

(*

Function: This program will correct some typing errors in a
    Modula-2 source file. The errors caught and corrected are
    those relating to the case sensitivity of Modula-2. Since
    keywords must be capitals, and identifiers are formed from
    series of words, usually with the first letter in capitals,
    many errors can be caused.
    In addition, when typing in source, constantly shifting can
    cause fatigue and is not friendly to people who cannot
    easily do shifting - arthritis, etc. To that end, this
    program will automatically convert any MODULA-2 keyword
    to uppercase. In addition, the first spelling of an
    identifier will be used and automatically substituted
    whenever a matching identifier is found regardless of
    what letters are upper- or lowercase. This latter point
    enforces the concept that it is better programming to use
    unique names and not allow (x,X) as two different
    variables.

Operation: The file 'casefix.dat' contains the list of Modula
    reserved words and common subroutine names. It can be added
    to anytime.

    The user is prompted for the source name and a target name.
    The program then reads the source, fixes the lower- to
    uppercase problems and creates the target. The user
    can then reedit the target, etc.

    There is not much checking done with the fileids given and
    the user simply types in the name: TRIAL.MOD

    The basic logic is:

        - set up reserved word list from casefix.dat
          in hash table linked lists off the table
        - set up source and target files
        - until the end of the source file scan for
          words - if in hash table, replace with master
                - if not in hash table, place in table

*)

FROM FileSystem IMPORT Lookup, Close, ReadChar, Response,
                    WriteChar, File;

```
FROM FileNames    IMPORT ReadFileName, FNParts, FNPartSet;

FROM InOut        IMPORT Write, WriteString, WriteCard, WriteLn;

FROM ListHandler IMPORT CreateList, CreateElement, InsertBefore,
                        Anchor, InsertAfter,
                        RemoveList;

FROM Terminal     IMPORT Read;

FROM SYSTEM       IMPORT ADDRESS, TSIZE, ADR;

CONST
    WordLength     = 24;
    HashModulus    = 32;
    MaxFileId      = 14;
    ReservedFileId = "C:CASEFIX.DAT";

TYPE
    WordToken       = ARRAY [0..WordLength-1] OF CHAR;

    FileId          = ARRAY [0..MaxFileId-1] OF CHAR;

    HashListPtrType = POINTER TO HashListElement;

    HashListElement = RECORD
        Prev            : ADDRESS;
        Next            : ADDRESS;
        Size            : CARDINAL;
        UpperCaseWord   : WordToken;
        SubstituteWord  : WordToken;
        END;

VAR
    AnchorPtr          : POINTER TO Anchor;
    BitBucket          : BOOLEAN;
    GlobalIndex        : CARDINAL;
    HashTable          : ARRAY [0..HashModulus-1] OF ADDRESS;
    InputChar          : CHAR;
    InputFileId        : FileId;
    InputFileIdParts   : FNPartSet;
    InputFile          : File;
    InputFile1         : File;
    InputSize          : CARDINAL;
    InputWord          : WordToken;
    NilAddress         : ADDRESS;
    OutputFile         : File;
    OutputFileId       : FileId;
    OutputFileIdParts  : FNPartSet;
    OutputWord         : WordToken;
    ReadAgain          : BOOLEAN;
    ReturnCode         : BOOLEAN;
```

```
    UpperWord              : WordToken;

PROCEDURE AddWord(      InsertAdr   : ADDRESS;
                        HashValue   : CARDINAL;
                    VAR ElementAdr  : ADDRESS;
                    VAR ReturnCode  : BOOLEAN);

    VAR
        ElementPtr : HashListPtrType;
        Index      : CARDINAL;

    BEGIN
        ReturnCode := FALSE;
        CreateElement(HashTable[HashValue],ElementPtr);
        IF ElementPtr <> NIL THEN
            FOR Index := 0 TO InputSize DO
                ElementPtr^.UpperCaseWord[Index]  :=
                        UpperWord[Index];
                ElementPtr^.SubstituteWord[Index] :=
                        InputWord[Index];
                END;
            ElementPtr^.Size := InputSize;
            InsertAfter(HashTable[HashValue],
                        ElementPtr,InsertAdr);
            ReturnCode := TRUE;
            ElementAdr := ElementPtr;
            END;
        RETURN;
    END AddWord;


PROCEDURE FindWord(VAR HashValue   : CARDINAL;
                   VAR InsertAdr    : ADDRESS;
                   VAR ReturnCode   : BOOLEAN);

    VAR
        AnchorPtr  : POINTER TO Anchor;
        ElementPtr : HashListPtrType;
        Index      : CARDINAL;
        Reset      : BOOLEAN;

    BEGIN
        HashValue := GetHash(InputWord,InputSize);
        IF HashTable[HashValue] = NIL THEN
            ReturnCode := FALSE;
            CreateList(TSIZE(HashListElement),
                        HashTable[HashValue]);
            InsertAdr  := NIL;
        ELSE
            AnchorPtr := HashTable[HashValue];
            IF AnchorPtr^.Ptr = NIL THEN
                ReturnCode := FALSE;
```

```
                    InsertAdr   := NIL;
            ELSE
                ElementPtr := AnchorPtr^.Ptr;
                Reset      := TRUE;
                LOOP
                    IF Reset THEN
                        Index := 0;
                        Reset := FALSE;
                        END;
                    IF UpperWord[Index] >
                            ElementPtr^.UpperCaseWord[Index]
                        THEN
                        IF ElementPtr^.Next = NIL THEN
                            InsertAdr   := ElementPtr;
                            ReturnCode := FALSE;
                            EXIT;
                            END;
                        Reset        := TRUE;
                        ElementPtr := ElementPtr^.Next;
                    ELSE
                        IF UpperWord[Index] <
                                ElementPtr^.UpperCaseWord[Index]
                            THEN
                            InsertAdr   := ElementPtr^.Prev;
                            ReturnCode := FALSE;
                            EXIT;
                            END;
                        IF (Index = InputSize) &
                            (Index = ElementPtr^.Size) THEN
                            InsertAdr   := ElementPtr;
                            ReturnCode := TRUE;
                            EXIT;
                            END;
                        Index := Index + 1;
                        IF (Index = InputSize + 1) &
                            (Index <= ElementPtr^.Size) THEN
                            InsertAdr   := ElementPtr^.Prev;
                            ReturnCode := FALSE;
                            EXIT;
                            END;
                        IF (Index <= InputSize) &
                            (Index = ElementPtr^.Size + 1)
                            THEN
                            IF ElementPtr^.Next = NIL THEN
                                InsertAdr   := ElementPtr;
                                ReturnCode := FALSE;
                                EXIT;
                                END;
                            Reset        := TRUE;
                            ElementPtr := ElementPtr^.Next;
                            END;
                        END;
```

```
                                END;
                        END;
                    END;
            END FindWord;


    PROCEDURE FixWord() : BOOLEAN;

        VAR
            ElementPtr : HashListPtrType;
            HashValue  : CARDINAL;
            Index      : CARDINAL;
            InsertPtr  : HashListPtrType;
            ReturnCode : BOOLEAN;

        BEGIN
            FindWord(HashValue,InsertPtr,ReturnCode);
            IF ReturnCode = TRUE THEN
                FOR Index := 0 TO InputSize DO
                    OutputWord[Index] :=
                            InsertPtr^.SubstituteWord[Index];
                    END;
            ELSE
                AddWord(InsertPtr,HashValue,ElementPtr,ReturnCode);
                IF ReturnCode THEN
                    FOR Index := 0 TO InputSize DO
                        OutputWord[Index] :=
                                ElementPtr^.SubstituteWord[Index];
                        END;
                    END;
                END;
            RETURN ReturnCode;
        END FixWord;


    PROCEDURE GetChar(VAR ch         : CHAR;
                      VAR ReturnCode : BOOLEAN);

        BEGIN
            ReturnCode    := TRUE;
            IF ReadAgain THEN
                ch        := InputChar;
                ReadAgain := FALSE;
            ELSE
                ReadChar(InputFile,InputChar);
                IF InputFile.res <> done THEN
                    ReturnCode := FALSE;
                    END;
                ch := InputChar;
                END;
        END GetChar;
```

```
PROCEDURE GetComment() : BOOLEAN;

    VAR
        NextChar   : CHAR;
        ReturnCode : BOOLEAN;

    BEGIN
        LOOP
            GetChar(NextChar,ReturnCode);
            IF ReturnCode = FALSE THEN
                EXIT;
                END;
            WriteItOut(NextChar);
            IF NextChar = "*" THEN
                GetChar(NextChar,ReturnCode);
                IF ReturnCode = FALSE THEN
                    EXIT;
                    END;
                IF NextChar = ")" THEN
                    WriteItOut(NextChar);
                    EXIT;
                    END;
                ReadAgain := TRUE;
            ELSIF NextChar = "(" THEN
                GetChar(NextChar,ReturnCode);
                IF ReturnCode = FALSE THEN
                    EXIT;
                    END;
                IF NextChar <> "*" THEN
                    ReadAgain := TRUE;
                ELSE
                    WriteItOut(NextChar);
                    IF GetComment() = FALSE THEN
                        ReturnCode := FALSE;
                        EXIT;
                        END;
                    END;
                END;
            END;
        RETURN ReturnCode;
    END GetComment;


PROCEDURE GetHash(    SourceWord : ARRAY OF CHAR;
                      SourceSize : CARDINAL        ) : CARDINAL;

    VAR
        Hash  : CARDINAL;
        Index : CARDINAL;

    BEGIN
```

```
        Hash := 0;
        FOR Index := 0 TO SourceSize DO
            Hash := Hash + ORD(SourceWord[Index]);
            END;
        Hash := Hash MOD HashModulus;
        RETURN Hash;
    END GetHash;


PROCEDURE GetWord() : BOOLEAN;

    VAR
        Index      : CARDINAL;
        NextChar   : CHAR;
        ReturnCode : BOOLEAN;

    BEGIN
        LOOP
            GetChar(NextChar,ReturnCode);
            IF ReturnCode = FALSE THEN
                EXIT;
                END;
            IF NextChar = "'" THEN
                REPEAT
                    WriteItOut(NextChar);
                    GetChar(NextChar,ReturnCode);
                    UNTIL (ReturnCode = FALSE) OR
                        (NextChar   = "'");
                IF ReturnCode = FALSE THEN
                    WriteString("Mismatched string spec");
                    EXIT;
                    END;
                WriteItOut(NextChar);
            ELSIF NextChar = '"' THEN
                REPEAT
                    WriteItOut(NextChar);
                    GetChar(NextChar,ReturnCode);
                    UNTIL (ReturnCode = FALSE) OR
                        (NextChar   = '"');
                IF ReturnCode = FALSE THEN
                    WriteString("Mismatched string spec");
                    EXIT;
                    END;
                WriteItOut(NextChar);
            ELSIF NextChar = '(' THEN
                WriteItOut(NextChar);
                GetChar(NextChar,ReturnCode);
                IF ReturnCode = FALSE THEN
                    WriteString("Open parens at end of file");
                    EXIT;
                    END;
                IF NextChar <> "*" THEN
```

```
                    ReadAgain := TRUE;
                ELSE
                    WriteItOut(NextChar);
                    IF GetComment() = FALSE THEN
                        WriteString("Mismatched comments");
                        ReturnCode := FALSE;
                        EXIT;
                        END;
                END;
        ELSIF ((NextChar >= "0") & (NextChar <= "9")) THEN
            REPEAT
                WriteItOut(NextChar);
                GetChar(NextChar,ReturnCode);
                UNTIL (ReturnCode = FALSE)OR
                (((NextChar >= "0") & (NextChar <= "9")) OR
                ((NextChar >= "A") & (NextChar <= "Z")) OR
                ((NextChar >= "a") & (NextChar <= "z"))
                = FALSE);
            IF ReturnCode THEN
                ReadAgain := TRUE;
                END;
        ELSIF ((NextChar >= "A") & (NextChar <= "Z")) OR
                ((NextChar >= "a") & (NextChar <= "z")) THEN
            InputSize := 0;
            REPEAT
                InputWord[InputSize] := NextChar;
                UpperWord[InputSize] := CAP(NextChar);
                InputSize := InputSize + 1;
                GetChar(NextChar,ReturnCode);
                UNTIL (ReturnCode = FALSE) OR
                 (((NextChar >= "0") & (NextChar <= "9")) OR
                ((NextChar >= "A") & (NextChar <= "Z")) OR
                ((NextChar >= "a") & (NextChar <= "z"))
                 = FALSE);
            IF ReturnCode = FALSE THEN
                WriteString("Premature end of file");
                EXIT;
                END;
            IF InputSize >= WordLength + 1 THEN
                WriteString("Identifier too long");
                ReturnCode := FALSE;
                EXIT;
                END;
            InputSize := InputSize - 1;
            ReadAgain := TRUE;
            EXIT;
        ELSE
            WriteItOut(NextChar);
            END;
        END;
    RETURN ReturnCode;
END GetWord;
```

```
PROCEDURE SetUpFiles() : BOOLEAN;

    VAR
        ReturnCode : BOOLEAN;

    BEGIN
        LOOP
            ReturnCode := FALSE;
            WriteString("Enter source file identifier: ");
            ReadFileName(InputFileId,"",InputFileIdParts);
            Read(InputChar);
            WriteLn;
            Lookup(InputFile,InputFileId,FALSE);
            IF InputFile.res = notdone THEN
                WriteString("Source file does not exist");
                WriteLn;
                EXIT;
                END;
            WriteString("Enter target file identifier: ");
            ReadFileName(OutputFileId,"",OutputFileIdParts);
            Read(InputChar);
            WriteLn;
            Lookup(OutputFile,OutputFileId,FALSE);
            IF OutputFile.res = done THEN
                WriteString("Target file already exists");
                WriteLn;
                Close(InputFile);
                Close(OutputFile);
                EXIT;
                END;
            Lookup(OutputFile,OutputFileId,TRUE);
            IF OutputFile.res = notdone THEN
                WriteString("Target file cannot be opened");
                WriteLn;
                Close(InputFile);
                EXIT;
                END;
            ReturnCode := TRUE;
            EXIT;
            END;
        RETURN ReturnCode;
    END SetUpFiles;

PROCEDURE SetUpReserved() : BOOLEAN;

    VAR
        ElementAdr : ADDRESS;
        HashValue  : CARDINAL;
        InsertAdr  : ADDRESS;
        ReturnCode : BOOLEAN;
```

```
    BEGIN
        ReturnCode := FALSE;
        Lookup(InputFile,ReservedFileId,FALSE);
        IF InputFile.res = notdone THEN
            WriteString("Reserved data file does not exist");
            WriteLn;
        ELSE
            ReturnCode := TRUE;
            LOOP
                IF GetWord() = FALSE THEN
                    ReturnCode := TRUE;
                    EXIT;
                    END;
                FindWord(HashValue,InsertAdr,ReturnCode);
                AddWord(InsertAdr,HashValue,
                        ElementAdr,ReturnCode);
                IF NOT ReturnCode THEN
                    EXIT;
                    END;
                END;
            IF (InputFile.eof = FALSE) THEN
                Close(InputFile);
                ReturnCode := FALSE;
            ELSE
                Close(InputFile);
                END;
            END;
        RETURN ReturnCode;
    END SetUpReserved;

PROCEDURE WriteItOut(    ch : CHAR);

    BEGIN
        IF (ch <> OC) & (NOT (BitBucket)) THEN
            WriteChar(OutputFile,ch);
            END;
    END WriteItOut;

BEGIN
    LOOP
        ReadAgain   := FALSE;
        InputSize   := 0;
        NilAddress := NIL;
        FOR GlobalIndex := 0 TO HashModulus-1 DO
            HashTable[GlobalIndex] := NilAddress;
            END;
        FOR GlobalIndex := 0 TO WordLength-1 DO
            InputWord[GlobalIndex] := " ";
            END;
        BitBucket := TRUE;
        IF SetUpReserved() = FALSE THEN
```

```
            EXIT;
            END;
        BitBucket := FALSE;
        IF SetUpFiles() = FALSE THEN
            EXIT;
            END;

    LOOP
        IF GetWord() = FALSE THEN
            EXIT;
            END;
        IF FixWord() = FALSE THEN
            EXIT;
            END;
        FOR GlobalIndex := 0 TO InputSize DO
            WriteItOut(OutputWord[GlobalIndex]);
            END;
        END;

    Close(InputFile);
    Close(OutputFile);
    EXIT;
    END;
FOR GlobalIndex := 0 TO HashModulus-1 DO
    IF HashTable[GlobalIndex] <> NIL THEN
        RemoveList(HashTable[GlobalIndex]);
    END;
    END;
END CaseFix.
```

CaseFix Data

AND ARRAY BEGIN BY CASE CONST DEFINITION
DIV DO ELSE ELSIF END EXIT EXPORT
FOR FROM IF IMPLEMENTATION IMPORT IN
LOOP MOD MODULE NOT OF OR POINTER
PROCEDURE QUALIFIED RECORD REPEAT RETURN SET THEN
TO TYPE UNTIL VAR WHILE WITH

ABS BITSET BOOLEAN CAP CARDINAL CHAR CHR
DEC DISPOSE EXCL FALSE FLOAT HALT HIGH
INC INCL INTEGER NEW NIL ODD ORD
PROC REAL TRUE TRUNC VAL

SYSTEM ADDRESS ADR SIZE TSIZE WORD

Storage ALLOCATE DEALLOCATE

InOut Write WriteInt WriteCard WriteLn WriteString
Read ReadInt ReadCard ReadString
EOL termCH

FileSystem File Flag Lookup Open Close
ReadChar WriteChar Response res done
notdone

FileNames FNParts FNPartSet ReadFileName

Count Value Letter Number Condition Temp
Index LocalIndex MaxInt MinInt MaxCard MinCard
Variable I J A B C
X Y Z Buffer BufferLen BufferAdr
K L M N Input Output
FileId Status ReturnCode Terminal InputFile OutputFile

D.3   Easy Input and Output - EasyIO

EasyIO Definition

```
DEFINITION MODULE EasyIO;

EXPORT QUALIFIED DispText, DispReal, DispInt, DispCard,
                 PromptText, PromptReal, PromptInt, PromptCard,
                 DispTextText, DispTextReal, DispTextInt,
                 DispTextCard, DispRealText, DispIntText,
                 DispCardText;

PROCEDURE DispText(    Output : ARRAY OF CHAR);

PROCEDURE DispReal(    Output : REAL);

PROCEDURE DispInt(    Output : INTEGER);

PROCEDURE DispCard(    Output : CARDINAL);

PROCEDURE PromptText(    Output : ARRAY OF CHAR;
                 VAR Input  : ARRAY OF CHAR;
                 VAR Ch     : CHAR);

PROCEDURE PromptReal(    Output : ARRAY OF CHAR;
                 VAR Input  : REAL;
                 VAR Ch     : CHAR);

PROCEDURE PromptInt(    Output : ARRAY OF CHAR;
                 VAR Input  : INTEGER;
                 VAR Ch     : CHAR);

PROCEDURE PromptCard(    Output : ARRAY OF CHAR;
                 VAR Input  : CARDINAL;
                 VAR Ch     : CHAR);

PROCEDURE DispTextText(    Output1 : ARRAY OF CHAR;
                           Output2 : ARRAY OF CHAR);

PROCEDURE DispTextReal(    Output1 : ARRAY OF CHAR;
                           Output2 : REAL);

PROCEDURE DispTextInt(    Output1 : ARRAY OF CHAR;
                          Output2 : INTEGER);

PROCEDURE DispTextCard(    Output1 : ARRAY OF CHAR;
                           Output2 : CARDINAL);

PROCEDURE DispRealText(    Output1 : REAL;
                           Output2 : ARRAY OF CHAR);

PROCEDURE DispIntText(    Output1 : INTEGER;
```

```
                              Output2 : ARRAY OF CHAR);

PROCEDURE DispCardText(    Output1 : CARDINAL;
                          Output2 : ARRAY OF CHAR);

END EasyIO.
```

EasyIO Module

```
IMPLEMENTATION MODULE EasyIO;

FROM InOut      IMPORT Write, Read, ReadCard, WriteCard, ReadInt,
                       WriteInt, ReadString,
                       WriteString, termCH, EOL, WriteLn;

FROM RealInOut IMPORT ReadReal, WriteReal;

PROCEDURE DispText(     Output : ARRAY OF CHAR);

    BEGIN
        WriteString(Output);
        WriteLn;
    END DispText;

PROCEDURE DispReal(     Output : REAL);

    BEGIN
        WriteReal(Output,8);
        WriteLn;
    END DispReal;

PROCEDURE DispInt(     Output : INTEGER);

    BEGIN
        WriteInt(Output,8);
        WriteLn;
    END DispInt;

PROCEDURE DispCard(     Output : CARDINAL);

    BEGIN
        WriteCard(Output,8);
        WriteLn;
    END DispCard;

PROCEDURE PromptText(     Output : ARRAY OF CHAR;
                      VAR Input  : ARRAY OF CHAR;
                      VAR Ch     : CHAR);

    BEGIN
        WriteString(Output);
        ReadString(Input);
        Ch := termCH;
        WriteLn;
    END PromptText;

PROCEDURE PromptReal(     Output : ARRAY OF CHAR;
                      VAR Input  : REAL;
                      VAR Ch     : CHAR);
```

```
        BEGIN
            WriteString(Output);
            ReadReal(Input);
            Ch := termCH;
            WriteLn;
        END PromptReal;

    PROCEDURE PromptInt(     Output : ARRAY OF CHAR;
                        VAR Input  : INTEGER;
                        VAR Ch     : CHAR);

        BEGIN
            WriteString(Output);
            ReadInt(Input);
            Ch := termCH;
            WriteLn;
        END PromptInt;

    PROCEDURE PromptCard(    Output : ARRAY OF CHAR;
                        VAR Input  : CARDINAL;
                        VAR Ch     : CHAR);

        BEGIN
            WriteString(Output);
            ReadCard(Input);
            Ch := termCH;
            WriteLn;
        END PromptCard;

    PROCEDURE DispTextText(    Output1 : ARRAY OF CHAR;
                               Output2 : ARRAY OF CHAR);

        BEGIN
            WriteString(Output1);
            WriteString(Output2);
            WriteLn;
        END DispTextText;

    PROCEDURE DispTextReal(    Output1 : ARRAY OF CHAR;
                               Output2 : REAL);

        BEGIN
            WriteString(Output1);
            WriteReal(Output2,8);
            WriteLn;
        END DispTextReal;

    PROCEDURE DispTextInt(    Output1 : ARRAY OF CHAR;
                              Output2 : INTEGER);

        BEGIN
```

```
            WriteString(Output1);
            WriteInt(Output2,8);
            WriteLn;
        END DispTextInt;

PROCEDURE DispTextCard(      Output1 : ARRAY OF CHAR;
                            Output2 : CARDINAL);

    BEGIN
        WriteString(Output1);
        WriteCard(Output2,8);
        WriteLn;
    END DispTextCard;

PROCEDURE DispRealText(      Output1 : REAL;
                            Output2 : ARRAY OF CHAR);

    BEGIN
        WriteReal(Output1,8);
        WriteString(Output2);
        WriteLn;
    END DispRealText;

PROCEDURE DispIntText(      Output1 : INTEGER;
                           Output2 : ARRAY OF CHAR);

    BEGIN
        WriteInt(Output1,8);
        WriteString(Output2);
        WriteLn;
    END DispIntText;

PROCEDURE DispCardText(      Output1 : CARDINAL;
                            Output2 : ARRAY OF CHAR);

    BEGIN
        WriteCard(Output1,8);
        WriteString(Output2);
        WriteLn;
    END DispCardText;

  BEGIN
  END EasyIO.
```

EasyIO Example

```
MODULE Easy;

FROM EasyIO IMPORT DispText, DispReal, DispInt, DispCard,
                   PromptText, PromptReal, PromptInt, PromptCard,
                   DispTextText, DispTextReal  DispTextInt,
                   DispTextCard, DispRealText, DispIntText,
                   DispCardText;

VAR
    Str1 : ARRAY [0..9] OF CHAR;
    Int1 : INTEGER;
    Real1 : REAL;
    Card1 : CARDINAL;
    EndCH : CHAR;

BEGIN
    DispText('This is first line from DispText');
    DispReal(1.0);
    DispInt(2);
    DispCard(3);
    PromptText('Enter string: ',Str1,EndCH);
    DispText(Str1);
    PromptReal('Enter real  : ',Real1,EndCH);
    DispReal(Real1);
    PromptInt('Enter int  : ',Int1,EndCH);
    DispInt(Int1);
    PromptCard('Enter card  : ',Card1,EndCH);
    DispCard(Card1);
    DispTextText('test1','test2');
    DispTextReal('real number',Real1);
    DispTextInt('int number',Int1);
    DispTextCard('card number',Card1);
    DispRealText(Real1,'was a real');
    DispIntText(Int1,'was a int');
    DispCardText(Card1,'was a card');
END Easy.
```

D.4   Dynamic Structures – ListHandler, TreeHandler

ListHandler Definition

```
DEFINITION MODULE ListHandler;


FROM SYSTEM  IMPORT ADDRESS;

EXPORT QUALIFIED CopyElement, CopyList, CreateElement,
                 CreateList, InsertAfter, InsertBefore,
                 InsertList, RemoveElement, RemoveList,
                 Anchor;

TYPE Anchor = RECORD
        Prev   : ADDRESS;
        Next   : ADDRESS;
        Size   : CARDINAL;
        Ptr    : ADDRESS;
        END;


PROCEDURE CopyElement(     AnchorAdr,
                           SourceAdr : ADDRESS;
                       VAR CopyAdr   : ADDRESS);

PROCEDURE CopyList(     AnchorAdr,
                        StartAdr,
                        EndAdr    : ADDRESS;
                    VAR CopyAdr   : ADDRESS);

PROCEDURE CreateElement(     AnchorAdr : ADDRESS;
                         VAR NewAdr    : ADDRESS);

PROCEDURE CreateList(     ElementSize : CARDINAL;
                      VAR AnchorAdr    : ADDRESS);

PROCEDURE InsertAfter(     AnchorAdr,
                           SourceAdr,
                           TargetAdr : ADDRESS);

PROCEDURE InsertBefore(     AnchorAdr,
                            SourceAdr,
                            TargetAdr : ADDRESS);

PROCEDURE InsertList(     AnchorAdr,
                          SourceAdr,
                          TargetAdr : ADDRESS);

PROCEDURE RemoveElement(     AnchorAdr,
                             SourceAdr : ADDRESS);
```

```
PROCEDURE RemoveList(    AnchorAdr : ADDRESS);

END ListHandler.
```

ListHandler Module

```
IMPLEMENTATION MODULE ListHandler;

(*

Function: The intention of this library is to provide a number
          of standard routines that perform the normal work of
          creating lists, and manipulating their elements.

Data Structures:

          All routines are independent of element keys, and data. It
          is assumed that each element is of the form:
```

```
                 -----------------------------
                 |  <-- Ptr to previous      |
                 |---------------------------|
                 |     Ptr to next     -->   |
                 |---------------------------|
                 |     any keys and data     |
                 |                .          |
                 |                .          |
                 |      .         .          |
                 -----------------------------
```

```
          The lists themself are maintained via a list of anchor
          elements that contain the maximum size of an element
          and a pointer to the first element in the list. The
          first element in the list points back to its anchor.
          The list handler routines are themselves used to create
          and maintain the list of lists.

          Pictorially, the data structure looks roughly like:
```

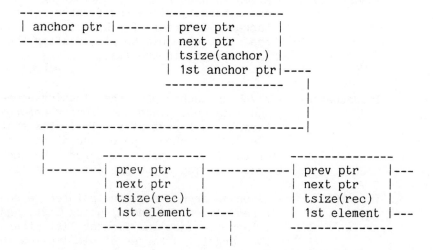

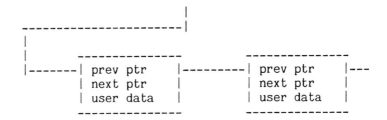

Routines:

       CopyElement   - given an anchor ptr and an element
pointer,
                        create a duplicate of the element and
                        return the new pointer - a pointer of NIL
                        indicates failure.

       CopyList   - given an anchor ptr, start ptr, and an end
                        pointer, all the elements in between will
                        be copied into a standalone list pointed
                        to by the return pointer. If insufficient
                        memory exists, all temporary elements will
                        be removed and a pointer value of NIL will
                        be returned. If the end pointer is NIL the
                        complete list following the start is
                        copied.

       CreateElement - given an anchor ptr, create an element
                       and return the pointer.

       CreateList   - given the maximum element size, allocate
                        a list and return the anchor ptr and a
                        pointer of NIL indicates failure.

       InsertAfter   - given an anchor ptr, the floating element
                        and a target, place the floater before the
                        target - a target of NIL indicates that
                        the floater should be placed after the
                        last element in the list.

       InsertBefore   - given an anchor ptr, the floating element
                        and a target, place the floater before the
                        target - a target of NIL indicates that
                        the floater should be placed at the front
                        of the list - inserting before the anchor
                        adds the floater to the end of the list.

       InsertList   - given an anchor ptr, the pointer to the
                        first element in the floating list, and
                        a target, place the floater list after
                        the target - a target of NIL implies the

```
                            end of the list.

   RemoveElement - given an anchor ptr and an element number,
                   remove the element from the list and then
                   deallocate the storage.

   RemoveList    - given an anchor ptr, remove all elements
                   and then mark the list unallocated.


*)

FROM SYSTEM  IMPORT ADR, ADDRESS, TSIZE;

FROM Storage IMPORT ALLOCATE, DEALLOCATE, Available;

TYPE
    Element = RECORD
        Prev   : ADDRESS;
        Next   : ADDRESS;
        END;

    ElementPtrType = POINTER TO Element;

VAR
    MasterAnchor     : Anchor;
    MasterAnchorPtr  : POINTER TO Anchor;


PROCEDURE CopyElement(     AnchorAdr : ADDRESS;
                           SourceAdr : ADDRESS;
                       VAR CopyAdr    : ADDRESS);

    VAR
        AnchorPtr : POINTER TO Anchor;
        CopyPtr   : ElementPtrType;
        EndAdr    : ADDRESS;
        TempCard  : CARDINAL;

    BEGIN
        CreateElement(AnchorAdr,CopyAdr);
        IF CopyAdr <> NIL THEN
            AnchorPtr := AnchorAdr;
            CopyPtr   := CopyAdr;
            TempCard  := AnchorPtr^.Size;
            EndAdr    := CopyAdr;
            INC(EndAdr,TempCard);
            REPEAT
                CopyAdr^   := SourceAdr^;
                INC(CopyAdr,1);
                INC(SourceAdr,1);
                UNTIL CopyAdr = EndAdr;
```

```
            CopyPtr^.Prev := NIL;
            CopyPtr^.Next := NIL;
            CopyAdr        := CopyPtr;
            END;
    END CopyElement;


PROCEDURE CopyList(     AnchorAdr : ADDRESS;
                        StartAdr  : ADDRESS;
                        EndAdr    : ADDRESS;
                    VAR CopyAdr   : ADDRESS);

    VAR
        SourcePtr    : ElementPtrType;
        LastCopyPtr  : ElementPtrType;
        NextCopyPtr  : ElementPtrType;

    BEGIN
        CopyElement(AnchorAdr,StartAdr,CopyAdr);
        SourcePtr := StartAdr;
        IF (CopyAdr           <> NIL)    &
           (StartAdr          <> EndAdr) &
           (SourcePtr^.Next <> NIL)      THEN
            LastCopyPtr := CopyAdr;
            LOOP
                CopyElement(AnchorAdr,SourcePtr^.Next,
                            NextCopyPtr);
                IF NextCopyPtr = NIL THEN
                    NextCopyPtr := CopyAdr;
                    WHILE NextCopyPtr <> NIL DO
                        NextCopyPtr := LastCopyPtr^.Prev;
                        RemoveElement(AnchorAdr,LastCopyPtr);
                        LastCopyPtr := NextCopyPtr;
                        END;
                    CopyAdr := NIL;
                    EXIT;
                    END;
                InsertAfter(NIL,NextCopyPtr,LastCopyPtr);
                LastCopyPtr := NextCopyPtr;
                SourcePtr   := SourcePtr^.Next;
                IF (SourcePtr = EndAdr) OR
                   (SourcePtr^.Next = NIL) THEN
                    EXIT;
                    END;
                END;
            END;
    END CopyList;


PROCEDURE CreateElement(    AnchorAdr : ADDRESS;
                        VAR NewAdr    : ADDRESS);
```

```
    VAR
        AnchorPtr : POINTER TO Anchor;
        NewPtr    : ElementPtrType;

    BEGIN
        AnchorPtr := AnchorAdr;
        NewAdr    := NIL;
        IF Available(AnchorPtr^.Size) THEN
            ALLOCATE(NewAdr,AnchorPtr^.Size);
            NewPtr       := NewAdr;
            NewPtr^.Prev := NIL;
            NewPtr^.Next := NIL;
            END;
    END CreateElement;


PROCEDURE CreateList(    ElementSize : CARDINAL;
                     VAR AnchorAdr   : ADDRESS);

    VAR
        AnchorPtr : POINTER TO Anchor;

    BEGIN
        CreateElement(MasterAnchorPtr,AnchorAdr);
        IF AnchorAdr <> NIL THEN
            AnchorPtr        := AnchorAdr;
            AnchorPtr^.Size := ElementSize;
            AnchorPtr^.Ptr  := NIL;
            InsertBefore(MasterAnchorPtr,AnchorAdr,NIL);
            END;
    END CreateList;


PROCEDURE InsertAfter(    AnchorAdr : ADDRESS;
                          SourceAdr : ADDRESS;
                          TargetAdr : ADDRESS);

    VAR
        AnchorPtr : POINTER TO Anchor;
        NextPtr   : ElementPtrType;
        SourcePtr : ElementPtrType;
        TargetPtr : ElementPtrType;

    BEGIN
        AnchorPtr  := AnchorAdr;
        SourcePtr := SourceAdr;
        TargetPtr := TargetAdr;
        IF TargetPtr = NIL THEN
            IF AnchorPtr^.Ptr = NIL THEN
                AnchorPtr^.Ptr     := SourceAdr;
                SourcePtr^.Prev := AnchorAdr;
            ELSE
```

```
                TargetPtr := AnchorPtr^.Ptr;
                WHILE TargetPtr^.Next <> NIL DO
                    TargetPtr := TargetPtr^.Next;
                    END;
                SourcePtr^.Prev := TargetPtr;
                TargetPtr^.Next := SourcePtr;
                SourcePtr^.Next := NIL;
                END;
        ELSE
            IF TargetPtr = AnchorAdr THEN
                IF AnchorPtr^.Ptr = NIL THEN
                    AnchorPtr^.Ptr    := SourcePtr;
                    SourcePtr^.Prev := AnchorAdr;
                ELSE
                    InsertBefore(AnchorAdr,SourcePtr,NIL);
                    END;
            ELSE
                IF TargetPtr^.Next = NIL THEN
                    TargetPtr^.Next := SourcePtr;
                    SourcePtr^.Prev := TargetPtr;
                ELSE
                    NextPtr            := TargetPtr^.Next;
                    TargetPtr^.Next := SourcePtr;
                    SourcePtr^.Prev := TargetPtr;
                    SourcePtr^.Next := NextPtr;
                    NextPtr^.Prev    := SourcePtr;
                    END;
                END;
            END;
    END InsertAfter;


PROCEDURE InsertBefore(     AnchorAdr : ADDRESS;
                           SourceAdr : ADDRESS;
                           TargetAdr : ADDRESS);

    VAR
        AnchorPtr : POINTER TO Anchor;
        PrevPtr   : ElementPtrType;
        SourcePtr : ElementPtrType;
        TargetPtr : ElementPtrType;

    BEGIN
        AnchorPtr := AnchorAdr;
        SourcePtr := SourceAdr;
        TargetPtr := TargetAdr;
        IF TargetPtr = NIL THEN
            IF AnchorPtr^.Ptr = NIL THEN
                AnchorPtr^.Ptr    := SourceAdr;
                SourcePtr^.Prev := AnchorAdr;
            ELSE
                TargetPtr            := AnchorPtr^.Ptr;
```

```
                    SourcePtr^.Prev := AnchorAdr;
                    SourcePtr^.Next := TargetPtr;
                    TargetPtr^.Prev := SourcePtr;
                    AnchorPtr^.Ptr  := SourcePtr;
                    END;
            ELSE
                IF TargetPtr = AnchorAdr THEN
                    InsertAfter(AnchorAdr,SourcePtr,NIL);
                ELSE
                    IF TargetPtr^.Prev = AnchorAdr THEN
                        AnchorPtr^.Ptr  := SourcePtr;
                        SourcePtr^.Prev := AnchorAdr;
                        SourcePtr^.Next := TargetPtr;
                        TargetPtr^.Prev := SourcePtr;
                    ELSE
                        PrevPtr            := TargetPtr^.Prev;
                        PrevPtr^.Next    := SourcePtr;
                        SourcePtr^.Prev := PrevPtr;
                        SourcePtr^.Next := TargetPtr;
                        TargetPtr^.Prev := SourcePtr;
                        END;
                    END;
                END;
        END InsertBefore;


PROCEDURE InsertList(      AnchorAdr : ADDRESS;
                          SourceAdr : ADDRESS;
                          TargetAdr : ADDRESS);

    VAR
        AnchorPtr : POINTER TO Anchor;
        LastPtr   : ElementPtrType;
        NextPtr   : ElementPtrType;
        SourcePtr : ElementPtrType;
        TargetPtr : ElementPtrType;

    BEGIN
        AnchorPtr := AnchorAdr;
        SourcePtr := SourceAdr;
        TargetPtr := TargetAdr;
        IF TargetPtr = NIL THEN
            IF AnchorPtr^.Ptr = NIL THEN
                AnchorPtr^.Ptr  := SourceAdr;
                SourcePtr^.Prev := AnchorAdr;
            ELSE
                TargetPtr := AnchorPtr^.Ptr;
                WHILE TargetPtr^.Next <> NIL DO
                    TargetPtr := TargetPtr^.Next;
                    END;
                SourcePtr^.Prev := TargetPtr;
                TargetPtr^.Next := SourcePtr;
```

```
                    END;
            ELSE
                LastPtr := SourcePtr;
                WHILE LastPtr^.Next <> NIL DO
                        LastPtr := LastPtr^.Next;
                END;
                IF TargetPtr = AnchorAdr THEN
                    IF AnchorPtr^.Ptr = NIL THEN
                        AnchorPtr^.Ptr   := SourcePtr;
                        SourcePtr^.Prev := AnchorAdr;
                    ELSE
                        NextPtr              := AnchorPtr^.Ptr;
                        LastPtr^.Next     := NextPtr;
                        SourcePtr^.Prev := TargetPtr;
                        AnchorPtr^.Ptr   := SourcePtr;
                        NextPtr^.Prev    := LastPtr;
                        END;
                ELSE
                    IF TargetPtr^.Next = NIL THEN
                        TargetPtr^.Next := SourcePtr;
                        SourcePtr^.Prev := TargetPtr;
                    ELSE
                        NextPtr              := TargetPtr^.Next;
                        TargetPtr^.Next := SourcePtr;
                        SourcePtr^.Prev := TargetPtr;
                        LastPtr^.Next     := NextPtr;
                        NextPtr^.Prev    := LastPtr;
                        END;
                    END;
                END;
        END InsertList;


    PROCEDURE RemoveElement(     AnchorAdr : ADDRESS;
                                 SourceAdr : ADDRESS);

        VAR
            AnchorPtr : POINTER TO Anchor;
            PrevPtr   : ElementPtrType;
            NextPtr   : ElementPtrType;
            SourcePtr : ElementPtrType;

        BEGIN
            AnchorPtr := AnchorAdr;
            SourcePtr := SourceAdr;
            PrevPtr   := SourcePtr^.Prev;
            NextPtr   := SourcePtr^.Next;
            IF NextPtr <> NIL THEN
                NextPtr^.Prev := PrevPtr;
                END;
            IF PrevPtr <> NIL THEN
                IF PrevPtr = AnchorAdr THEN
```

```
                AnchorPtr^.Ptr := NextPtr;
            ELSE
                PrevPtr^.Next := NextPtr;
                END;
            END;
        DEALLOCATE(SourceAdr,AnchorPtr^.Size);
    END RemoveElement;


PROCEDURE RemoveList(    AnchorAdr : ADDRESS);

    VAR
        AnchorPtr : POINTER TO Anchor;

    BEGIN
        AnchorPtr := AnchorAdr;
        WHILE AnchorPtr^.Ptr <> NIL DO
            RemoveElement(AnchorPtr,AnchorPtr^.Ptr);
            END;
        RemoveElement(MasterAnchorPtr,AnchorPtr);
    END RemoveList;


BEGIN
    MasterAnchorPtr        := ADR(MasterAnchor);
    MasterAnchorPtr^.Prev := ADR(MasterAnchorPtr);
    MasterAnchorPtr^.Next := NIL;
    MasterAnchorPtr^.Size := TSIZE(Anchor);
    MasterAnchorPtr^.Ptr   := NIL;
END ListHandler.
```

ListHelp Definition

DEFINITION MODULE ListHelp;

FROM ListHandler IMPORT Anchor;

FROM SYSTEM   IMPORT ADDRESS;

EXPORT QUALIFIED Display, DisplayAnchor,
                 DisplayElement, DisplayList;

PROCEDURE Display(MemAdr : ADDRESS;
                      Size   : CARDINAL);

PROCEDURE DisplayAnchor(AnchorAdr : ADDRESS);

PROCEDURE DisplayElement(ElementAdr : ADDRESS;
                             DataSize   : CARDINAL);
PROCEDURE DisplayList(AnchorAdr : ADDRESS;
                          DataSize : CARDINAL);

END ListHelp.

ListHelp Module

```
IMPLEMENTATION MODULE ListHelp;

(*

Function: This library contains a number of useful subroutines
        for the debugging of linked lists. They should be used
        with ListHandler routines. They will display an area of
        memory, a single element, or a complete list. All data
        is displayed in hex.

Routines:
        Display      - from a specified address, display 'n' words

        DisplayAnchor  - display anchor block

        DisplayElement - display individual element

        DisplayList    - using the above, display a whole list

*)

FROM InOut        IMPORT WriteString, WriteHex, WriteLn;
FROM ListHandler  IMPORT Anchor;
FROM SYSTEM       IMPORT ADDRESS,WORD,ADR;

TYPE
    SampleElement = RECORD
        Prev : ADDRESS;
        Next : ADDRESS;
        Data : CHAR;
        END;

PROCEDURE Display(    MemAdr : ADDRESS;
                      Size   : CARDINAL);

    BEGIN
        WHILE Size <> 0 DO
            WriteHex(CARDINAL(MemAdr^), 6);
            INC(MemAdr, 1);
            DEC(Size);
            END;
    END Display;

PROCEDURE DisplayAnchor(    AnchorAdr : ADDRESS);

    VAR
        AnchorPtr : POINTER TO Anchor;

    BEGIN
        AnchorPtr := AnchorAdr;
```

```
            WriteString("R is at:");
            Display(ADR(AnchorPtr),1);
            WriteString(" P:");
            Display(ADR(AnchorPtr^.Prev),1);
            WriteString(" N:");
            Display(ADR(AnchorPtr^.Next),1);
            WriteString(" S:");
            Display(ADR(AnchorPtr^.Size),1);
            WriteString(" E:");
            Display(ADR(AnchorPtr^.Ptr),1);
            WriteLn;
        END DisplayAnchor;

PROCEDURE DisplayElement(     ElementAdr : ADDRESS;
                              DataSize   : CARDINAL);

    VAR
        ElementPtr : POINTER TO SampleElement;

    BEGIN
        ElementPtr := ElementAdr;
        WriteString("E is at:");
        Display(ADR(ElementPtr),1);
        WriteString(" P:");
        Display(ADR(ElementPtr^.Prev),1);
        WriteString(" N:");
        Display(ADR(ElementPtr^.Next),1);
        WriteString(" D:");
        Display(ADR(ElementPtr^.Data),DataSize);
        WriteLn;
    END DisplayElement;

PROCEDURE DisplayList(     AnchorAdr : ADDRESS;
                           DataSize  : CARDINAL);

    VAR
        AnchorPtr  : POINTER TO Anchor;
        ElementPtr : POINTER TO Anchor;

    BEGIN
        WriteString("List:");
        WriteLn;
        AnchorPtr := AnchorAdr;
        DisplayAnchor(AnchorPtr);
        IF AnchorPtr^.Ptr <> NIL THEN
            ElementPtr := AnchorPtr^.Ptr;
            REPEAT
                DisplayElement(ElementPtr,DataSize);
                ElementPtr := ElementPtr^.Next;
                UNTIL ElementPtr = NIL;
            END;
    END DisplayList;
```

```
BEGIN
END ListHelp.
```

TreeHandler Definition

```
DEFINITION MODULE TreeHandler;


FROM SYSTEM       IMPORT ADDRESS;

FROM ListHandler IMPORT Anchor;

EXPORT QUALIFIED Node, NodeWithKey, Family, AddLeaf, CopyNode,
                 CopyTree, CreateNode, CreateTree, FindNode,
                 LocateParent, LocateRtn, PrintTreeIn,
                 PrintTreePre, RemoveLeaf, RemoveNode,
                 FindRtn, PrintTreePost, RemoveRtn,
                 RemoveTree, SearchAndDestroyNode;

TYPE
    Node = RECORD
        Left    : ADDRESS;
        Right   : ADDRESS;
        END;

    NodeWithKey = RECORD
        Left    : ADDRESS;
        Right   : ADDRESS;
        Key     : CARDINAL;
        END;

    Family = (LeftChild,RightChild,Parent,Ancestor,Orphan);


PROCEDURE AddLeaf(      SourceAdr : ADDRESS;
                       TargetAdr : ADDRESS;
                       NodeCode  : Family);


PROCEDURE CopyNode(      AnchorAdr : ADDRESS;
                        SourceAdr : ADDRESS;
                   VAR CopyAdr    : ADDRESS);


PROCEDURE CopyTree(      AnchorAdr : ADDRESS;
                        StartAdr  : ADDRESS;
                   VAR CopyAdr    : ADDRESS);


PROCEDURE CreateNode(    AnchorAdr : ADDRESS;
                    VAR NewAdr    : ADDRESS);


PROCEDURE CreateTree(    NodeSize  : CARDINAL;
                    VAR AnchorAdr : ADDRESS);
```

```
PROCEDURE FindNode(     AnchorAdr : ADDRESS;
                        SearchKey : CARDINAL;
                    VAR ReturnAdr : ADDRESS;
                    VAR NodeCode  : Family);


PROCEDURE FindRtn(     NodeAdr    : ADDRESS;
                       TestKey    : CARDINAL;
                   VAR ReturnAdr  : ADDRESS;
                   VAR NodeCode   : Family);


PROCEDURE LocateParent(     AnchorAdr : ADDRESS;
                            SearchKey : CARDINAL;
                        VAR ReturnAdr : ADDRESS;
                        VAR NodeCode  : Family);


PROCEDURE LocateRtn(     NodeAdr    : ADDRESS;
                         TestKey    : CARDINAL;
                     VAR ReturnAdr  : ADDRESS;
                     VAR NodeCode   : Family);


PROCEDURE PrintTreeIn(     AnchorAdr : ADDRESS;
                           SourceAdr : ADDRESS);


PROCEDURE PrintTreePost(     AnchorAdr: ADDRESS;
                             SourceAdr: ADDRESS);


PROCEDURE PrintTreePre(     AnchorAdr : ADDRESS;
                            SourceAdr : ADDRESS);


PROCEDURE RemoveLeaf(     AnchorAdr : ADDRESS;
                          SourceAdr : ADDRESS;
                          NodeCode  : Family);


PROCEDURE RemoveNode(     AnchorAdr : ADDRESS;
                          TargetAdr : ADDRESS;
                      VAR NewAdr     : ADDRESS);


PROCEDURE RemoveRtn(     AnchorAdr : ADDRESS;
                         SourceAdr : ADDRESS);
```

```
PROCEDURE RemoveTree(      AnchorAdr : ADDRESS;
                           SourceAdr : ADDRESS);


PROCEDURE SearchAndDestroyNode(      AnchorAdr : ADDRESS;
                                     TestKey   : CARDINAL)
                         : BOOLEAN;

END TreeHandler.
```

TreeHandler Module

IMPLEMENTATION MODULE TreeHandler;

(*

Function: The intention of this library is to provide a number
   of standard routines that perform the normal work of
   creating trees and manipulating their nodes.

Data Structures:

   All of the routines are independent of additional data
   following the key. The Find and Print routines supplied
   assume that the key is cardinal. The nodes are assumed
   to have the following form:

```
    --------------------------
   | <-- Ptr to left          |
   |--------------------------|
   |      Ptr to right   -->  |
   |--------------------------|
   |      Node Key            |
   |--------------------------|
   |      any other data      |
   |              .           |
   |              .           |
   |              .           |
    --------------------------
```

   The trees are maintained via a list of anchor
   elements that contain the maximum size of a node
   and a pointer to the root of the tree.

Routines:

   AddLeaf   - given the floating node ptr, a target,
                    and the node code, add node to tree.

   CopyNode   - given an anchor ptr and a node pointer,
                    create a duplicate of the node and
                    return the new pointer - a pointer of NIL
                    indicates failure.

   CopyTree   - given an anchor ptr and a node pointer, copy
                    all the nodes in the tree formed by the node.
                    A standalone tree is created and is pointed
                    to by the return pointer. If insufficient
                    memory exists, all temporary nodes will
                    be removed and a pointer value of NIL will
                    be returned.

CreateNode   - given an anchor ptr, create a node
                and return the pointer. A pointer of NIL
                indicates a failure.

CreateTree   - given the maximum node size, allocate
                a tree and return the anchor ptr. A
                pointer of NIL indicates failure.

FindNode   - given an anchor ptr, Key compare procedure,
                and a key, the tree will be searched with the
                ptr indicating the matching node or where the
                node should go, node code indicates where the
                value should go if it is not the parent.

FindRtn   - recursive routine for FindNode.

LocateParent   - for a specified key, find the parent of
                the node that matches the key.

LocateRtn   - recursive routine for LocateParent.

PrintTreeIn   - given an anchor ptr and a node ptr, print
                the tree starting at the node in in-fix
                order. A node ptr = to the anchor pointer
                will print the whole tree.

PrintTreePost   - given an anchor ptr and a node ptr, print
                the tree starting at the node in post-fix
                order. A node ptr = to the anchor pointer
                will print the whole tree.

PrintTreePre   - given an anchor ptr and a node ptr, print
                the tree starting at the node in pre-fix
                order. A node ptr = to the anchor pointer
                will print the whole tree.

RemoveLeaf   - given an anchor ptr, a node ptr, and a node
                code, remove the leaf or ancestor - removing
                the ancestor removes the list.

RemoveNode   - given an anchor and address of node to remove
                the tree is shuffled and the appropriate node
                address is returned.

RemoveRtn   - traversing the tree, nodes are nipped off
                and the space deallocated (recursive).

RemoveTree   - first all nodes are removed; then the anchor
                is deallocated (if source = anchor) else just
                the tree pointed to is removed. If source =
                nil, this is same as source = anchor (uses
                RemoveRtn, RemoveLeaf).

```
        SearchAndDestroyNode - precisely as it says, give it a key
                      and the node matching the key will be
                      destroyed. The tree will be re-shuffled.

*)

FROM InOut        IMPORT WriteCard;

FROM SYSTEM       IMPORT ADDRESS;

FROM Storage      IMPORT ALLOCATE, DEALLOCATE, Available;

FROM ListHandler IMPORT CreateList, RemoveList, Anchor;

TYPE
    NodePtr = POINTER TO Node;

    NodeWithKeyPtrType = POINTER TO NodeWithKey;


PROCEDURE AddLeaf(     SourceAdr : ADDRESS;
                       TargetAdr : ADDRESS;
                       NodeCode  : Family);

    VAR
        TargetPtr : NodePtr;
        AnchorPtr : POINTER TO Anchor;

    BEGIN
        TargetPtr := TargetAdr;
        IF NodeCode = Ancestor THEN
            AnchorPtr := TargetAdr;
            AnchorPtr^.Ptr := SourceAdr;
        ELSIF NodeCode = RightChild THEN
            TargetPtr^.Right := SourceAdr;
        ELSE
            TargetPtr^.Left := SourceAdr;
            END;
    END AddLeaf;


PROCEDURE CopyNode(     AnchorAdr : ADDRESS;
                        SourceAdr : ADDRESS;
                    VAR CopyAdr    : ADDRESS);

    VAR
        AnchorPtr : POINTER TO Anchor;
        CopyPtr   : NodePtr;
        EndAdr    : ADDRESS;
        TempCard  : CARDINAL;
```

```
    BEGIN
        CreateNode(AnchorAdr,CopyAdr);
        IF CopyAdr <> NIL THEN
            AnchorPtr := AnchorAdr;
            CopyPtr   := CopyAdr;
            TempCard  := AnchorPtr^.Size;
            EndAdr    := CopyAdr;
            INC(EndAdr,TempCard);
            REPEAT
                CopyAdr^  := SourceAdr^;
                INC(CopyAdr,1);
                INC(SourceAdr,1);
                UNTIL CopyAdr = EndAdr;
            CopyPtr^.Left  := NIL;
            CopyPtr^.Right := NIL;
            CopyAdr        := CopyPtr;
            END;
    END CopyNode;


    PROCEDURE CopyTree(     AnchorAdr : ADDRESS;
                            StartAdr  : ADDRESS;
                        VAR CopyAdr   : ADDRESS);

    VAR
        SourcePtr    : NodePtr;
        CopyPtr      : NodePtr;
        RightCopyPtr : NodePtr;
        LeftCopyPtr  : NodePtr;

    BEGIN
        LeftCopyPtr  := NIL;
        RightCopyPtr := NIL;
        SourcePtr    := StartAdr;
        LOOP
            IF SourcePtr^.Left <> NIL THEN
                CopyTree(AnchorAdr,SourcePtr^.Left,LeftCopyPtr);
                IF LeftCopyPtr = NIL THEN
                    EXIT;
                    END;
                END;
            IF SourcePtr^.Right <> NIL THEN
                CopyTree(AnchorAdr,SourcePtr^.Right,
                        RightCopyPtr);
                IF RightCopyPtr = NIL THEN
                    IF SourcePtr^.Left <> NIL THEN
                        RemoveTree(AnchorAdr,LeftCopyPtr);
                        EXIT;
                        END;
                    END;
                END;
            CopyNode(AnchorAdr,StartAdr,CopyAdr);
```

```
                IF CopyAdr = NIL THEN
                    IF LeftCopyPtr <> NIL THEN
                        RemoveTree(AnchorAdr,LeftCopyPtr);
                        END;
                    IF RightCopyPtr <> NIL THEN
                        RemoveTree(AnchorAdr,RightCopyPtr);
                        END;
                    EXIT;
                    END;
                CopyPtr          := CopyAdr;
                CopyPtr^.Left    := LeftCopyPtr;
                CopyPtr^.Right   := RightCopyPtr;
                EXIT;
                END;
        END CopyTree;


PROCEDURE CreateNode(     AnchorAdr : ADDRESS;
                      VAR NewAdr    : ADDRESS);

    VAR
        AnchorPtr : POINTER TO Anchor;
        NewPtr    : NodePtr;

    BEGIN
        AnchorPtr := AnchorAdr;
        NewAdr    := NIL;
        IF Available(AnchorPtr^.Size) THEN
            ALLOCATE(NewAdr,AnchorPtr^.Size);
            NewPtr          := NewAdr;
            NewPtr^.Left  := NIL;
            NewPtr^.Right := NIL;
            END;
        END CreateNode;


PROCEDURE CreateTree(     NodeSize  : CARDINAL;
                      VAR AnchorAdr : ADDRESS);

    VAR
        AnchorPtr : POINTER TO Anchor;

    BEGIN
        CreateList(NodeSize,AnchorAdr);
        END CreateTree;


PROCEDURE FindNode(     AnchorAdr : ADDRESS;
                        SearchKey : CARDINAL;
                    VAR ReturnAdr : ADDRESS;
                    VAR NodeCode  : Family);
```

```
    VAR
        AnchorPtr  : POINTER TO Anchor;

    BEGIN
        AnchorPtr := AnchorAdr;
        IF AnchorPtr^.Ptr = NIL THEN
            ReturnAdr := AnchorPtr;
            NodeCode  := Ancestor;
        ELSE
            FindRtn(AnchorPtr^.Ptr,SearchKey,ReturnAdr,
                    NodeCode);
            END;
    END FindNode;


PROCEDURE FindRtn(     NodeAdr    : ADDRESS;
                       TestKey    : CARDINAL;
                   VAR ReturnAdr : ADDRESS;
                   VAR NodeCode  : Family);

    VAR
        NodePtr : NodeWithKeyPtrType;

    BEGIN
        NodePtr   := NodeAdr;
        NodeCode  := Parent;
        ReturnAdr := NodeAdr;
        IF NodePtr^.Key > TestKey THEN
            IF NodePtr^.Left = NIL THEN
                NodeCode := LeftChild;
            ELSE
                FindRtn(NodePtr^.Left,TestKey,ReturnAdr,
                        NodeCode);
                END;
        ELSIF NodePtr^.Key < TestKey THEN
            IF NodePtr^.Right = NIL THEN
                NodeCode := RightChild;
            ELSE
                FindRtn(NodePtr^.Right,TestKey,ReturnAdr,
                        NodeCode);
                END;
            END;
    END FindRtn;


PROCEDURE LocateParent(     AnchorAdr : ADDRESS;
                            SearchKey : CARDINAL;
                        VAR ReturnAdr : ADDRESS;
                        VAR NodeCode  : Family);

    VAR
        AnchorPtr  : POINTER TO Anchor;
```

```
    BEGIN
        AnchorPtr := AnchorAdr;
        IF AnchorPtr^.Ptr = NIL THEN
            ReturnAdr := NIL;
            NodeCode  := Orphan;
        ELSE
            LocateRtn(AnchorPtr^.Ptr,SearchKey,ReturnAdr,
                    NodeCode);
        END;
    END LocateParent;


PROCEDURE LocateRtn(     NodeAdr    : ADDRESS;
                         TestKey    : CARDINAL;
                     VAR ReturnAdr  : ADDRESS;
                     VAR NodeCode   : Family);

    VAR
        NodePtr : NodeWithKeyPtrType;

    BEGIN
        NodePtr   := NodeAdr;
        ReturnAdr := NIL;
        IF NodePtr^.Key = TestKey THEN
            NodeCode  := Ancestor;
            ReturnAdr := NIL;
        ELSIF NodePtr^.Key > TestKey THEN
            IF NodePtr^.Left = NIL THEN
                NodeCode := Orphan;
            ELSE
                LocateRtn(NodePtr^.Left,TestKey,ReturnAdr,
                        NodeCode);
                IF (NodeCode = Ancestor) & (ReturnAdr = NIL)
                    THEN
                    NodeCode  := LeftChild;
                    ReturnAdr := NodePtr;
                    END;
            END;
        ELSIF NodePtr^.Key < TestKey THEN
            IF NodePtr^.Right = NIL THEN
                NodeCode := Orphan;
            ELSE
                LocateRtn(NodePtr^.Right,TestKey,ReturnAdr,
                        NodeCode);
                IF (NodeCode = Ancestor) & (ReturnAdr = NIL)
                    THEN
                    NodeCode  := RightChild;
                    ReturnAdr := NodePtr;
                    END;
            END;
        END;
```

```
        VAR
            AnchorPtr : POINTER TO Anchor;
            SourcePtr : NodeWithKeyPtrType;

        BEGIN
            IF AnchorAdr = SourceAdr THEN
                AnchorPtr := AnchorAdr;
                SourcePtr := AnchorPtr^.Ptr;
            ELSE
                SourcePtr := SourceAdr;
                END;
            IF SourcePtr <> NIL THEN
                PrintTreeIn(AnchorAdr,SourcePtr^.Left);
                WriteCard(SourcePtr^.Key,6);
                PrintTreeIn(AnchorAdr,SourcePtr^.Right);
                END;
            END PrintTreeIn;


    PROCEDURE PrintTreePost(    AnchorAdr: ADDRESS;
                                SourceAdr: ADDRESS);

        VAR
            AnchorPtr : POINTER TO Anchor;
            SourcePtr : NodeWithKeyPtrType;

        BEGIN
            IF AnchorAdr = SourceAdr THEN
                AnchorPtr := AnchorAdr;
                SourcePtr := AnchorPtr^.Ptr;
            ELSE
                SourcePtr := SourceAdr;
                END;
            IF SourcePtr <> NIL THEN
                PrintTreePost(AnchorAdr,SourcePtr^.Left);
                PrintTreePost(AnchorAdr,SourcePtr^.Right);
                WriteCard(SourcePtr^.Key,6);
                END;
            END PrintTreePost;


    PROCEDURE PrintTreePre(    AnchorAdr : ADDRESS;
                               SourceAdr : ADDRESS);

        VAR
            AnchorPtr : POINTER TO Anchor;
        END LocateRtn;


    PROCEDURE PrintTreeIn(    AnchorAdr : ADDRESS;
                              S
```

```
            SourcePtr : NodeWithKeyPtrType;

        BEGIN
            IF AnchorAdr = SourceAdr THEN
                AnchorPtr := AnchorAdr;
                SourcePtr := AnchorPtr^.Ptr;
            ELSE
                SourcePtr := SourceAdr;
                END;
            IF SourcePtr <> NIL THEN
                WriteCard(SourcePtr^.Key,6);
                PrintTreePre(AnchorAdr,SourcePtr^.Left);
                PrintTreePre(AnchorAdr,SourcePtr^.Right);
                END;
            END PrintTreePre;


PROCEDURE RemoveLeaf(    AnchorAdr : ADDRESS;
                        SourceAdr : ADDRESS;
                        NodeCode  : Family);

    VAR
        AnchorPtr : POINTER TO Anchor;
        SourcePtr : NodePtr;

    BEGIN
        AnchorPtr := AnchorAdr;
        SourcePtr := SourceAdr;
        IF NodeCode = Ancestor THEN
            IF AnchorPtr^.Ptr <> NIL THEN
                RemoveRtn(AnchorAdr,AnchorPtr^.Ptr);
                AnchorPtr^.Ptr := NIL;
                END;
            RemoveList(AnchorPtr);
        ELSE
            IF NodeCode = Parent THEN
                DEALLOCATE(SourcePtr,AnchorPtr^.Size);
            ELSIF NodeCode = LeftChild THEN
                DEALLOCATE(SourcePtr^.Left,AnchorPtr^.Size);
                SourcePtr^.Left := NIL;
            ELSE
                DEALLOCATE(SourcePtr^.Right,AnchorPtr^.Size);
                SourcePtr^.Right := NIL;
                END;
            END;
        END RemoveLeaf;


PROCEDURE RemoveNode(    AnchorAdr : ADDRESS;
                        TargetAdr : ADDRESS;
                    VAR NewAdr    : ADDRESS);
```

```
    VAR
        TargetPtr : NodePtr;
        NewPtr    : NodePtr;
        TempPtr   : NodePtr;

    BEGIN
        TargetPtr := TargetAdr;
        IF (TargetPtr^.Right = NIL) & (TargetPtr^.Left = NIL)
            THEN
            NewAdr := NIL;
        ELSIF TargetPtr^.Right = NIL THEN
            NewAdr := TargetPtr^.Left;
        ELSIF TargetPtr^.Left = NIL THEN
            NewAdr := TargetPtr^.Right;
        ELSE
            TempPtr := TargetPtr^.Left;
            WHILE TempPtr^.Right <> NIL DO
                TempPtr := TempPtr^.Right;
                END;
            TempPtr^.Right := TargetPtr^.Right;
            NewAdr          := TargetPtr^.Left;
            END;
        RemoveLeaf(AnchorAdr,TargetAdr,Parent);
    END RemoveNode;


PROCEDURE RemoveRtn(     AnchorAdr : ADDRESS;
                         SourceAdr : ADDRESS);

    VAR
        SourcePtr : NodePtr;

    BEGIN
        SourcePtr := SourceAdr;
        IF SourcePtr^.Left <> NIL THEN
            RemoveRtn(AnchorAdr,SourcePtr^.Left);
            END;
        IF SourcePtr^.Right <> NIL THEN
            RemoveRtn(AnchorAdr,SourcePtr^.Right);
            END;
        RemoveLeaf(AnchorAdr,SourcePtr,Parent);
    END RemoveRtn;


PROCEDURE RemoveTree(     AnchorAdr : ADDRESS;
                          SourceAdr : ADDRESS);

    VAR
        AnchorPtr : POINTER TO Anchor;

    BEGIN
        IF (AnchorAdr = SourceAdr) OR
```

```
                    (SourceAdr = NIL) THEN
                       RemoveLeaf(AnchorAdr,SourceAdr,Ancestor);
                 ELSE
                       RemoveRtn(AnchorAdr,SourceAdr);
                 END;
            END RemoveTree;


PROCEDURE SearchAndDestroyNode(       AnchorAdr : ADDRESS;
                                      TestKey   : CARDINAL)
                               : BOOLEAN;

    VAR
        AnchorPtr  : POINTER TO Anchor;
        NewPtr     : NodePtr;
        ParentPtr  : NodePtr;
        NodeCode   : Family;
        ReturnCode : BOOLEAN;

    BEGIN
        ReturnCode := TRUE;
        LocateParent(AnchorAdr,TestKey,ParentPtr,NodeCode);
        IF NodeCode = Orphan THEN
            ReturnCode := FALSE;
        ELSIF NodeCode = Ancestor THEN
            AnchorPtr := AnchorAdr;
            RemoveNode(AnchorAdr,AnchorPtr^.Ptr,NewPtr);
            AnchorPtr^.Ptr := NewPtr;
        ELSIF NodeCode = RightChild THEN
            RemoveNode(AnchorAdr,ParentPtr^.Right,NewPtr);
            ParentPtr^.Right := NewPtr;
        ELSIF NodeCode = LeftChild THEN
            RemoveNode(AnchorAdr,ParentPtr^.Left,NewPtr);
            ParentPtr^.Left := NewPtr;
            END;
        RETURN ReturnCode;
    END SearchAndDestroyNode;

BEGIN
END TreeHandler.
```

TreeHandler Example

```
MODULE TreeTest;

FROM TreeHandler IMPORT CreateTree, CreateNode, NodeWithKey,
                        PrintTreePost,PrintTreePre, PrintTreeIn,
                        RemoveTree, AddLeaf, Family, FindNode;

FROM InOut          IMPORT WriteLn, WriteString;

FROM SYSTEM         IMPORT TSIZE, ADDRESS;

VAR
    MyTree    : ADDRESS;
    NodePtr   : POINTER TO NodeWithKey;
    ParentPtr : POINTER TO NodeWithKey;
    NodeCode  : Family;

PROCEDURE BuildTree(    Key : CARDINAL);

    BEGIN
        CreateNode(MyTree,NodePtr);
        NodePtr^.Key := Key;
        FindNode(MyTree,NodePtr^.Key,ParentPtr,NodeCode);
        AddLeaf(NodePtr,ParentPtr,NodeCode);
    END BuildTree;

BEGIN
    CreateTree(TSIZE(NodeWithKey),MyTree);
    BuildTree(6);
    BuildTree(2);
    BuildTree(22);
    BuildTree(3);
    BuildTree(9);
    BuildTree(7);
    BuildTree(8);
    BuildTree(5);
    BuildTree(4);
    BuildTree(1);
    WriteString("Build:    6,2,22,3,9,7,8,5,4,1");
    WriteLn;
    WriteString("In-Fix:   ");
    PrintTreeIn(MyTree,MyTree);
    WriteLn;
    WriteString("Pre-Fix:  ");
    PrintTreePre(MyTree,MyTree);
    WriteLn;
    WriteString("Post-Fix: ");
    PrintTreePost(MyTree,MyTree);
    RemoveTree(MyTree,MyTree);
END TreeTest.
```

D.5   Coroutines - Processes

```
IMPLEMENTATION MODULE Processes;

(* This module corresponds to the standard suggested by N. Wirth
   and is closely followed by the various implementations.
   We have retained the original naming and logic wherever
   possible.
*)

FROM SYSTEM  IMPORT ADDRESS,PROCESS,NEWPROCESS,TRANSFER,TSIZE;

FROM Storage IMPORT ALLOCATE;

TYPE
    SIGNAL = POINTER TO ProcessDescriptor;

    ProcessDescriptor = RECORD
        NextSignal   : SIGNAL; (* ring *)
        WaitingQueue : SIGNAL; (* Queue of waiting processes *)
        Coroutine    : PROCESS;
        ReadyState   : BOOLEAN;
        END;

VAR
    CallingProcess : SIGNAL;   (* current process *)


PROCEDURE StartProcess(    P     : PROC;
                           WsSize : CARDINAL);

    VAR PrevProcess : SIGNAL;
        WsAdr       : ADDRESS;(* work space address *)

    BEGIN
        PrevProcess := CallingProcess;
        ALLOCATE(WsAdr,WsSize);
        ALLOCATE(CallingProcess,TSIZE(ProcessDescriptor));
        WITH CallingProcess^ DO
            NextSignal                 := PrevProcess^.NextSignal;
            PrevProcess^.NextSignal := CallingProcess;
            ReadyState                 := TRUE;
            WaitingQueue               := NIL;
            END;
        NEWPROCESS(P,WsAdr,WsSize,CallingProcess^.Coroutine);
        TRANSFER(PrevProcess^.Coroutine,
                 CallingProcess^.Coroutine);
    END StartProcess;

PROCEDURE SEND (VAR SentSignal : SIGNAL);

    VAR
```

```
            SendingProcess: SIGNAL;

    BEGIN
        IF SentSignal <> NIL THEN
            SendingProcess := CallingProcess;
            CallingProcess := SentSignal;
            WITH CallingProcess^ DO
                SentSignal    := WaitingQueue;
                ReadyState    := TRUE;
                WaitingQueue  := NIL;
                END;
            TRANSFER(SendingProcess^.Coroutine,
                    CallingProcess^.Coroutine);
            END;
    END SEND;

PROCEDURE WAIT(VAR WaitedForSignal : SIGNAL);

    VAR
        ThisSignal : SIGNAL;
        NextSignal : SIGNAL;

    BEGIN (* insert CallingProcess in WaitingQueue for signal *)
        IF WaitedForSignal = NIL THEN
            WaitedForSignal := CallingProcess;
        ELSE
            ThisSignal := WaitedForSignal;
            NextSignal := ThisSignal^.WaitingQueue;
            WHILE NextSignal <> NIL DO
                ThisSignal := NextSignal;
                NextSignal := ThisSignal^.WaitingQueue;
                END;
            ThisSignal^.WaitingQueue := CallingProcess;
            END;
        ThisSignal := CallingProcess;
        REPEAT
            CallingProcess := CallingProcess^.NextSignal
            UNTIL CallingProcess^.ReadyState;
        IF CallingProcess = ThisSignal THEN
            (* deadlock *)
            HALT;
            END;
        ThisSignal^.ReadyState := FALSE;
        TRANSFER(ThisSignal^.Coroutine,
                CallingProcess^.Coroutine);
    END WAIT;


PROCEDURE Awaited(    SignalToCheck : SIGNAL) : BOOLEAN;

    BEGIN
        RETURN (SignalToCheck <> NIL);
```

```
    END Awaited;


PROCEDURE Init(VAR SignalToInit : SIGNAL);

    BEGIN
        SignalToInit := NIL;
    END Init;


BEGIN
    ALLOCATE(CallingProcess,TSIZE(ProcessDescriptor));
    WITH CallingProcess^ DO
        NextSignal   := CallingProcess;
        ReadyState   := TRUE;
        WaitingQueue := NIL;
        END;
END Processes.
```

D.6   Direct Access Input and Output – DirectIO

```
MODULE DirectIO;
```

(* This module illustrates the basic capabilities of direct-
access input and output using the Logitech version. The
main logic is:

- prompt for the name of the direct access file to create
- prompt for the initial records from the screen
- build the direct access file
- reset the file
- print the file in sequential order
- update a record
- print the file again

In this example, the key is equivalent to the record number.

Many of the subroutines have been implemented in a generic
fashion and can be easily used in other programs.
The Logitech calls use two cardinal values to position the
direct access file. The high value is used to index past
MaxCard and is interpreted as high*MaxCard. The IO routines
have been implemented as BOOLEAN procedures to simplify error
handling.

The following subroutines are provided:

    CalcPos   - given a record number and size,
                           return the high and low values
                           for direct access.

    CreateFile   - given a file and a number of
                           records, obtain input and fill the
                           file.

    DisplayRecord   - given a key/record number, obtain
                           the record from the file and display
                           it on the screen.

    DisplayAllRecords - display file.

    InputFields   - given a record number, prompt the
                           user via the crt for the record
                           contents.

    ReadRecord   - given a file, record number, record
                           size, and buffer address; locate the
                           record in the file and place the
                           record contents in the buffer.

    SetUpFile   - given an empty file, the

```
                         user is prompted for the file
                         identifier and the file is then opened.

    WriteRecord          - given a file, record number, record
                         size, and buffer address; locate the
                         record in the file and place the
                         buffer contents in the record.

*)

FROM FileSystem IMPORT Lookup, Close, ReadChar, ReadNBytes,
                       WriteNBytes, SetRead, SetWrite,
                       SetModify, SetOpen, Reset, SetPos,
                       GetPos, Length,
                       WriteChar, File, Response;

FROM FileNames  IMPORT ReadFileName, FNParts, FNPartSet;

FROM InOut      IMPORT Write, WriteString, WriteLn,
                       WriteInt, ReadInt, WriteCard, ReadCard,
                       ReadString;

FROM Terminal   IMPORT Read;

FROM SYSTEM     IMPORT WORD, TSIZE, ADR, ADDRESS, SIZE;

TYPE
    SampleRecord = RECORD
        Key    : INTEGER;
        Name   : ARRAY [0..11] OF CHAR;
        Amount : CARDINAL;
        Date   : CARDINAL;
        END;

VAR
    Buffer            : SampleRecord; (* input-output area *)
    DirectFile        : File;         (* the data file     *)
    RecSize           : CARDINAL;     (* length of a rec   *)
    RecNumber         : CARDINAL;     (* reference number  *)
    RecPtr            : ADDRESS;      (* location of a rec *)
    RecCount          : CARDINAL;     (* records/file      *)

PROCEDURE CalcPos(     RecordNumber : CARDINAL;
                       RecordSize   : CARDINAL;
                   VAR High         : CARDINAL;
                   VAR Low          : CARDINAL);

    CONST
        MaxCard = 65535;

    VAR
        RecPerChunk : CARDINAL;
```

```
    BEGIN
        RecPerChunk := MaxCard DIV RecordSize;
        High := RecordNumber DIV RecPerChunk;
        Low  := ((RecordNumber MOD RecPerChunk) - 1)
                * RecordSize;
    END CalcPos;

PROCEDURE CreateFile(VAR DataFile    : File;
                         NumOfRecords : CARDINAL) : BOOLEAN;

    VAR
        LocalIndex    : CARDINAL;
        NBytes        : CARDINAL;
        RecordNumber  : CARDINAL;
        RecordSize    : CARDINAL;
        RecordAdr     : ADDRESS;
        ReturnCode    : BOOLEAN;

    BEGIN
        ReturnCode := FALSE;
        LOOP
            FOR LocalIndex := 1 TO NumOfRecords DO
                InputFields(LocalIndex,RecordSize,RecordAdr);
                IF NOT WriteRecord(
                        DataFile,LocalIndex,RecordSize,RecordAdr)
                    THEN EXIT;
                    END;
                END;
            ReturnCode := TRUE;
            EXIT;
            END;
        RETURN ReturnCode;
    END CreateFile;

PROCEDURE DisplayRecord(    RecordNumber : CARDINAL) : BOOLEAN;

    VAR
        ReturnCode : BOOLEAN;

    BEGIN
        ReturnCode := FALSE;
        IF ReadRecord(DirectFile,RecordNumber,SIZE(Buffer),
            ADR(Buffer)) THEN
            WITH Buffer DO
                WriteInt(Key,8);
                Write(" ");
                WriteString(Name);
                WriteCard(Amount,8);
                WriteCard(Date,8);
                END;
            WriteLn;
```

```
            ReturnCode := TRUE;
            END;
        RETURN ReturnCode;
    END DisplayRecord;

PROCEDURE DisplayAllRecords () : BOOLEAN;

    VAR
        ReturnCode : BOOLEAN;
        LocalIndex : CARDINAL;

    BEGIN
        ReturnCode := TRUE;
        FOR LocalIndex := 1 TO RecCount DO
            IF NOT DisplayRecord(LocalIndex) THEN
                ReturnCode := FALSE;
                END;
            END;
        RETURN ReturnCode;
    END DisplayAllRecords;

PROCEDURE InputFields(    RecordNumber : CARDINAL;
                     VAR RecordSize   : CARDINAL;
                     VAR RecordPtr    : ADDRESS);

    BEGIN
        WriteString("Name(CHAR) Amount(CARD) Date(CARD): ");
        WITH Buffer DO
            Key := RecordNumber;
            RecordNumber := Key;
            ReadString(Name);
            Write(" ");
            ReadCard(Amount);
            Write(" ");
            ReadCard(Date);
            END;
        WriteLn;
        RecordPtr  := ADR(Buffer);
        RecordSize := SIZE(Buffer);
    END InputFields;

PROCEDURE ReadRecord(VAR DataFile     : File;
                         RecordNumber  : CARDINAL;
                         RecordSize    : CARDINAL;
                         BufferAddress : ADDRESS) : BOOLEAN;

    VAR
        High       : CARDINAL;
        Low        : CARDINAL;
        NBytes     : CARDINAL;
        ReturnCode : BOOLEAN;
```

```
    BEGIN
        ReturnCode := FALSE;
        LOOP
            SetRead(DataFile);
            IF DataFile.res <> done THEN EXIT END;
            CalcPos(RecordNumber,RecordSize,High,Low);
            SetPos(DataFile,High,Low);
            IF DataFile.res <> done THEN EXIT END;
            ReadNBytes(DataFile,BufferAddress,
                        RecordSize,NBytes);
            IF DataFile.res <> done THEN EXIT END;
            ReturnCode := TRUE;
            EXIT;
            END;
        RETURN ReturnCode;
    END ReadRecord;

PROCEDURE SetUpFile(VAR DataFile : File) : BOOLEAN;

    VAR
        ReturnCode  : BOOLEAN;
        InputChar   : CHAR;
        FileId      : ARRAY[0..14] OF CHAR;
        FileIdParts : FNPartSet;

    BEGIN
        LOOP
            ReturnCode := FALSE;
            WriteString("Enter file identifier: ");
            ReadFileName(FileId,"",FileIdParts);
            Read(InputChar);   (* logitech peculiarity *)
            WriteLn;
            Lookup(DataFile,FileId,FALSE);
            IF DataFile.res = done THEN
                WriteString("Target file already exists");
                WriteLn;
                Close(DataFile);
                EXIT;
                END;
            Lookup(DataFile,FileId,TRUE);
            IF DataFile.res = notdone THEN
                WriteString("Target file cannot be opened");
                WriteLn;
                EXIT;
                END;
            ReturnCode := TRUE;
            EXIT;
            END;
        RETURN ReturnCode;
    END SetUpFile;

PROCEDURE WriteRecord(VAR DataFile      : File;
```

```
                          RecordNumber  : CARDINAL;
                          RecordSize    : CARDINAL;
                          BufferAddress : ADDRESS) : BOOLEAN;

    VAR
        High       : CARDINAL;
        Low        : CARDINAL;
        NBytes     : CARDINAL;
        ReturnCode : BOOLEAN;

    BEGIN
        ReturnCode := FALSE;
        LOOP
            SetWrite(DataFile);
            IF DataFile.res <> done THEN EXIT END;
            CalcPos(RecordNumber,RecordSize,High,Low);
            SetPos(DataFile,High,Low);
            IF DataFile.res <> done THEN EXIT END;
            WriteNBytes(DataFile,BufferAddress,
                        RecordSize,NBytes);
            IF DataFile.res <> done THEN EXIT END;
            ReturnCode := TRUE;
            EXIT;
            END;
        RETURN ReturnCode;
    END WriteRecord;

BEGIN
    LOOP
        IF NOT SetUpFile(DirectFile) THEN EXIT END;

        WriteString("Five records will be created");
        WriteLn;
        RecCount := 5;
        IF NOT CreateFile(DirectFile,RecCount) THEN EXIT END;
        Reset(DirectFile);
        IF DirectFile.res <> done THEN EXIT END;
        IF NOT DisplayAllRecords() THEN EXIT END;

        WriteString('Enter record number to update: ');
        ReadCard(RecNumber);
        WriteLn;
        InputFields(RecNumber,RecSize,RecPtr);
        IF NOT WriteRecord(DirectFile,RecNumber,
                           RecSize,RecPtr) THEN
            EXIT;
            END;
        IF NOT DisplayAllRecords() THEN EXIT END;
        EXIT; (* LOOP *)
        END;
END DirectIO.
```

Appendix E

GRAPHICS

E.1 Introduction

The listings in this chapter include Modula-2 source code which are the foundations for performing graphics on the IBM PC using the standard IBM color graphics card and color monitor.

Pertinent information about the IBM color controller is found in the comments contained within the program listings. The Graphics module contains a number of routines that show how pixels on a graphics screen are manipulated and how to perform memory-mapped I/O with the display registers. It further demonstrates how to use arrays to build tables at initialization time in order to reduce execution-time overhead.

The third listing is a short demonstration program that shows how to use the basic routines to produce shapes, lines and colors.

The source code is available on a diskette from the authors. Information is found in the Preface.

E.2 Graphics Definition

```
DEFINITION MODULE Graphics;

FROM SYSTEM IMPORT ADDRESS;

EXPORT QUALIFIED BackGroundColors, COLOR, MODE, Palette,
                 FillRectangle, Rectangle,
                 ClearScreen, DisplayDot, Fill, Line,
                 ReadDot, SetBackGroundColor, SetClipArea,
                 SetMode, SetPalette, Pause,

                 (* the following are more internal in nature
                    and are exported for convenience *)
                 TempBlank, DisplayPixel, InitGraphics,
                 ScanLeft, ScanRight,
                 GraphicsSet, GraphicsReset;

TYPE
    BackGroundColors   = (Black,Blue,Green,Cyan,Red,Magenta,
                          Brown,White,Gray,LtBlue,LtGreen,LtCyan,
                          LtRed,LtMagenta,Yellow,HiWhite);
    COLOR              = [0..3];
    MODE               = (replace,invert,paint,erase);
    Palette            = (GrnRedYlw,CynMagWht);

PROCEDURE ClearScreen(    ColorParm : COLOR);

PROCEDURE DisplayDot(    X         : INTEGER;
                         Y         : INTEGER;
                         ColorParm : COLOR;
                         ModeParm  : MODE);

PROCEDURE DisplayPixel(    X         : CARDINAL;
                           Y         : CARDINAL;
                           ColorParm : COLOR;
                           ModeParm  : MODE);

PROCEDURE Fill(    X1              : INTEGER;
                   Y1              : INTEGER;
                   FillColorParm   : COLOR;
                   BorderColorParm : COLOR);

PROCEDURE FillRectangle(    X1            : INTEGER;
                            Y1            : INTEGER;
                            X2            : INTEGER;
                            Y2            : INTEGER;
                            FillColorParm : COLOR);

PROCEDURE GraphicsReset();

PROCEDURE GraphicsSet();
```

```
PROCEDURE InitGraphics();

PROCEDURE Line(     X1          : INTEGER;
                    Y1          : INTEGER;
                    X2          : INTEGER;
                    Y2          : INTEGER;
                    ColorParm : COLOR;
                    ModeParm  : MODE);

PROCEDURE Pause(    Count : CARDINAL);

PROCEDURE ReadDot(    X : CARDINAL;
                      Y : CARDINAL) : COLOR;

PROCEDURE Rectangle(    X1          : INTEGER;
                        Y1          : INTEGER;
                        X2          : INTEGER;
                        Y2          : INTEGER;
                        ColorParm : COLOR;
                        ModeParm  : MODE);

PROCEDURE ScanLeft(     X1              : CARDINAL;
                        Y1              : CARDINAL;
                        FillColorParm   : COLOR;
                        BorderColorParm : COLOR);

PROCEDURE ScanRight(    X1              : CARDINAL;
                        Y1              : CARDINAL;
                        FillColorParm   : COLOR;
                        BorderColorParm : COLOR);

PROCEDURE SetBackGroundColor(    BkGrnd : BackGroundColors);

PROCEDURE SetClipArea(    XLeft   : CARDINAL;
                          YTop    : CARDINAL;
                          XRight  : CARDINAL;
                          YBottom : CARDINAL);

PROCEDURE SetMode(    ModeParm : CARDINAL);

PROCEDURE SetPalette(    PaletteParm : Palette);

PROCEDURE TempBlank;

END Graphics.
```

E.3 Graphics Module

IMPLEMENTATION MODULE Graphics;

(* This module supplies the basic interfaces to the IBM color
graphics (medium resolution). It is an example of using SETs to
manipulate bits in a byte and of using the port interface
routines in the Logitech implementation.

The calling sequence has been designed to be as close as
possible to graphics routines supplied by MRI with its
interpreter. Not all of the routines are supplied and it
is left up to the reader to further experiment and implement
other routines.

Most of the algorithms and PC related graphics data in this
program were obtained from "Applied Concepts in MicroComputer
Graphics" by Bruce A. ArtWick (Prentice-Hall, Inc, Englewood
Cliffs,
N.J., 1984).

FUNCTIONS:

```
ClearScreen      export   - reset entire screen to a color
DisplayDot       export   - sets a specific dot (in clip area) on
DisplayPixel     internal - does dirty work of setting pixels
Fill             export   - fill simple enclosed area with color
FillRectangle    export   - draw and fill a rectangle
GraphicsReset    internal - resets screen chip to alpha mode
GraphicsSet      internal - sets screen chip to graphics mode
InitGraphics     internal - sets up all of the optimization arrays
Line             export   - draws a line
Pause            export   - times out for a while
ReadDot          export   - returns color of selected pixel
Rectangle        export   - draw rectangle
ScanLeft         internal - used by fill...
ScanRight        internal -                    ...
SetBackGroundColor export  - sets border and background color
SetClipArea      export   - determines viewing area
SetMode          export   - choose alpha or graphics
SetPalette       export   - choose one of two color sets
TempBlank        internal - temp. blank screen to prevent glitches
Test             internal - test routine
```

CRT CHARACTERISTICS:

The IBM CRT color graphics characteristics are:

Start of CRT memory is B8000(Hex).

Each byte references 4 pixels (2 bits each).

CRT origin is the upper left corner (0,0).

Lower right corner is (320,200).

In the memory, each row is stored contiguously (0,i) to (320,i).

Each row takes up 80 bytes.

Even numbered rows are stored together (1 following 0 etc.)
    starting at B8000 and going until B91F0.

Odd numbered rows start at BA000.

There are 16 background colors that can be selected.
    Black,Blue,Green,Cyan,Red,Magenta,Brown,White,Gray,
    LtBlue,LtGreen,LtCyan,LtRed,LtMagenta,Yellow,HiWhite

Only four colors can be displayed on top of the
    background at any one time.

The colors are further grouped into 2 bunches, called palettes.

One or the other palette can be chosen. The two palettes are:
    Palette 0 - 00 backgrnd   01 Green   10 Red   11 Yellow
    Palette 1 - 00 backgrnd   01 Cyan   10 Magenta   11 White

The CRT controller chip must be set for graphics mode and
then reset for alpha. Internal routines are included that
do that.

Register for selecting chip's register - 3D4
Register for holding value is - 3D5

When switching modes, the video and color bursts are turned
off to prevent glitches on the screen.

The two normally (Write Only) registers used to manipulate
the screen characteristics are:

ColorSelectRegister (at 3B8)
ModeControlRegister (at 3B9)

with the following bit layouts:

ColorSelectRegister:

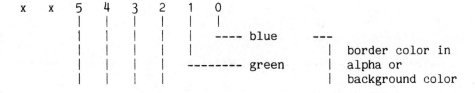

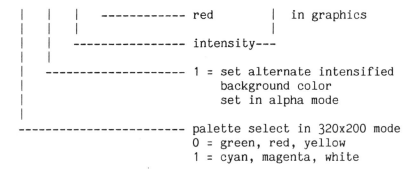

```
                |    |    |   ------------ red          |   in graphics
                |    |    |                             |
                |    |    ---------------- intensity---
                |    |
                |    -------------------- 1 = set alternate intensified
                |                             background color
                |                             set in alpha mode
                |
                ------------------------- palette select in 320x200 mode
                                          0 = green, red, yellow
                                          1 = cyan, magenta, white
```

ModeControlRegister:

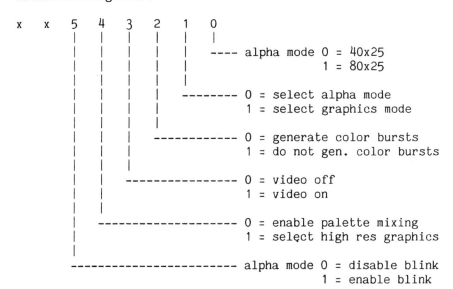

```
   x    x    5    4    3    2    1    0
             |    |    |    |    |    |
             |    |    |    |    |    ---- alpha mode 0 = 40x25
             |    |    |    |    |                    1 = 80x25
             |    |    |    |    |
             |    |    |    |    -------- 0 = select alpha mode
             |    |    |    |             1 = select graphics mode
             |    |    |    |
             |    |    |    ------------ 0 = generate color bursts
             |    |    |                 1 = do not gen. color bursts
             |    |    |
             |    |    ---------------- 0 = video off
             |    |                      1 = video on
             |    |
             |    -------------------- 0 = enable palette mixing
             |                          1 = select high res graphics
             |
             ------------------------- alpha mode 0 = disable blink
                                                  1 = enable blink
```

When using the screen in color alpha mode, there are two
bytes per character used. The upper left corner of the
screen starts at B8000 and just keeps on going until all of
the 80x25 lines are accounted for. The first byte per
screen position contains the ASCII representation of the
character. The second byte contains the attributes -
background (up to 8), character colour (up to 16), and
whether or not the character should blink. There are
a total of 256 possible combinations.

```
        bits 0 - 3 - character colour
        bits 4 - 6 - background
        bit  7     - blink/no blink
```

****

Throughout this module, there are a number of data structures
and techniques used. The basic technique is to calcuate data
once, put it into an array and later index to find it.

This approach is used for translating the X,Y co-ordinates into
the screen memory map, and since each pixel is 2 bits out of 8,
the mask indicating which set of bits is also generated. The
arrays XIndex and YIndex are initialized when the program is
loaded.

The values stored into the screen control register to select
the different screen modes are stored into the ScreenMode array
so that they can be indexed later.

The different bit patterns placed into the control register to
select the background colors are placed into the BkColor array
for later indexing.

A great deal of work is done with a pixel and several arrays
are used to isolate a pixel's two bits from the other three
pixels stored in the byte. The IsolatePixel array is used to
clear the other pixels, leaving the party we are interested
in - usually followed in the logic with a right shift to make
the bits right justified in the byte. The ResetPixel array is
used to leave the other pixels alone while zeroing the one we
are interested in.

To quickly and, or, add, invert a pixel's color depends on its
current color, and which position in the byte are its two bits.
The ColorGrid array is a two dimensional array that allows
indexing by pixel position and color and returns the appropriate
mask.

All the preceding arrays are used to make Graphics run quickly
and reduce the amount of discrete logic that would be needed
if the program was not table based.

DisplayPixel is an annotated routine in Graphics that describes
how some of the arrays are used in conjunction with memory
mapping to set pixels to specific colors or states.

It should be noted that computer graphics is not terribly
difficult but it is messy and complicated. It is very easy
to get the wrong result or no result.

```
*)
FROM InOut  IMPORT Write, Read, WriteString, WriteCard, WriteLn,
                   WriteHex;

FROM SYSTEM IMPORT ADDRESS, TSIZE, ADR, BYTE, WORD, OUTBYTE;

TYPE
```

```
    ByteSet                = SET OF [0..7];

CONST
    ColorBank              = 16384;        (* 8k in each memory bank *)
    ColorOutputPort        = 03D9H;
    DefaultClipXLeft       = 0;
    DefaultClipYTop        = 0;
    MediumResX             = 320;
    DefaultClipXRight      = MediumResX-1;
    MediumResY             = 200;
    DefaultClipYBottom     = MediumResY-1;
    LeftMost               = 0;            (* pixel position in byte *)
    MiddleLeft             = 1;            (* pixel position in byte *)
    MiddleRight            = 2;            (* pixel position in byte *)
    ModeOutputPort         = 03D8H;
    Mode40x25MA            = 2CH;              (*monochrome alpha*)
    Mode40x25CA            = 28H;              (*color       alpha*)
    Mode80x25MA            = 2DH;              (*monochrome alpha*)
    Mode80x25CA            = 29H;              (*color       alpha*)
    Mode320x200MG          = 0EH;              (*monochrome graphics*)
    Mode320x200CG          = 0AH;              (*color       graphics*)
    Mode640x200MG          = 1EH;              (*color       graphics*)
    PointerPort            = 03D4H;
    RightMost              = 3;            (* pixel position in byte *)
    ValuePort              = 03D5H;

VAR
    BkColor                : ARRAY [0..15] OF ByteSet;
    ClipXLeft              : CARDINAL;
    ClipXRight             : CARDINAL;
    ClipYTop               : CARDINAL;
    ClipYBottom            : CARDINAL;
    ColorGrid              : ARRAY [0..3],[0..3] OF ByteSet;
    CrtBank[0B000H:8000H]  : ARRAY [0..ColorBank-1] OF CHAR;
    GlobalMode             : CARDINAL;
    IsolatePixel           : ARRAY [0..3] OF ByteSet;
    MasterColorSelect      : ByteSet;
    ResetPixel             : ARRAY [0..3] OF ByteSet;
    ScreenModes            : ARRAY [0..6] OF CHAR;
    XIndex                 : ARRAY [0..MediumResX-1],
                                   [0..1] OF CARDINAL;
    YIndex                 : ARRAY [0..MediumResY-1] OF CARDINAL;


PROCEDURE ClearScreen(    ColorParm : COLOR);

    VAR
        Index      : CARDINAL;
        ByteColor  : CHAR;

    BEGIN
        TempBlank;
```

```
          CASE GlobalMode OF
              0 : (* alpha 40x25 black and white *)
            | 1 : (* alpha 40x25 color          *)
            | 2 : (* alpha 80x25 black and white *)
            | 3 : (* alpha 80x25 color          *)
                  FOR Index := 0 TO (ColorBank - 2) BY 2 DO
                      CrtBank[Index]   := CHR(020H);
                      CrtBank[Index+1] := CHR(007H);
                      END;
                  GraphicsReset;
            | 4 : (* med res color graphics       *)
                  (* create one byte of solid color
                     for resetting screen *)
                  CASE ColorParm OF
                      0 : ByteColor := CHR(0);
                    | 1 : ByteColor := CHR(85);
                    | 2 : ByteColor := CHR(170);
                    | 3 : ByteColor := CHR(255);
                    END;

                  (* go through screen memory making everything
                     same color *)
                  FOR Index := 0 TO (ColorBank - 1) BY 1 DO
                      CrtBank[Index] := ByteColor;
                      END;
            | 5 : (* med res bWATFIV   graphics      *)
            | 6 : (* high res bWATFIV graphics        *)
            END;
            OUTBYTE(ModeOutputPort,ScreenModes[GlobalMode]);
      END ClearScreen;

PROCEDURE DisplayDot(     X          : INTEGER;
                          Y          : INTEGER;
                          ColorParm  : COLOR;
                          ModeParm   : MODE);

    BEGIN
        (* check for clipping and then turn on pixel *)

        IF (CARDINAL(X) >= ClipXLeft)   &
           (CARDINAL(X) <= ClipXRight)  &
           (CARDINAL(Y) >= ClipYTop)    &
           (CARDINAL(Y) <= ClipYBottom) THEN
            DisplayPixel(CARDINAL(X),CARDINAL(Y),
                         ColorParm,ModeParm);
            END;
    END DisplayDot;

        (* ***********************************************
         *                                              *
         *   Annotated routine explaining arrays, etc  *
         *                                              *
```

```
             ********************************************** *)

PROCEDURE DisplayPixel(     X          : CARDINAL;
                            Y          : CARDINAL;
                            ColorParm  : COLOR;
                            ModeParm   : MODE);

   (* a lot of the logic in the following code is due to
      the way bytes and words are stored. playing with bytes and
      (that means only 8 bits) takes a bit of doing.           *)

   VAR
       Offset      : CARDINAL;   (* offset into memory map *)
       MaskIndex   : CARDINAL;   (* index into mask arrays *)
       Temp        : ByteSet;    (* temporary 16 bit set *)
       Temp1       : ByteSet;    (* temporary 8 bit set value *)

   BEGIN

       (* from XIndex obtain the value that will be used to
          index into a number of arrays that represents if the
          pixel is in left, middleleft, middleright, right
          position in the byte *)
       MaskIndex   := XIndex[X,1];

       (* add the X coordinate offset to the Y offset - this is
          due to the way the memory map is laid out *)
       Offset := YIndex[Y] + XIndex[X,0];

       (* the following gyrations are due to Modula's type
          setting characteristics and the Logitech implementation.
          That is, set operations only work on sets (i.e. 16 bits)
          and we only want to work on 8 bits. Characters stored
          in an array, take up only 8 bits and are stored
          contiguously - thus we can index off beginning of the
          array and fetch any one byte we like. However, we must
          then convert this to a 16 bit entity if we wish to
          perform set operations. After doing the set operations,
          we must then convert back to 8 bit type so we can store
          value in array.   *)

       Temp := ByteSet(ORD(CrtBank[Offset]));

       (* there are four possible actions that can be done to
          a pixel and the following case statement implements
          each one individually *)
       CASE ModeParm OF
            replace :
                   (* replace destination pixel with new color *)

                   (* zero out the pixel's two bits
                      we are interested in *)
```

```
        Temp := Temp * ResetPixel[MaskIndex];

        (* set the two bits to the value in the
           array by an OR *)
        Temp := Temp +
                ColorGrid[ColorParm][MaskIndex];

| invert  :
        (* invert the destination pixel if match *)

        (* leave the pixel's bits standing alone *)
        Temp1 := Temp * IsolatePixel[MaskIndex];

        (* see if the bits match those in the table *)
        IF Temp1 = ColorGrid[ColorParm][MaskIndex]
           THEN
           (* zero out the two bits *)
           Temp := Temp * ResetPixel[MaskIndex];

           (* OR in the inverted (or opposite) color
              bits where 3-0, 2-1 are opposites *)
           Temp := Temp +
                   ColorGrid[3-ColorParm][MaskIndex];

        END;

| paint   :
        (* new color is added to old one *)

        (* leave the pixel's bits standing alone *)
        Temp1 := Temp * IsolatePixel[MaskIndex];

        (* get both bit masks, add them together, we
           might get carry, so we are not done yet! *)
        Temp1 := ByteSet(CARDINAL(Temp1) +
           CARDINAL(ColorGrid[ColorParm][MaskIndex]));

        (* pull out of the byte, the two bits we want
           thus taking care of carry and the like *)
        Temp1 := Temp1 * IsolatePixel[MaskIndex];

        (* zero out pixel's bits in orginal byte *)
        Temp := Temp * ResetPixel[MaskIndex];

        (* add both patterns together, effectively
           overlaying them *)
        Temp := Temp1 + Temp;

| erase   :
        (* dest. is cleared where source = set bits *)

        (* leave the pixel's bits standing alone *)
```

```
                    Temp1 := Temp * IsolatePixel[MaskIndex];

                    (* see if a color match on our two bits *)
                    IF Temp1 = ColorGrid[ColorParm][MaskIndex]
                        THEN
                        (* turn off the bits so the background
                            color will show *)
                        Temp := Temp * ResetPixel[MaskIndex];

                    END;
            END;
        (* we must now return the 16 bit value back to the
            screen memory bank *)
        CrtBank[Offset] := CHR(CARDINAL(Temp));
    END DisplayPixel;


PROCEDURE Fill(     X1                : INTEGER;
                    Y1                : INTEGER;
                    FillColorParm   : COLOR;
                    BorderColorParm : COLOR);

    VAR
        X               : CARDINAL;
        Y               : CARDINAL;

    BEGIN
        LOOP
            X := CARDINAL(X1);
            Y := CARDINAL(Y1);
            IF (X < ClipXLeft)    OR
               (X > ClipXRight)   OR
               (Y < ClipYTop)OR
               (Y > ClipYBottom) THEN
                EXIT;
                END;
            Y := Y + 1;
            LOOP
                IF (Y = 0) OR (Y = ClipYTop)   THEN
                    EXIT;
                    END;
                Y := Y - 1;
                IF (ReadDot(X,Y) = BorderColorParm) THEN
                    EXIT;
                    END;
                ScanRight(X,Y,FillColorParm,BorderColorParm);
                ScanLeft(X,Y,FillColorParm,BorderColorParm);
                END;
            X := CARDINAL(X1);
            Y := CARDINAL(Y1);
            LOOP
                IF (Y = MediumResY - 1) OR
```

```
                         (Y = ClipYBottom)  THEN
                            EXIT;
                            END;
                      Y := Y + 1;
                      IF (ReadDot(X,Y) = BorderColorParm) THEN
                            EXIT;
                            END;
                      ScanRight(X,Y,FillColorParm,BorderColorParm);
                      ScanLeft(X,Y,FillColorParm,BorderColorParm);
                      END;
                  EXIT;
                  END;
        END Fill;


PROCEDURE FillRectangle(     X1              : INTEGER;
                             Y1              : INTEGER;
                             X2              : INTEGER;
                             Y2              : INTEGER;
                             FillColorParm : COLOR);
        VAR
            IndexX : INTEGER;
            IndexY : INTEGER;

        BEGIN
            FOR IndexY := Y1 TO Y2 DO
                FOR IndexX := X1 TO X2 DO
                    DisplayDot(IndexX,IndexY,FillColorParm,replace);
                    END;
                END;
        END FillRectangle;


PROCEDURE GraphicsReset();

        BEGIN
        (* set up the 6845 CRT controller chip for 80x25 alpha *)

            OUTBYTE(PointerPort, 00H);(* horizontal total *)
            OUTBYTE(ValuePort,   71H);
            OUTBYTE(PointerPort, 01H);(* horizontal displayed *)
            OUTBYTE(ValuePort,   50H);
            OUTBYTE(PointerPort, 02H);(* horizontal sync position *)
            OUTBYTE(ValuePort,   5AH);
            OUTBYTE(PointerPort, 04H);(* vertical total *)
            OUTBYTE(ValuePort,   1FH);
            OUTBYTE(PointerPort, 06H);(* vertical displayed *)
            OUTBYTE(ValuePort,   19H);
            OUTBYTE(PointerPort, 07H);(* vertical synch position *)
            OUTBYTE(ValuePort,   1CH);
            OUTBYTE(PointerPort, 09H);(* max scan line address *)
            OUTBYTE(ValuePort,   07H);
```

```
    END GraphicsReset;


PROCEDURE GraphicsSet();

    BEGIN
    (* set up the 6845 CRT controller chip for graphics modes *)

        OUTBYTE(PointerPort, 00H);(* horizontal total *)
        OUTBYTE(ValuePort,   38H);
        OUTBYTE(PointerPort, 01H);(* horizontal displayed *)
        OUTBYTE(ValuePort,   28H);
        OUTBYTE(PointerPort, 02H);(* horizontal sync position *)
        OUTBYTE(ValuePort,   2DH);
        OUTBYTE(PointerPort, 04H);(* vertical total *)
        OUTBYTE(ValuePort,   7FH);
        OUTBYTE(PointerPort, 06H);(* vertical displayed *)
        OUTBYTE(ValuePort,   64H);
        OUTBYTE(PointerPort, 07H);(* vertical synch position *)
        OUTBYTE(ValuePort,   70H);
        OUTBYTE(PointerPort, 09H);(* max scan line address *)
        OUTBYTE(ValuePort,   01H);
    END GraphicsSet;


PROCEDURE InitGraphics();

    VAR
        Index     : CARDINAL;
        Offset    : CARDINAL;
        Offset1   : CARDINAL;

    BEGIN
        (* build index tables for even and odd scan lines *)
        Offset  := 0;
        Offset1 := 8192;
        FOR Index :=0 TO MediumResY - 2 BY 2 DO
            YIndex[Index]   := Offset;
            Offset          := Offset + 80;
            YIndex[Index+1] := Offset1;
            Offset1         := Offset1 + 80;
            END;

        (* build index table for offsetting x values *)
        Offset := 0;
        FOR Index :=0 TO MediumResX-4 BY 4 DO
            XIndex[Index  ,0] := Offset;
            XIndex[Index+1,0] := Offset;
            XIndex[Index+2,0] := Offset;
            XIndex[Index+3,0] := Offset;
            Offset            := Offset + 1;
            XIndex[Index  ,1] := LeftMost;
```

```
        XIndex[Index+1,1] := MiddleLeft;
        XIndex[Index+2,1] := MiddleRight;
        XIndex[Index+3,1] := RightMost;
        END;

    (* set up default viewing area *)
    ClipXLeft           := DefaultClipXLeft;
    ClipXRight          := DefaultClipXRight;
    ClipYTop            := DefaultClipYTop;
    ClipYBottom         := DefaultClipYBottom;

    (* set up array for SetMode function *)
    ScreenModes[0]      := CHAR(Mode40x25MA);
    ScreenModes[1]      := CHAR(Mode40x25CA);
    ScreenModes[2]      := CHAR(Mode80x25MA);
    ScreenModes[3]      := CHAR(Mode80x25CA);
    ScreenModes[4]      := CHAR(Mode320x200CG);
    ScreenModes[5]      := CHAR(Mode320x200MG);
    ScreenModes[6]      := CHAR(Mode640x200MG);

(* set up array for background colors *)
    BkColor[0]  := ByteSet{         };  (* black     0000 *)
    BkColor[1]  := ByteSet{       0};   (* blue      0001 *)
    BkColor[2]  := ByteSet{     1  };   (* green     0010 *)
    BkColor[3]  := ByteSet{     1,0};   (* cyan      0011 *)
    BkColor[4]  := ByteSet{   2     };  (* red       0100 *)
    BkColor[5]  := ByteSet{   2,  0};   (* magenta   0101 *)
    BkColor[6]  := ByteSet{   2,1  };   (* brown     0110 *)
    BkColor[7]  := ByteSet{   2,1,0};   (* white     0111 *)
    BkColor[8]  := ByteSet{3        };  (* gray      1000 *)
    BkColor[9]  := ByteSet{3,     0};   (* ltblue    1001 *)
    BkColor[10] := ByteSet{3,   1  };   (* ltgreen   1010 *)
    BkColor[11] := ByteSet{3,   1,0};   (* ltcyan    1011 *)
    BkColor[12] := ByteSet{3,2     };   (* ltred     1100 *)
    BkColor[13] := ByteSet{3,2,   0};   (* ltmagenta 1101 *)
    BkColor[14] := ByteSet{3,2,1  };    (* yellow    1110 *)
    BkColor[15] := ByteSet{3,2,1,0};    (* hiwhite   1111 *)

    (* isolate array is used to 'and' out all other bits *)
    IsolatePixel[0] := ByteSet{7,6}; (* 11000000 *)
    IsolatePixel[1] := ByteSet{5,4}; (* 00110000 *)
    IsolatePixel[2] := ByteSet{3,2}; (* 00001100 *)
    IsolatePixel[3] := ByteSet{1,0}; (* 00001111 *)

    (* reset is used to set to zero a selected pixel *)
    ResetPixel[0] := ByteSet{    5,4,3,2,1,0};(* 00111111 *)
    ResetPixel[1] := ByteSet{7,6,    3,2,1,0};(* 11001111 *)
    ResetPixel[2] := ByteSet{7,6,5,4,    1,0};(* 11110011 *)
    ResetPixel[3] := ByteSet{7,6,5,4,3,2    };(* 11111100 *)

    (* the color grid is a 2x2 matrix for setting colors
    0..3 in left, middle left, middle right, right pixel
```

```
        slots via 'ands' and it is also used to compare a color
        against the isolated pixel *)
        ColorGrid[0][0] := ByteSet{};    (* 00000000 *)
        ColorGrid[1][0] := ByteSet{6};   (* 01000000 *)
        ColorGrid[2][0] := ByteSet{7};   (* 10000000 *)
        ColorGrid[3][0] := ByteSet{7,6}; (* 11000000 *)
        ColorGrid[0][1] := ByteSet{};    (* 00000000 *)
        ColorGrid[1][1] := ByteSet{4};   (* 00010000 *)
        ColorGrid[2][1] := ByteSet{5};   (* 00100000 *)
        ColorGrid[3][1] := ByteSet{5,4}; (* 00110000 *)
        ColorGrid[0][2] := ByteSet{};    (* 00000000 *)
        ColorGrid[1][2] := ByteSet{2};   (* 00000100 *)
        ColorGrid[2][2] := ByteSet{3};   (* 00001000 *)
        ColorGrid[3][2] := ByteSet{3,2}; (* 00001100 *)
        ColorGrid[0][3] := ByteSet{};    (* 00000000 *)
        ColorGrid[1][3] := ByteSet{0};   (* 00000001 *)
        ColorGrid[2][3] := ByteSet{1};   (* 00000010 *)
        ColorGrid[3][3] := ByteSet{1,0}; (* 00000011 *)

        (* set up initial color select history value *)
        MasterColorSelect  := ByteSet{5};
        GlobalMode         := Mode80x25CA;
    END InitGraphics;


PROCEDURE Line(    X1          : INTEGER;
                   Y1          : INTEGER;
                   X2          : INTEGER;
                   Y2          : INTEGER;
                   ColorParm : COLOR;
                   ModeParm  : MODE);

    VAR
        ErrorFactor : INTEGER;
        XMove       : INTEGER;
        YMove       : INTEGER;
        dx          : INTEGER;
        dy          : INTEGER;

    BEGIN
        ErrorFactor := 0;    (* set line tracking error to 0 *)
        XMove       := 1;    (* indicate movement to right   *)
        YMove       := 1;    (* indicate movement is up      *)

        (* generate x movement constant *)
        dx := X2 - X1;
        IF dx < 0 THEN
            (* left x movement *)
            XMove := -1;
            dx    := -dx;
        ELSIF dx = 0 THEN
            (* vertical movement *)
```

```
            ErrorFactor := -1;
            END;

        (* generate y movement constant *)
        dy := Y2 - Y1;
        IF dy < 0 THEN
            (* left y movement *)
            YMove := -1;
            dy    := -dy;
            END;

        (* line generation loop *)
        LOOP
            DisplayDot(X1,Y1,ColorParm,ModeParm);
            IF (X1 = X2) & (Y1 = Y2) THEN
                (* x,y at final values *)
                EXIT;
                END;
            IF ErrorFactor < 0 THEN
                (* negative tracking error *)
                Y1           := Y1 + YMove;
                ErrorFactor := ErrorFactor + dx;
            ELSE
                (* positive tracking error *)
                X1           := X1 + XMove;
                ErrorFactor := ErrorFactor - dy;
                END;
            END;
    END Line;


PROCEDURE Pause(    Count : CARDINAL);

    CONST
        BigCard        = 40000;

    VAR
        LocalCount    : CARDINAL;
        NumberSeconds : CARDINAL;
        InnerCount    : CARDINAL;

    BEGIN
        (* pause system for rough number of seconds *)

        NumberSeconds := Count DIV 2;
        FOR LocalCount := 0 TO NumberSeconds DO
            FOR InnerCount := 0 TO BigCard DO
                END;
            FOR InnerCount := 0 TO BigCard DO
                END;
            END;
    END Pause;
```

```
PROCEDURE ReadDot(    X : CARDINAL;
                      Y : CARDINAL) : COLOR;

    VAR
        Offset      : CARDINAL;
        MaskIndex   : CARDINAL;
        Temp        : ByteSet;
        ReturnColor : COLOR;

    BEGIN
        (* get address of byte containing pixel, isolate pixel's
        two bits, essentially right justify the bits via DIV,
        then convert to color type for returning *)
        MaskIndex := XIndex[X,1];
        Offset    := YIndex[Y] + XIndex[X,0];
        Temp      := ByteSet(ORD(CrtBank[Offset]));

        CASE MaskIndex OF
            LeftMost    :
                    Temp := Temp * IsolatePixel[LeftMost];
                    ReturnColor := COLOR(CARDINAL(Temp) DIV 64);
            | MiddleLeft   :
                    Temp := Temp * IsolatePixel[MiddleLeft];
                    ReturnColor := COLOR(CARDINAL(Temp) DIV 16);
            | MiddleRight :
                    Temp := Temp * IsolatePixel[MiddleRight];
                    ReturnColor := COLOR(CARDINAL(Temp) DIV 4);
            | RightMost   :
                    Temp := Temp * IsolatePixel[MiddleRight];
                    ReturnColor := COLOR(Temp);
            END;
        RETURN ReturnColor;
    END ReadDot;


PROCEDURE Rectangle(    X1        : INTEGER;
                        Y1        : INTEGER;
                        X2        : INTEGER;
                        Y2        : INTEGER;
                        ColorParm : COLOR;
                        ModeParm  : MODE);
    VAR
        Index : INTEGER;

    BEGIN
        FOR Index := X1 TO X2 DO
            DisplayDot(Index,Y1,ColorParm,ModeParm);
            DisplayDot(Index,Y2,ColorParm,ModeParm);
            END;
        FOR Index := Y1 TO Y2 DO
```

```
            DisplayDot(X1,Index,ColorParm,ModeParm);
            DisplayDot(X2,Index,ColorParm,ModeParm);
            END;
    END Rectangle;


PROCEDURE ScanLeft(     X1                : CARDINAL;
                        Y1                : CARDINAL;
                        FillColorParm     : COLOR;
                        BorderColorParm : COLOR);

    BEGIN
        LOOP
            IF X1 = 0 THEN
                EXIT;
                END;
            X1 := X1 - 1;
            IF (ReadDot(X1,Y1) = BorderColorParm) OR
                (X1 < ClipXLeft) THEN
                EXIT;
                END;
            DisplayDot(X1,Y1,FillColorParm,replace);
            END;
    END ScanLeft;


PROCEDURE ScanRight(    X1                : CARDINAL;
                        Y1                : CARDINAL;
                        FillColorParm     : COLOR;
                        BorderColorParm : COLOR);
    VAR
        SafeX1 : CARDINAL;
        SafeY1 : CARDINAL;

    BEGIN
        SafeX1 := X1;
        SafeY1 := Y1;
        LOOP
            IF X1 = MediumResX - 1 THEN
                EXIT;
                END;
            X1 := X1 + 1;
            IF (ReadDot(X1,Y1) = BorderColorParm) OR
                (X1 > ClipXRight) THEN
                EXIT;
                END;
            DisplayDot(X1,Y1,FillColorParm,replace);
            END;
        DisplayDot(SafeX1,SafeY1,FillColorParm,replace);
    END ScanRight;
```

```
PROCEDURE SetBackGroundColor(BkGrnd : BackGroundColors);

    BEGIN
        (* keep leftmost 4 bits as is, then change background *)

        MasterColorSelect := MasterColorSelect *
                             ByteSet{4,5,6,7};
        MasterColorSelect := MasterColorSelect +
                             BkColor[ORD(BkGrnd)];
        OUTBYTE(ColorOutputPort,MasterColorSelect);
    END SetBackGroundColor;


PROCEDURE SetClipArea(    XLeft   : CARDINAL;
                          YTop    : CARDINAL;
                          XRight  : CARDINAL;
                          YBottom : CARDINAL);

    BEGIN
        ClipXLeft   := XLeft;
        ClipYTop    := YTop;
        ClipXRight  := XRight;
        ClipYBottom := YBottom;
    END SetClipArea;


PROCEDURE SetMode(ModeParm : CARDINAL);

    VAR
        Index : CARDINAL;

    BEGIN
        GlobalMode := ModeParm;
        CASE ModeParm OF
                0:      (* alpha 40x25 black and white *)
              | 1:      (* alpha 40x25 color           *)
              | 2:      (* alpha 80x25 black and white *)
              | 3:      (* alpha 80x25 color           *)
                TempBlank;
                FOR Index := 0 TO (ColorBank - 2) BY 2 DO
                    CrtBank[Index]   := CHR(020H);
                    CrtBank[Index+1] := CHR(007H);
                    END;
                GraphicsReset;
                SetBackGroundColor(Black);
                OUTBYTE(ModeOutputPort,ScreenModes[GlobalMode]);
              | 4:      (* med res color graphics      *)
                GraphicsSet;
                SetBackGroundColor(Black);
                ClearScreen(0);
              | 5:      (* med res bWATFIV   graphics   *)
              | 6:      (* high res bWATFIV graphics   *)
```

```
            END;
        END SetMode;


PROCEDURE SetPalette(PaletteParm : Palette);

    BEGIN
        (* keep all but mode bit, then set it *)

        MasterColorSelect := MasterColorSelect *
                            ByteSet{0,1,2,3,4,6,7};
        IF PaletteParm = GrnRedYlw THEN
            MasterColorSelect := MasterColorSelect + ByteSet{};
        ELSE
            MasterColorSelect := MasterColorSelect + ByteSet{5};
            END;
        OUTBYTE(ColorOutputPort,MasterColorSelect);
    END SetPalette;


PROCEDURE TempBlank;

    BEGIN
        (* turn off video and color bursts so
            no glitches on screen *)

        OUTBYTE(ModeOutputPort,06H);
    END TempBlank;

BEGIN
    InitGraphics;
END Graphics.
```

E.4 Graphics Example

```
MODULE Demo;

FROM InOut    IMPORT Read;

FROM Graphics IMPORT BackGroundColors, COLOR, MODE, Palette,
                    FillRectangle, Rectangle,
                    ClearScreen, DisplayDot, Fill, Line,
                    ReadDot, SetBackGroundColor, SetClipArea,
                    SetMode, SetPalette, Pause;

VAR
    Index     : INTEGER;
    InputChar : CHAR;
    Value     : INTEGER;
    CrtBank[0B000H:8000H] : ARRAY [0..16384] OF CHAR;
```

```
BEGIN

    SetMode(4);
    SetPalette(GrnRedYlw);
    SetBackGroundColor(Blue);
    ClearScreen(0);
    Pause(5);
    ClearScreen(1);
    Pause(5);
    ClearScreen(2);
    Pause(5);
    ClearScreen(3);
    Pause(5);
    ClearScreen(0);

    (* display a rectangle and then pause *)
    FOR Index := 50 TO 250 DO
        DisplayDot(Index,75,0,invert);
        DisplayDot(Index,150,0,invert);
        END;
    FOR Index := 75 TO 150 DO
        DisplayDot(50,Index,0,invert);
        DisplayDot(250,Index,0,invert);
        END;
    Read(InputChar);

    (* fill in the rectangle *)
    Fill(100,100,2,3);

    (* draw a second one *)
    Rectangle(10,10,40,50,2,replace);

    (* draw and fill a third and then pause *)
    FillRectangle(90,90,150,199,3);
    Read(InputChar);

    (* clear the screen, and draw a box *)
    ClearScreen(2);
    FillRectangle(25,25,75,75,1);

    (* set a clip area and draw a second box *)
    SetClipArea(50,50,150,150);
    FillRectangle(25,25,75,75,3);

    (* reset the clip area and draw moire patterns, then pause
       the different colours on the screen are due to the paint
       option and the individual pixels being hit several times
       while drawing the lines *)
    SetClipArea(1,1,320,200);
    FOR Index := 1 TO 200 BY 10 DO
        Line(100,100,300,Index,1,replace);
        END;
```

```
    FOR Index := 1 TO 200 BY 10 DO
        Line(300,100,100,Index,1,replace);
        END;
    Read(InputChar);

    (* give a taste for color alpha mode *)
    SetMode(3);
    Value := 0;
    FOR Index := 0 TO 511 BY 2 DO
        CrtBank[Index] := "A";
        CrtBank[Index+1] := CHR(Value);
        Value := Value + 1;
        END;
    Read(InputChar);
    ClearScreen(0);
END Demo.
```

Appendix F

PROGRAMMING STYLE SUMMARY

F.1 Introduction

The following are general programming guidelines that will result in clear, concise, and understandable Modula-2 programs. In addition to the suggestions mentioned in the body of the book and repeated here, there are extra guidelines that relate to programming "industrial strength" software. In industry, there are many factors that affect the cost of developing and maintaining software – programming style is one of these.

Programming style affects the reusing of code, training of staff, debugging, testing, code reviews, and documentation. Good style does not mean that there is a good design, or that the code works and is good. Good style just means that it will be easier to work with and might remain in use longer. There are some programmers that will sacrifice user functionality for a pretty program – they are hacks. The best programmers are those that acknowledge that the purpose of programming is to deliver something that someone will use and be happy with – regardless of the internals.

Guidelines are just guidelines and are not meant to be applied in a dogmatic sense. Use them where appropriate and do not use them where they will create problems or are nonsense.

F.2 Style GuideLines

Goal of Style

1. To make programs readable, understandable, and maintainable past the first writing and debugging of the module.

2. To make the scope of algorithms clear.

3. To make variable usage self-evident.

4. To minimize the number of lines modified when a change takes place in the future as it surely must.

5. To make sure that significant program facts are not hidden in a cloud of punctuation, statement formation and "cuteness".

6. To avoid the "I cannot figure it out, I will just rewrite it" syndrome.

Identifiers

1. Use meaningful names. For example, use GrossPay and NetPay instead of X and Y.

2. Use mixed case unless your keyboard has uppercase only. For example, use Count in preference to COUNT. Experiments have shown that mixed case is more readable.

3. Use word pairs or word triples. Capitalize the first letter in each word as in "LastYearToDate."

4. Avoid names similar to the reserved words, standard identifiers and library components. For example, don't use Loop, If, Real, Halt as variable names.

5. Avoid using the same name with different cases in the same program.

Constant Declarations

1. Use a single CONST declaration in a procedure or module and put it ahead of all other declarations.

2. Use meaningful identifiers.

3. Indent and vertically align all constant identifiers and within reason vertically align the equal signs.

4. When there is a large number of identifiers, put them in alphabetic order.

Type Declarations

1. In general, use a single TYPE declaration within a procedure or module. Put it after the CONST declaration and ahead of the VAR declaration.

2. Use meaningful type names that have the suffixes:

   o "Type" for an enumerated type

   o "Range" for a subrange identifier

   o "Array", "Record", "Set" and "Ptr" for declarations of array, record, set and pointer types respectively

3. Indent and vertically align the type identifiers and, when reasonable, the equal signs.

4. If there are many types declare them in alphabetic order.

Variable Declarations

1. In general, use a single variable declaration in a procedure or module. Put it after the TYPE declaration.

2. Use meaningful variable names.

3. Indent and vertically align the identifiers and, when reasonable, the colons preceding the types.

4. If there are many variables, declare them in alphabetic order.

5. Refer to multidimensional arrays throughout the program in a consistent fashion.

6. Do not use a variable for more than one purpose. It is better to create a second variable to perform the second function. Doubling up of functions causes a number of problems, including the creation of a meaningful name.

7. Use a suffix to aid in understanding variable usage or restrictions. For example, use "Adr" on addresses to highlight restricted capabilities.

Record Declarations

1. Use the suffix "Rec" or "Record" in a record type identifier.

2. Indent and vertically align the field names and "END". Where reasonable, align the colons in the field declarations.

3. If more than one field has the same type, define the field type separately and put each field name on a separate line.

Record Variants

1. Even though optional, use a tagfield. Without it there is nothing in a record to indicate which variant is being used; hence knowledge of which fields are present would have to be determined by other means.

2. Indent and align the start of each case selector list. If one or more of these lists are lengthy, indent the start of the field list on the line below the case selector list.

3. If the case logic is extensive, insert a blank line between cases.

4. Vertically align the case separator characters, ELSE (if used) and END.

Pointers

1. Pointer types. Use the suffix "Ptr" in the name of a pointer type.

2. Pointer variables. Use names appropriate to the objects (variables) being created.

Comments

1. Common sense should be used when inserting comments. They should point out exceptions, special logic, or hidden meanings.

2. Long comments. Put a box around comments that are particularly important. Alternatively, align the '(*' and '*)' on the left and indent the comment.

3. Each procedure and module heading should be followed by a comment describing the purpose of the unit. Other information may include the author, the date, and the meaning of objects imported, exported or passed to and from the procedure or module.

4. If a program contains a large number of variables, it is preferable to order variables alphabetically.

5. Where possible and reasonable, align the beginning of all comments at a particular position on an input line.

6. In long structured statements, follow the END with a comment containing the reserved word that began the statement.

7. Develop your own style of commenting and use it consistently.

Statements

1. Long statements should be wrapped at an operator or comma or other punctuation character and indented beneath the first line.

Assignment Statement

1. A program is more visually pleasing if the assignment operators in a sequence of assignment statements are vertically aligned.

2. If there is a long sequence of simple assignments, arrange them in a tabular format.

3. Place a ";" on all assignment, END statements, and procedure calls.

IF Statement

1. Indentation. Vertically align the IF, each ELSIF and ELSE. Indent each statement sequence and END.

2. When the IF statement specifies a single, simple action to be performed when a condition is true, you can state the IF all on one line. If the action has importance, the IF statement should be on several lines highlighting the action.

3. Although empty statement sequences following IF, ELSIF and ELSE are permitted, it is not good programming style.

4. Omit the ELSE clause if nothing is to be done when the preceding condition(s) is false.

CASE Statement

1. Consistent vertical alignment of the components of the CASE statement makes the structure more visible. In particular, align the case label separators, ELSE, and END. Align the colons delimiting the end of each case-label-list.

2. If a case-label-list is lengthy, start the associated statement sequence on the line below the case-label-list.

3. Use CASE when the value of the expression is limited to a relatively small number of known, discrete values. If the values are widely dispersed or may vary from one run to another, use an IF statement with ELSIF clauses to separate the cases.

4. When the case logic is lengthy, insert a blank line between cases.

5. Include the ELSE clause to guard against execution-time errors.

LOOP and EXIT Statements

1. Indent and vertically align the start of each statement in the statement sequence with END.

2. If there is a single condition that terminates loop execution and this condition can be tested either at the beginning or end of the statement sequence, use a WHILE or REPEAT statement respectively. Use LOOP when one of several conditions can cause loop termination or when the exit condition cannot be evaluated until the middle of the loop. More generally, use LOOP when it will simplify the programming logic.

WHILE Statement

1. Vertically align and indent the statement sequence and END.

2. A WHILE statement should be used when it may be necessary to skip all executions of a statement sequence.

REPEAT Statement

1. Indent and vertically align the statement sequence and UNTIL.

2. Use a REPEAT statement when the statement sequence must be executed once or when it is natural to check for loop repetition at the end of the sequence.

FOR Statement

1. Indent and vertically align the statement sequence with END.

2. Use the FOR statement to express simple loops that can be controlled by a counter.

Procedures

1. If the procedure does not return a value but can result in an error, make the procedure into a BOOLEAN function.

2. Indent and align VAR, CONST, TYPE, BEGIN, and END statements.

3. Indent nested procedures and place a line of asterisks before and after the procedure.

4. A procedure may be used to remove "lunch-box" code from important algorithms to ensure the logic is clear, even if the procedure is only called from one location.

5. A procedure may be used to package a generic function that is used in two or more locations in the program.

6. A procedure may be used to package functions that "start from scratch", "do a specific task", and then "return to caller".

7. A simple test for functionality should be applied to procedures: describe the procedure function in one sentence without using the word "and".

8. Procedures should fit on one or two pages. If they are larger, functionality and logic should be reviewed.

Formal Parameter List

1. When declaring a formal parameter list, each parameter should appear on a separate line.

2. Vertically align each instance of "VAR". Leave four blank spaces before the start of each value parameter identifier.

3. Be consistent with the order of VAR parameters and the value parameter declarations.

4. Do not use a parameter for more than one purpose. It is better to create a second parameter to perform the second function. Doubling up of functions causes a number of problems.

RETURN Statement

1. Unless logic is convoluted and complex, use only one RETURN statement and make it the last statement in the procedure body.

2. Do not use a RETURN statement with nonfunction procedures; let the procedure exit from the "bottom" of the procedure body.

Program Modules

1. Align the MODULE, IMPORT, EXPORT, VAR, CONST, TYPE, BEGIN, END and PROCEDURE statements and indent the module body.

2. Develop and use a style consistently that will result in reusable logic and can be easily maintained.

Definition Modules

1. Align the MODULE, IMPORT, VAR, CONST, TYPE, and PROCEDURE statements.

2. In multideveloper situations, code the definition modules prior to coding and debugging the implementation modules.

3. Types, constants, and procedures are good objects to export. Variable sharing should be done carefully.

4. Keep the number of things exported down to what is needed and avoid exporting things for the sake of exporting.

5. Export simple generic functions and let the user join them together in his own way. This may be done in conjunction with exporting higher-level routines.

6. When functions are being exported that perform "parameter setup" "data verification", "the actual work", and then "cleanup"; export all levels so that other programs can bypass or make use of the internal levels if they want.

Implementation Modules

1. Align the MODULE, IMPORT, EXPORT, VAR, CONST, TYPE, PROCEDURE, BEGIN, and END statements and indent the module body.

2. Use logical groupings for the procedures placed in implementation modules. Data abstraction, functional subsystems, and common utilities are examples of good reasons for grouping procedures.

3. Where applicable, separate functions into different procedures for "parameter setup". "data verification", "work" and "cleanup".

Local Modules

1. Indent local modules and place a line of asterisks around them to highlight their presence.

2. Do not use local modules unless their need and use is obvious and is indeed better than using appropriate global variables.

3. Avoid using the same identifier in local modules for different objects.

Appendix G

SOFTWARE DESIGN AND DEVELOPMENT

This appendix provides an overview of the discipline called "software engineering". It identifies and defines the main activities associated with software development. Greater detail is provided on the topic of software design and program development.

G.1   Computer Engineering

Computer Systems Engineering. Most new applications of computers begin with a somewhat fuzzy definition of desired function. Following a feasibility study which may include any or all of legal, environmental, profitability, personnel and technology considerations, a decision to proceed to a detailed functional statement may be made.

Systems architects and product management personnel together with end users prepare a document called a functional specification. The functional specification is a thorough description of the external interfaces, user interfaces, and any technical constraints placed upon the product such as compatibility, migration, performance, installation criteria, and quality goals. This document covers both hardware and software and is concerned with the "what" and not the "how". In parallel with the creation of the functional description, hardware and software planning is carried out that identifies the resources needed, schedules, and preliminary cost estimates. Issues such as training, maintenance costs, publications, and field support are covered in the planning process.

As the product is defined, further engineering studies are conducted in both hardware and software to analyze prototype ideas, state of the art in particular disciplines, technological trends, and availability of suitable components.

Hardware Engineering. This activity involves answering questions such as the following:

o What kinds of hardware best perform the required functions?

o What hardware is available for purchase, lease, or rent? What is the cost?

o What kind of hardware interfaces and networks are needed?

o Is suitable hardware already in use by the company?

o Is any custom hardware needed? What is the lead time for designing and building it?

o What are the technological risks associated with choosing the identified hardware?

o What are the associated design and manufacturing costs for supporting a specific software-hardware architecture?

Software, unlike hardware is logical rather than physical. Software studies and planning at this stage would include:

o What is a reasonable direction to follow – third party contracts, do it yourself, or stay with "of the shelf"?

o What software is currently available – languages, tools, libraries – and how stable is it – are you to be a pioneer?

o What familiarity does current personnel have with the languages and tools?

o What impact do the choices being made by the hardware engineers have on software architecture, implementation strategy, and future growth?

The information obtained during the engineering studies is used in the the functional specifications and planning documents.

Following the preparation and approval of the functional specification and project plan, hardware and software engineering continues with each discipline having its own requirements and steps to follow. The hardware analysis proceeds with detailed hardware specifications, reliability analysis, field support analysis, manufacturability analysis and cost estimation. followed by feasibility models, preproduction models, and finally production models. The period of time required to develop product requirements and detailed functional specifications may extend anywhere from one-quarter to one-third of the initial development cycle.

Software Engineering. Software, unlike hardware is logical rather than physical. With software, costs are associated with planning and development rather than manufacturing. Software does not wear out, rust, or mildew and software maintenance often includes modification and enhancement.

Software engineering involves the planning, developing, and maintaining activities in the software life cycle. Specifically:

o Planning includes statements of scope, resource analysis, cost estimating, and scheduling. The results of the planning activity are project plans that are used throughout the development and are refined as the project continues. Major events and activities are planned and estimated from the very beginning and microlevel planning is performed as the activities progress.

o Requirement analysis is the step between the concept and the design activities. Its purposes are to provide a complete description of the information and its flow, detailed functional descriptions, and the appropriate validation criteria. Attention is paid to who will use the software, in what environment, for what purpose, and with what amount of background and training. Other questions that should be asked are: What are the interrelationships between functions? How is a function initiated? How is a function terminated? What does the function mean to the user?

o Software design encompasses preliminary design, detailed design, coding and testing. Section G.2 contains more information.

o Software testing. Further details are found in Section G.3.

o Software maintenance involves much more than just corrective maintenance (fixing program bugs). There is also adaptive maintenance (modification of software to interface with new hardware or software environments). Perfective maintenance activities are those that modify, enhance, or extend program function. Preventative software maintenance means changing software with the purpose of making future enhancements and maintenance activities easier.

G.2   Software Design

Design is the process of applying various techniques and principles for the purpose of defining a system in sufficient detail to permit its realization. Software design transforms requirements into a representation of software. The software design phase may take approximately one-third of the initial development cycle.

Preliminary Design

The inputs to preliminary design are the functional requirements and information flows and structures. The output is a specification of the software structure.

Good software design should exhibit the following characteristics. It should:

o have a hierarchical organization

o be modular. It should be partitioned into components that perform specific functions and subfunctions

o have cohesiveness (single-mindedness) and, to the extent possible, independence from other modules.

Two of the common approaches for mapping information flows and structures onto software structure are data-flow-oriented design and data-structure-oriented design. Details of data-flow-oriented design can be found in E. Yourdon's book "Techniques of Program Structure and Design", (Prentice-Hall, Inc., Englewood Cliffs, N.J., 1975). Data-structured-oriented design is strongly advocated and well-explained by M. A. Jackson in "Principles of Program Design", (Academic Press, New York, 1975). Roger S. Pressman describes these and other methodologies in "Software Engineering: A Practitioner's Approach", (McGraw-Hill, New York, 1982).

There are other conceptual design methods and each has merit in a particular situation. The key is to use and understand several of the methods and know when to apply one versus another. The methods should be applied consistently and knowingly. The first time a method is used will be experimental and it will take several projects before all of the benefits will be obtained. As observed at a software engineering conference – it may not make a significant difference which method is used, as long as one is.

The authors personally use Jackson's data structure design method (also called data modelling) extensively and believe that modelling the data results in software that is more robust and easier to maintain.

There are three main outputs of the preliminary design phase. First are descriptions of the software modules. These include descriptions of the function, interface, and data organization of each module. The second output is the file and external data specification including record descriptions, access methods, and file cross-reference details. The third output is the test plan which details the procedures for testing the software.

Detailed Design

The preliminary design specifies the modules and module interfaces needed to achieve the objective. Detailed design focuses on the within module specifications and representation. It emphasizes procedure and logic and is the final step preceding coding.

A number of tools are suitable for representing program logic. An excellent overview of diagrammatic aids for depicting data relationships, software structures and logic flow is found in J. Martin and P. McClure's book "Diagramming Techniques for Analysts and Programmers", (Prentice-Hall Inc., Englewood Cliffs, 1985). An ideal tool should indicate flow of control, processing function, data organization and implementation details. No one tool is best in all respects.

In particular, graphical design tools include program flowcharts and box diagrams. The most common tabular representation of logic is a decision table. IBM developed and refined the use of its HIPO (Hierarchical Input Output Organization) detailed design tool. As well, a number of "design languages" have been proposed and used with varying degrees of success.

Keep in mind that the various design tools are notational methods that give organization and shape to a design. Using a particular design tool for annotating a design will not produce a proper and good design but will help in determining if it is good.

Coding Guidelines

This section provides guidelines that assist the production of high-quality programs.

Stepwise Refinement. Stepwise refinement is a form of top down or outside-in strategy for producing increasingly detailed specifications of logic. It proceeds by expressing the total logic in terms of a few simple steps. Subsequently each step is decomposed into a series of steps explaining how the step's objective can be achieved. This refinement process continues until all logic is expressed at a level of detail that allows direct translation into programming language statements.

Program Documentation. Internal documentation of source code is what we have called program style. It includes choice of identifiers, comments, and visual structure. Extensive style guidelines are provided throughout the book and summarized in Appendix F.

Each unit of source code should include a statement of purpose, description of arguments and parameters, a list of procedures called, the author(s) and date of creation, a dated list of modifications, and any assumptions and exceptions.

Input-Output Considerations. Input-output style will depend on whether the program interface with the user is batch mode or interactive. For batched input, the organization of data, error-checking and recovery logic and report formatting require detailed consideration. When the style of use is interactive, attention must be paid to input prompts, extensive error checking, consistency of the interface and user-friendliness. Regardless of the mode the following should be done.

o Validate all input values.

o Check combinations of inputs for consistency.

o Keep input formats simple.

o Use sentinel values to indicate the end of input data.

o Label outputs and make report formats consistent.

G.3   Software Testing

Most programmers are egotistical enough to believe that their programs will be correct. This is a triumph of faith over reason. Tests should be designed at the same time the software is designed. The software tests should attempt to demolish the software and ignore any assumptions of correctness. Good tests have a high probability of finding an error.

Black box Versus White box Testing. Any engineered product that has a well-defined function can be tested in one of two ways. A black box test is done at the interface level. Each test has different inputs; the outputs are compared with that defined by the functional requirement. White box testing on the other hand requires knowledge of the internal workings of the software. Test inputs are designed to exercise every logic path in the module. Although in theory white box testing could guarantee 100 percent correctness, the number of possible logic paths in a nontrivial program unit may be in the billions.

Unit Versus Integration Testing. Each logical component in a software system should be tested. This is called unit testing and white or black box testing can be used with each unit. Unit testing does not uncover errors in communication between software subsystems or functions.

Such errors may mean data is lost; one module affects the correctness of another; or combined functions may not collectively produce a higher-level function. Integrated testing is a means of assembling software units and uncovering interface errors. There are two fundamental strategies – top down and bottom up.

Top-Down Integration. In this approach, modules are assembled beginning with the highest level of control in the software hierarchy and moving downward. Program stubs are written to simulate the function performed by the next lower level in the hierarchy. As each interface passes the tests, the program stub is replaced by the full-function module. When all program stubs have been replaced successfully the testing process is complete.

Bottom-Up Integration. Using this strategy, assembling and testing begin with the lowest level in the software hierarchy. Integration and testing are performed from the bottom up resulting in larger and larger logical units. Bottom-up integration requires writing test drivers rather than program stubs as in the top-down approach.

There are advantages and disadvantages to both approaches. The authors recommend top-down design but bottom-up integration and testing. The best choice depends on the particular system and in many cases a combination of the two methods may be the best solution.

G.4   Common Execution Errors

Getting a clean compile and seeing the first test case run correctly is just the tip of the iceberg. Computers are devices that take what you say literally. They never do what you mean, but only what they are told. They rarely invent things. This characteristic of computers is the part that some programmers find intriguing during the debug and test phase. Since the computer does not graciously overlook human error, the name of the game is perfection. Have you covered all situations and of the ones you think are covered, are they really covered?

The following are some items that you should consider as you program:

o When using arrays starting with index 0, make sure that the subscript is one less than the ordinal position of the desired element

o Remember to assign NIL to pointers when the object referenced is deleted.

o Always check for NIL pointers before using the contents of an address field.

o At boundaries, >=, >, and = have significantly different meanings.

o Initialize all fields in data structures.

o If a routine provides a return code or status, use it.

o Remember to put things back to the way you were passed them if you decide to terminate abnormally.

o Watch for terminating a loop when a buffer is not full; using origin 0 or < instead of <= may cause this.

o Remember to allow for partial buffers and partial blocks at the end of files or transmissions; files and transmitted data seldom end exactly with a full buffer.

o Be careful with negative or double negative logic – the computer will not be confused, but you may be.

o Avoid using a variable for two different purposes.

o Avoid hanging IFs; use the ELSE clause – your routine may be passed an unexpected value.

o Order the parameters in a parameter list so that all input-only parameters precede parameters whose values may be modified by the called routine.

G.5   Debugging Approach

1. Spend some time at a desk and look at the program. Play computer and think about parameters being passed to the program and what would happen. Many bugs can be found and corrected before the software is typed in, compiled, or executed.

2. Declare a BOOLEAN variable called Debug and include statements in your program of the form:

        IF Debug THEN ...

3. Give careful choice to the data used to test your progam.

4. Check your implementation documentation to see what debugging aids such as statement traces, memory dumps, memory maps, cross-reference listings, etc. are provided.

5. During the testing phase always use automatic compiler options to check ranges, subscripts, stack test, index test, etc.

6. Use a bottom-up testing approach to reduce the number of stubs required.

7. Place test data in a file and use this as input rather than entering test data interactively. This provides controlled and repeatable test runs.

8. Place test output data in a file and compare the results of subsequent runs.

Appendix H

DIFFERENCES BETWEEN MODULA-2 AND PASCAL

H.1   Introduction

This appendix is of particular interest to the person who knows the Pascal programming language. It describes the most important differences between Modula-2 and Pascal.

Niklaus Wirth, the designer of Modula-2, also designed the Pascal language. Pascal was originally designed to teach the principles of computer programming. Its strengths were quickly recognized not only by educators but also by commercial organizations. Consequently, the usage of Pascal grew exponentially. Many attempts were made to use Pascal in ways that were not initially intended by Wirth. The original form of the language had several deficiencies that implementors have attempted to remedy in different ways with varying degrees of success. Some current implementations such as Borland's Turbo Pascal are excellent.

Modula-2, though similar in many ways to Pascal, was not designed with the purpose of correcting Pascal's shortcomings. Instead, while building on Pascal's strengths, it extended the role of the language in two opposite directions.

o Modula-2 is suitable for expressing both the design and implementation of large software systems involving many people.

o Modula-2 includes facilities for low-level programming that can eliminate the need for assembly language programming.

The two sections that follow describe, respectively, new features in Modula-2 vis-a-vis Pascal and similarities with Pascal.

H.2   New Features in Modula-2

Modules

Concepts. A module resembles a Pascal procedure. One of the most important differences concerns the lifetime and visibility of locally-declared objects. In Pascal, the rule is "you-can-see-out-but-you-can't-see-in". In Modula-2, objects are explicitly imported and exported thus permitting much better control of visibility. The second significant difference concerns existence. In Pascal, a procedure "disappears" when it terminates execution. A module however, once activated, remains "alive" for the lifetime of the program.

Separate versus Independent Compilation. Some implementations of Pascal permit procedures to be compiled independently of programs that call them. Facilities are provided for checking parameter compatibility at execution time. Modula-2 on the other hand, performs intermodule import and export checking at compile time. This traps many programming errors at an early stage in the program development cycle. Thus modules are compiled separately but not independently.

Definition and Implementation Modules. A separately compiled module has two component modules -- a definition module which is public, and an implementation module which is private. The definition module is the interface to other modules. The implementation module performs the task. Knowledge of the definition module is all that is required in order to use it. Thus proprietary code can be hidden from users if a user does not need to know the details.

Utility Modules. Some implementations of Pascal supply a library of Pascal subroutines. In Pascal, these subroutines are not required to run Pascal programs. In Modula-2, on the other hand, the language contains no predefined procedures for input-output, memory management or arithmetic procedures. Instead, these facilities are obtained from a library of service modules accompanying every Modula-2 system.

Using a module library to provide essential services results in a smaller, simpler language and open-ended functionality since you can expand the library indefinitely. The disadvantages include the requirement that all programs must import needed services and that Modula-2 programs cannot be moved from machine to machine unless the required library modules are present. Nonetheless, the advantages far outweigh the disadvantages.

Low-Level Programming

Pascal is a high level language that does not permit you to:

o directly address specific memory locations

o examine and manipulate bit patterns representing a value

o communicate directly with devices in order to mask and/or service device interrupts

Although machine-dependent programming should be avoided where possible, some systems software absolutely requires it. Through the SYSTEM module, Modula-2 provides facilities for interfacing directly with the hardware. Chapter 12 describes Modula-2's low-level facilities.

Concurrent Programming

Concurrent programming involves two or more sequences of instructions executing simultaneously. Even though computers contain only one instruction processor, concurrent programming can be simulated in software. Modula-2 provides facilities that allow you to define concurrent processes. Communication between these parallel processes or coroutines is accomplished using semaphores (signals). Concurrent programming facilities are described in Chapter 9.

Procedure Variables

A procedure variable is one that can be assigned the name of a procedure. Their existence makes it easy to write general routines that use a passed procedure to calculate internal values. Procedure variables are described in Chapter 8.

H.3   Differences Between Modula-2 and Pascal

The structure, vocabulary and syntax of Modula-2 is similar in many ways to that of Pascal. The following information is not intended to be rigorous but rather to give an overview of the salient differences.

The pedagogical style of this section is that of a tutorial for a Pascal programmer who wants to learn what is different in Modula-2. While there may be some Modula-2 programmers who need to learn Pascal, there are far more Pascal programmers who are changing to Modula-2

Identifiers

Modula-2 identifiers are case sensitive. "END", "End", "end", and "eND" are different in Modula-2. All characters in Modula-2 identifiers (not just the first eight, sixteen, etc.) are significant.

Symbols

Modula-2 contains thirty-five reserved words compared to Pascal's twenty-two. These are listed in Appendix A.

Modula-2 uses the symbols "|", "&" and "#" as a case separator, boolean "and" and not equals respectively.

Comments

The character pairs "(*" and "*)" delimit comments. Braces (curly brackets) are not an acceptable alternative. Comments may be nested.

Constants

Declarations. Constant declarations may include expressions in the definition. The constant identifier may be used anywhere the constant is valid. Set constants can be defined.

Integers. Modula-2 distinguishes between CARDINALs (nonnegative integers) and INTEGERs (positive and negative whole numbers). The values in these types overlap and are assignment compatible within the overlap. Integer constants can also be defined as hexadecimal or octal values.

REAL. Real constants have the same syntax in Modula-2 as in Pascal. Only "E" (not "D") can be used to define an exponent as in 123.45E-6.

CHAR. Either single or double quotes can delimit a single character or character string. A single character can also be used as a character string of length 1.

Sets. Modula-2 has a predefined type called BITSET which on most microcomputers has the base type [0..15]. Braces (curly brackets) delimit set constants as in {1,3,11}.

Types

Modula-2 includes the types CARDINAL (nonnegative integers) and PROC (for procedure variables), ADDRESS (memory addresses) and WORD (generic two-byte type) as well as INTEGER, REAL, CHAR and BOOLEAN.

The VAL procedure is provided to extract the n'th value in an enumerated type.

Subrange definitions require square brackets as part of the definition.

Array definitions do not enclose the index type within square brackets unless the index type is a subrange definition (see previous paragraph).

Record structures are more flexible in Modula-2. They may contain several variant parts. Fixed fields do not need to precede a variant segment. Expressions are permitted in case label lists. An optional ELSE part applies to unspecified tag field values.

Pointer types are defined using the reserved words POINTER TO rather than the caret symbol.

Expressions

Modula-2 does not permit values of different types to be mixed in arithmetic expressions. Type conversion functions must be used to achieve a homogeneous expression.

Function procedures may return values of any type. Functions that have no parameters must be written with an empty parameter list as in F().

Conditional Evaluation. The second operand of a Boolean expression involving either AND or OR is conditionally evaluated. For example, in the following expressions, X is not evaluated at execution time.

        TRUE   OR   X   FALSE   AND   X

Statements

Compound Statements. The assignment statement, the procedure call RETURN and EXIT are the only noncompound statements in Modula-2. All compound statements except REPEAT end with "END". REPEAT ends with "UNTIL".

GOTO. Modula-2 has no GOTO statement nor does it have statement labels.

LOOP/EXIT. Modula-2 has a general loop statement. EXIT may be used anywhere within the loop.

RETURN. The RETURN statement returns from a procedure and also is used to return the function value as in "RETURN X".

FOR. The FOR statement uses negative step values instead of DOWNTO.

WITH. The WITH statement may unqualify only one record structure at a time thus nested WITHs may be required.

CASE. The CASE statement uses the case separator symbol "|" to separate cases. ELSE may be used to process undefined values of the case expression.

IF. The IF statement permits one or more ELSIF clauses to be part of the statement.

Procedures and Functions

Functions. There is no FUNCTION declaration in Modula-2. Instead, a procedure header that is a function appends the type of the function value to the end of the procedure header, follows:

        PROCEDURE F(X: REAL) : REAL

The RETURN statement is used to return the function value to the calling block.

Open Array Parameters. To permit arrays of unspecified dimensions to be processed by procedures, Modula-2 includes an open array type of parameter. An example is

        PROCEDURE StringLength (X: ARRAY OF CHAR): CARDINAL

The standard procedure HIGH can be used to determine the number of elements in an open array.

Standard Procedures

Modula-2 includes many of the standard procedures in Pascal. Appendix A has a complete list.

Some differences are:

o Modula-2 has INC and DEC procedures to increment and decrement ordinal valued variables. There is no PRED or SUCC function.

o Modula-2 has INCL and EXCL to add or remove a value from a set.

o The HALT procedure can be called to terminate execution.

Blocks

There are no ordering restrictions on the order of declarations within a block.

The block identifier must appear after the END that terminates the block.

Blocks are components of modules as well as procedures.

Input-Output

Modula-2 contains no built-in facilities for performing data transfers between memory and external devices. There is no FILE type in Modula-2.

Instead Modula-2 provides input-output services through procedures found in a library of modules which is part of every implementation. The desired procedures must be imported into every module needing them.

The procedures found with most implementations have limited formatting capability and process only one value per procedure call.

Appendix I

MODULA-2 IMPLEMENTATIONS

I.1   Preamble

Prior to the creation of this book, the authors purchased and used three different implementations of the Modula-2 language. Each implementation differs with respect to its style, procedures supplied and documentation. All implementations had simple debugging aids and other utilities included to assist the programmer. The comments which follow are admittedly subjective and reflect the status of the implementation at the time of writing.

The vendors were:

Logitech Inc.
805 Veterans Blvd.
Redwood City, CA 94063, USA

Modula Corporation (formerly Modula Research Institute – MRI)
950 N. University Ave.
Provo, Utah 84604, USA

Interface Technologies Corporation
3336 Richmond, Suite 200
Houston, Texas 77098, USA

Since implementations differ, selecting the one which is best depends on what type of computing system you have, how much you know about computing, what you already do with the computer, and what you want to do with Modula-2. Because various implementations are not source code or library compatible, converting between implementations is lengthy, costly, and frustrating. Thus the first purchase must be made carefully.

Logitech

This implementation is our choice especially if you have a computer system and are using it for a variety of programming tasks. You should know about the classic style of computer programming that includes editing (with the editor of your choice), compiling, linking, and separate execution. You should also be interested in developing significant applications with Modula-2. This implementation generates native code. The authors consider the Logitech implementation the most professional. It was chosen for programming the examples in the book.

Modula Corporation:

If your situation has characteristics similar to those described in the preceding paragraph, but you are not fluent with separate compilation, linking, and executing, the Modula Corporation version is a good bet. It has several limitations with respect to program and data size but it is unlikely that you would encounter such problems. Because of the address size, it is very difficult to address screen memory for instance which is well beyond 64K. However, it is possible to start with the Modula Corporation version and migrate to Logitech later. With the Modula Corporation version, you create the source program with the editor of your choosing and then enter the interpreting environment to "compile" and then execute the program.

Interface Technologies

If you are just starting your programming career and have just bought a new personal computer and wish to learn about programming and Modula-2 in a well-protected and guided fashion, the Interface Technologies version may be appropriate. The implementation has a special editor that assists you in the writing of your Modula-2 source code. It has a number of menus that lead the user through the programming tasks, file maintenance, and system interfacing. However, if you are seriously interested in learning how to program and want to be able to program in a variety of programming languages, you may not wish to use this implementation since it is so closely linked with Modula-2 in every way. Furthermore, if you plan to write a number of Modula-2 programs, you may quickly outgrow this version with its hand-holding approach. A reasonable alternative is to purchase a separate editor and the Modula Corporation implementation.

I.2   Implementation Incompatibilities

There is an interesting problem with Modula-2 that also occurs with other programming languages having widespread use. The problem is one of compatibility and portability of code across the various Modula-2 implementations. With Modula-2's separation of language and support libraries, any program that imports data types, procedures, or functions may have to be changed in order to run using a different implementation.

When transporting previously working source code to a different implementation, correcting incompatibilities can be very time consuming. It can often take longer to convert and recertify code than it took to debug the original code. This is due to having built code bottom up, debugging as you go with test beds, stubs, and harnesses. It is easier to build something from the ground up and get it working than tackle a large piece of software in its entirety and get it working. Some of the incompatibilities are caught during compilation but others are logic incompatibilities and only manifest themselves when the code is executed.

The nucleus of the language comprises various data types, statements, operators, and functions. In large measure it is compatible across the various implementations. Problems arise when implementations restrict the complexity and size of expressions. When converting or "porting" code between implementations, these restrictions are minor and can easily be accommodated. Such incompatibilities are usually caught during compilation.

If you write programs that do not use file devices and do not use low-level features of the machine, then you will have a fairly easy time converting between implementations. However, you may still discover that the function located in a certain library is found somewhere else or in fact is not provided. You will find that the procedure has fewer or more parameters than the one you were using. Several procedure calls will be required where one sufficed. The data structures and naming conventions will force you to edit and change source code since they will not be exactly the same as before. How the procedure performs its task may differ from one implementation to another and you cannot rely on certain return codes and responses being set in the same order or meaning the same thing. This list may appear long and pessimistic. It is!

We have used several implementations of Modula-2. When you are beginning to use Modula-2, you will probably have just one implementation. As you gain experience or require certain capabilities, you may find yourself buying a different implementation and are then faced with what may be a massive conversion effort. For example, we initially wrote the CaseFix utility usingr the Modula Corporation's implementation and then converted it to Logitech. There were six unique problems that occurred. They are summarized in the following paragraph.

There are differences in the way ADDRESS and CARDINAL are handled. There are a different number of parameters on the ReadFileName procedure. In Logitech you must include an extra procedure call to clear the terminator key after using the ReadFileName routine. The version of Logitech we were using had an implementation restriction that would not handle the syntax 'array[cardinal variable] := NIL'. The way status codes were set and what was needed to be checked for differed on the Lookup procedure. The way a file was handled at EOF was also different on the ReadChar. If you had to go through this for every one of your source files, we think you would see our point. The best (or worst) solution may be the cradle-to-death committment -- once you have one implementation, stay with it for better or worse and live with its deficiencies.

An alternative is to write your own virtual I/O and system interface library and force all of your input and output and system calls to be made through this filter. This approach makes it easier to migrate source code and makes the majority of your code portable.

I.3   Version Incompatibilities

The "Second, Corrected Edition" of N. Wirth's "Programming in Modula-2", (Springer-Verlag, Berlin Heidelberg, 1983) set the language standard for the various software vendors. In 1985, N. Wirth issued the "Third, Corrected Edition" making a number of changes to the language syntax. The lag between specification and implementation is common to all programming languages. The delay is necessary to allow software vendors to modify the compilers to accomodate the new definition.

Throughout this book, implementation independent features have reflected the third edition of the language except where otherwise noted. The vendor dependent features and the live code in the appendixes use the Logitech implementation of the second edition. Every attempt has been made to provide debugged, working code wherever possible.

If you find yourself between versions, a number of items will be incompatible between the two. Specifically in the third edition:

1. ConstExpressions are allowed to be any general expression. FUNCTION calls were not allowed in Version 2.

2. The ADDRESS type replaced the PROCESS type on the TRANSFER, IOTRANSFER, and NEWPROCESS procedures.

3. The NEW and DISPOSE synonyms for ALLOCATE and DEALLOCATE are system specific and may not be supported.

4. Long integers and reals are recognized as types in Modula-2. The details are system specific.

5. Subranges can be specified as having a specific type.

6. The identifier following CASE in a RECORD type declaration is optional.

7. The variant in a RECORD type declaration may be empty.

8. A case in a CASE statement may be empty.

9. The TSIZE procedure returns the size in a system specific type. It is not restricted to CARDINAL.

10. A DEFINITION module does not have "EXPORT QUALIFIED".

11. MIN and MAX procedures are standard.

12. The SIZE procedure, formerly imported from SYSTEM, is standard. The SIZE procedure allows types to be passed in addition to variables.

13. A string having a single character is compatible with the CHAR type.

14. In the FOR statement, the starting value and ending value must be compatible with the looping variable. The increment must be either INTEGER or CARDINAL.

15. The < > and & characters are not considered standard synonyms for # and AND.

16. The type of a formal variable parameter must be identical, not just compatible, with its actual parameter.

INDEX

Date Due

Due	Returned	Due	Returned
AUG 0 3 1987	JUN 3 0 1987	JUL 2 1 1989	
AUG 1 8 1987	AUG 1 8 1987		
SEP 0 9 1987	SEP 0 9 1987	SEP 1 9 1989	AUG 1 1 1989
SEP 3 0 1987	OCT 0 3 1987	OCT 2 1 1989	OCT 2 0 ...
OCT 2 6 1987	OCT 2 3 1987	FEB. 0 2 1990	FEB 0 7 1990
NOV 1 9 1987		FEB 2 8 1990	
DEC 0 4 1987		MAR 2 6 1988	
DEC 0 6 1987	JAN 0 5 1988	APR 1 7 1990	APR 2 3 1990
MAR 0 7 1988		JUL 0 2 1990	JAN 1 8 1990
APR 2 6 1988		JUL 1 7 1990	
JUN 2 7 1988	MAY 3 1 1988	AUG 0 6 1990	AUG 0 6 1990
AUG 0 1 1988	AUG 0 2 1988	OCT 2 2 1990	SEP 0 7 1990
OCT 0 5 1988	OCT 0 4 1988	NOV 1 2 1990	SEP 1 8 1990
OCT 2 8 1988	OCT 1 8 1988	NOV 2 7 1990	NOV 1 3 1990
NOV 0 7 1988	NOV 0 7 1988	DEC 1 4 1990	DEC 0 3 1990
NOV 2 8 1988	NOV 2 8 1988	DEC 1 4 1990	DEC 0 3 1990
JAN 2 5 1989	JAN 2 5 1989		
FEB 1 9 1989	FEB 1 9 1989		
MAR 1 6 1989	APR 1 0 1989		
MAY 2 6 1989	MAY 2 5 1990		